D1596283

Minneapolis Teamsters Strike of 1934

Minneapolis Teamsters Strike of 1934

Philip Korth

Michigan State University Press
East Lansing
1995

All Michigan State University Press books are produced on paper which
meets the requirements of American National Standard of Information
Sciences—Permanence of paper for printed materials ANSI Z39.48-1984.

Michigan State University Press
East Lansing, Michigan 48823-5202

03 02 01 00 99 98 97 96 95 1 2 3 4 5 6 7 8 9

Library of Congress Cataloging-in-Publication Data

Korth, Philip A., 1936-
    Minneapolis teamsters strike of 1934 / Philip Korth
        p.   cm.
    Includes bibliographical references and index.
    ISBN 0-87013-385-3
    1. Truck Drivers' Strike, Minneapolis, Minn., 1934. I. Title.
HD5325.M7952 1934.M65 1995
331.89'281388324'09776579—dc20

                                                        94-46315
                                                        CIP

Contents

Preface

MY INTEREST IN THE Minneapolis teamsters' strike of 1934 arose during graduate school at the University of Minnesota when I enrolled in Hyman Berman's Labor History course. I expanded a paper I wrote for that course to meet requirements for a Master of Arts degree in the American Studies Program, and felt I had gone about as far as I wanted to go on the subject. When I began to teach a course in American Radical Thought at Michigan State University, and when I became active in organizing faculty for collective bargaining there, my interest in the topic renewed. I also became interested in the period of the Great Depression more generally, and began a research task with a goal of understanding 1934 and the major strikes that year in Toledo, San Francisco and Minneapolis.

I was enabled to pursue my initial plan to conduct oral histories of participants and observers by support from the Rockefeller Foundation, and in consecutive summers I hired undergraduate students I had taught in Michigan State University's James Madison College to travel first to Toledo and then to Minneapolis to record those histories. The first set of interviews provided the core of *I Remember Like Today: The Auto-Lite Strike of 1934* (1988) which I wrote with Margaret Beegle, one of the students who helped collect interviews. The second set of interviews has provided substance to this book.

To the people we recorded in the course of preparing this book we offer a special word of thanks. Their contributions give life to a complex event and help us preserve their experiences and add not only color, but understanding to an event rapidly fading from living memory. I have edited their interviews with care, preserving their language, tone and point of view. Interviews in chapters titled "Voices" express each point of view; I did not attempt to corroborate them. I selected portions of some interviews for use in narrative chapters because they expressed points succinctly and eloquently, they advanced the narrative, and they were corroborated by documentary evidence, or by at least one other interview.

A work like this, which held my attention off and on for many years, has incurred debts which this book purports to repay. I hope that those who have supported my research and encouraged my writing will find it at least a modest reward for their indispensable help. The ledger listing these debts begins with Dr. Hyman Berman, who introduced me to the history of American workers. He remains a skilled and inspiring historian, and a personal friend. Lucille Kane, now retired from the Minnesota Historical Society, guided a young and naive graduate student on his initial foray through the manuscript archives she so ably managed. Dr. George Tselos, fellow graduate student at Minnesota and now Archivist with the National Park Service at the Edison National Historic Site, has remained a friend with a common interest in this strike. His dissertation *The Minneapolis Labor Movement in the 1930s* and our discussions about it helped me crystalize my interpretation. His permission, freely offered, to use oral histories he recorded with Vincent Dunne upholds the highest standards of scholarly cooperation and support. These three colleagues helped me lay out groundwork in fact and document that underpins this entire work.

This research was supported at a crucial time by the Rockefeller Foundation, which provided the resources to locate, contact and interview the people whose recollections add so much to our understanding of the complex events this book aspires to recreate. Peter Wood and Michael Novak, program officers at Rockefeller, guided me through the intricacies of foundation funding. Most recently, Michigan State University provided a grant that allowed me released time so I could concentrate on gathering all the material, sorting it and presenting it in a coherent and understandable way. Money, in academia, equals time, and time free to pursue research and writing is a scarce commodity for a writing instructor.

Janet Topolsky and Philip Fishman, both undergraduate students in James Madison College, helped locate individuals to be interviewed, and scheduled and conducted many interviews that appear in this book. They both did a fine, professional job.

Recording an oral history is easier than transcribing the recording. Linda Douglas, Sue Cunningham, and Judy Easterbrook fought through unfortunate background noises and uneven diction to produce precise, accurate transcripts.

Organizing this manuscript into a book has been ably handled by the MSU Press, particularly by Julie Loehr. It has benefitted from the editing skills of Kristine Blakeslee

A number of my colleagues read all or portions of the manuscript and offered useful, sound advice both about content and style. Joseleyne Slade Tien and Milton Powell read portions of this manuscript and tolerated my distraction and dereliction of duty as their fellow administrator in the Department of American Thought and Language. Others facilitated archival research: Steve Nielsen at the Minnesota Historical Society; the Local History staff at the Minneapolis Public Library; Rev. Thomas E. Blantz, C.S.C.; Joseph Howerton and Tab Lewis at the National Archives.

The bravest, most determined support, and most detailed review of this manuscript came from Reed Baird, Bruce Curtis and James McClintock, colleagues whose editing skill and generosity of spirit enabled me to see this project through to its end. I could offer no clearer demonstration that writing is a collaborative activity than the unflagging efforts these friends brought to support my project. I wrote and revised and they read and responded, suggesting clarifications, raised objections, and offered language all in an effort to improve the quality of my work. Exemplary colleagues!

Let me conclude my acknowledgments by absolving all whose spirit touched this work. I accepted all advice given me, but shamelessly did not implement it all. The virtues of this book I willingly share with them; the mistakes are all mine.

Chronology

1933

November   Local 574 launches an organizing drive in the Minneapolis coal yards.

1934

January 5   Meeting sponsored by the Minneapolis-St. Paul Regional Labor Board between Local 574 and coal yard dealers.

February 2   Local 574 votes to strike February 7 unless employers recognize the union.

February 7   Strike begins.

February 9   Local 574 drops all demands except recognition.

February 10   Strikers return to work believing they have won recognition.

February 14, 15   Elections in coal yards.

Early March   Citizens Alliance calls meeting of Minneapolis employers to warn of impending union drive.

April 30   Local 574 presents demands to eleven trucking firms.

                Employers form a committee that grows to 166 firms who designate Joseph R. Cochran as spokesman.

May 1   Meeting sponsored by Regional Labor Board between Local 574 and employer representatives.

May 14   Local 574 votes to strike on May 16.

May 16   Strike begins.

May 18   Governor Olson attempts to mediate the dispute and end the strike.

May 19   Clash between police and strikers in the Market district. Strikers dispersed.

                Committee of 25 recruits Special Deputies.

May 21   Clash between police and strikers with inconclusive result. Thirty-seven injured.

May 22   "Battle of Deputies Run" between strikers and police and special deputies. Police and deputies driven from Market district. Two special deputies killed.

May 23   Governor Olson secures a 48 hour truce and attempts to mediate the dispute.

May 25   Agreement reached between Local 574 and the 166 employers.

May 31   Agreement signed.

June 14   Local 574 informs Minneapolis-St. Paul Regional Labor Board that employers are not living up to the May 31 agreement.

June 16   Employers deny the charges.

July 6	Local 574 rallies support for a strike through a mass meeting at the Parade Grounds. Workers set a deadline of July 11 for a strike.
	E. H. Dunnigan, U.S. Conciliator arrives at the request of Minn. Senator Henrik Shipstead.
July 7	Regional Labor Board issues interpretation of May 31 agreement concerning "employees."
July 11	Workers vote for strike to commence midnight Monday, July 16.
July 15	Meeting at Wesley Church of workers opposed to a strike.
July 16	Workers confirm strike and endorse leadership at evening meeting.
July 17	Strike begins.
	Rev. Francis J. Haas, representing the National Labor Relations Board, arrives in Minneapolis.
July 19	Police escort truck with "Hospital Supplies" without incident.
	Governor Olson and Father Haas believe they have secured a 48 hour truce with Chief Johannes.
July 20	"Bloody Friday." Police open fire on strikers wounding 67 and killing two.
July 21	Chief Johannes announces temporary halt to convoying trucks.
July 25	Rev. Francis J. Haas and E. H. Dunnigan issue their plan for a settlement which becomes known as the Haas-Dunnigan Plan.
July 26	Governor Olson Declares Martial Law and institutes a permit system for delivery trucks.
August 1	National Guard raids strike headquarters.

August 3   National Guard raids Citizens Alliance
              headquarters.

August 5   Gov. Olson orders General Walsh to revoke all
              trucking permits and to institutes a new permit
              system based on agreement to sign the Haas-
              Dunnigan Plan.

August 6   Olson successfully defends his declaration of
              martial law against an employer requested
              injunction.

August 8   F. D. Roosevelt visits Rochester, Minn., and labor
              delegation submits its account of the strike to him
              through Louis Howe.

              Jesse Jones, head of the Reconstruction Finance
              Corporation puts Father Haas in touch with C. T.
              Jaffray who represents the RFC in Minneapolis.

August 13   Haas and Dunnigan take a revised EAC proposal to
              the Committee of 100, which supports the union's
              bargaining team and rejects it.

August 17   P. A. Donoghue from NLRB arrives in Minneapolis
              to conduct representation elections.

August 18   Jesse Jones calls Barton who contacts A. W. Strong,
              president of the Citizens Alliance.

August 19   EAC modifies its proposal.

August 21   EAC votes 155 to 3 to ratify the proposal. Union
              ratifies proposal in a mass meeting that night.

August 22   Strike ends.

Introduction

THE UNITED STATES SANK deeply into the Great Depression in the year 1933. Gross national product had fallen from 103 billion in 1929 to 58 billion in 1932.[1] Over twelve million Americans were unemployed in 1933.[2] Fear and uncertainty haunted workers despite President Franklin Delano Roosevelt's reassurance that "the only thing we have to fear, is fear itself." Workers knew that something had gone terribly wrong. Forces beyond their control had deprived them of jobs, the source of their livelihoods and their respectability. Franklin D. Roosevelt declared that none should starve, but few felt certain that the federal government's newly-enacted and untried system of economic and social reform could meet such an impossibly massive need. Part-time work at subsistence wages and soup lines etched daily a stark reality for thousands of workers in Minneapolis.

Workers across the globe suffered the Great Depression and turned in some places to strident voices of reaction for solutions. In Germany Adolf Hitler had been elected Chancellor, promising food, jobs, stability, and restored pride to German workers. To the middle classes he promised to end the communist threat, to restore law and order, and to raise Germany again to its rightful place among world powers. With the death of Paul von Hindenberg on August 2, 1934, Hitler silenced dissent and tightened his grip on the German state; his supporters believed that Adolf Hitler understood the needs of working people, and so they yielded to his dictatorship.

Unrest in the United States exploded sporadically in both rural and urban America. Initially the disaffected internalized their plight more often than they found fault with the system. If they had tried harder, worked harder, behaved more responsibly and with greater focus or purpose, they believed, their circumstances would be different. The flaw, they felt, was in themselves, and not the stars. However, as the impact of the Depression broadened, as, for example, foreclosures on farm mortgages increased, organization augmented and then displaced individual acts of resistance. In the case of farm mortgage foreclosures, individual acts evolved into organized responses to sheriffs' sales. On the date of the foreclosure sale, local farmers would gather for the sheriff's auction to bid one dollar for a farm, and to see that no one bid more. Thus they would rescue a farm for the farmer who had mixed his sweat with the good earth. These local responses led to broader organization and eventually in Minnesota to the Farm Holiday Association, which fought foreclosures directly through intimidation of bidders, and indirectly through lobbying in the halls of the state legislature and in the office of the Governor. Workers fought wage reductions and deterioration of working conditions directly through local organizations that eventually reached out to state and national labor unions. In their search for leaders to rescue them from despair, these dissidents reluctantly turned to the political arena.

Politicians, Americans historically believed, offered mixed blessings. More often excoriated than praised, politicians offered a breathtaking array of solutions. Republican President Herbert Hoover appealed to self-help and rugged individualism during the campaign of 1932 striking poignantly responsive chords across the land, but most Americans had come to understand that they lacked the power to end the Depression individually. In a close election, workers turned to Democrat Franklin D. Roosevelt who promised to intervene in the economy and ease the suffering of average people caught up in this system gone awry. Some American workers rallied to the call of political radicals, some to reactionaries. In the main, however, they turned to each other and to the American union tradition that sought protection through their own voluntary, united efforts. They chose labor unions generated by workers' solidarity to solve their problems, rather than separate political organization.

A wave of strikes greater than any spring in the previous decade greeted President Roosevelt within weeks of his inauguration in 1933. Even before passage of Roosevelt's proposed National Recovery Act workers responded to a perception that Washington had now a more favorable attitude toward unions than previous administrations. They were encouraged by creation of the NRA and a National Labor Board in 1933. However, 1934 became the crucial year for the emergence of a new national policy on industrial relations, a policy designed to respond to large scale worker protest. "Workers involved in disputes beginning in May 1934 were over three times the number involved in May 1933, and those involved in disputes in effect at the end of May 1934 were seven times those at the end of May 1933."[3] Three major strikes, one on the West coast and two in the midwest, demonstrated the weaknesses of these new agencies, the intransigence of employers, and the determination of workers to gain mastery over their own destinies. In Toledo, Ohio, workers confronted the automobile parts industry and organized the Electric Auto-Lite company through a new automobile workers union. In San Francisco, workers organized a general strike confronting employers and vigilantes in the course of organizing longshoremen. In Minneapolis truck drivers and helpers confronted their employers and the Citizens Alliance and defeated them in a bitter strike that created a powerful local Teamsters union and energized union organization throughout the region.

Although skilled workers knew unions existed, unskilled workers may not have known much about their actual structure and functioning. The tradition of workers creating organizations for self-help and self-protection has been traced to the medieval guild system, under which craftsmen banded together to protect standards, to establish a living income, to protect their markets, to create an apprenticeship system to train and certify craftsmen, and to limit the number of practitioners in the craft. They organized fraternal rituals to dramatize their commitments through the power of symbol. These rituals also distinguished one group of craftsmen from other workers. This tradition, expressed most clearly in nineteenth century unions such as the Knights of St. Crispin (shoemakers), The Sons of Vulcan (puddlers), and the national Noble Order of the Knights of Labor, had given way to less metaphoric names by 1934, but brotherhood and fraternal rituals continued to provide a model that bound workers together. To this tradition workers turned in 1934, feeling that only solidarity offered hope of self defense.

This craft tradition offered an ambiguous legacy, however, for the semi-skilled or unskilled worker had difficulty identifying his or her place in it. Driving a coal truck might require sufficient special skill to form a basis for craft identification, but with what craft could his helper who carried the coal identify? What about the laborer who helped load the truck for delivery? Did the weighmaster who worked in the same yard as the driver, the helper, and the laborer belong to the same craft of coal deliverers? Where should one draw the line for membership? More importantly, should union organizers draw a line at all; should they not welcome into membership *anyone* who worked in the coal yard? As we shall see, these proved lively questions in Minneapolis in 1934.

The political climate in 1934 offered renewed hope to both organized and unorganized workers. During the twenties their attempts to organize had met stiff, determined resistance, often with the blessing of, or sponsored by the state. In 1934 even the question of a union's legality had not been settled. It proved a question upon whose answer workers were unwilling to wait. Roosevelt appealed to a growing impatience, a desire for action to confront the Depression. The path Roosevelt's programs would or should take was not self-evident. Among his earliest approaches, Roosevelt secured Congressional approval of the National Industrial Recovery Act and the Emergency Relief Act, with goals and structure that sought to restore the lost harmony between work and success that Americans believed to be their birthright.

The NIRA set aside anti-trust laws and allowed industries to create "codes" (agreements between employers in a single industry that divided up their market), and set prices and wages, in the hope that sooner, rather than later, industry would recover and benefit the people. In the meantime, the ERA offered subsistence relief to the people, and the Civilian Works Administration and the Civilian Conservation Corps found work for idle hands through public construction and conservation projects. The starving would be fed and the unemployed given jobs.

American workers who believed in self-sufficiency as fully as the middle class could readily accept the various temporary work projects, but they had to confront their own sense of self when they decided whether to accept relief—charity, they called it. Work programs like the CWA and CCC were not hand-outs, but they did not employ everyone, so the worker had to swallow pride in order to get groceries from relief agencies. The personal anguish this caused lurks just below the surface in those who experienced it fifty years ago, as any one who has conducted oral histories from this period can attest.

Possibilities for organized self-help emerged in the NIRA, however, for among its provisions, Section 7a, read:

> Every code of fair competition, agreement and license approved, prescribed, or issued under this title shall contain the following conditions: 1) That employees shall have the right to organize and bargain collectively through representatives of their own choosing, and shall be free from the interference, restraint, or coercion of employers of labor, or their agents, in the designation of such representatives or in self-organization or in other concerted activities for the purpose of collective bargaining or other mutual aid or protection; 2) That no employee and no one seeking employment shall be required as a condition of employment to join any company union or to refrain from joining, organizing, or assisting a labor organization of his own choosing; and 3) That employers shall comply with the maximum hours of labor, minimum rates of pay, and other conditions of employment, approved or prescribed by the President.

This section had historical precedent in both the Sherman (1890) and Clayton (1914) Anti-Trust Acts which contained provisions that declared unions were not conspiracies in restraint of trade, and which affirmed workers' rights to organize. Neither had proven effective protection for workers. Although labor's right to organize was not expressly illegal in 1934, employers had attempted through the courts to break unions and imprison labor leaders under conspiracy laws, anti-syndicalism laws and anti-trust laws throughout the 1920s. Courts issued injunctions against labor, invoking Sherman and Clayton themselves. The *American Steel Foundries vs. Tri-City Trades and Labor Council* case (1921), tried under the Clayton Act before the Supreme Court, determined that picketing was unlawful except that the courts would allow "peaceful picketing," consisting of one former employee placed at a plant's entrance. The Red Jacket Coal case (1927),[4] upheld "yellow dog" contracts that forced workers to agree not to join or form unions, and "went so far as to forbid all attempts to organize coal miners."[5] Secondary boycotts had been declared illegal. The Supreme Court in the Bedford case (1927) broadened the definition. Workers and their leaders ran considerable risk of fine or imprisonment as late as 1932 when the Norris-LaGuardia Act attempted to restrict injunctions and to establish fair employment practices.[6]

The inclusion of Section 7a in the NIRA represented a legislative compromise between employers who sought freedom from anti-trust laws, and labor unions who sought assurances that workers would be protected. Drafted, reportedly, by staff members of the Brookings Institute and inserted in the bill by Senator Robert Wagner, it helped secure passage of the NRA.[7] It may also have reflected growing public support for the workers' right to organize unions of their own choosing.

Employers' anti-labor activities had proven effective, for only a small percentage of the American labor force enjoyed organization before the adoption of the NIRA. During the 1920s membership in the American Federation of Labor declined steadily from over four million in 1920 to a low of 2,100,000 in 1933.[8] Employer resistance, direct or in employee representation plans initiated by employers, such as company unions, may account for much of this decline. However, the AFL, committed to a policy of craft autonomy, was reluctant to organize semi-skilled or unskilled laborers, frustrating its industrial unionist members, to whom that policy appeared antiquated and inappropriate. Workers in search of state or national union backing often found only reluctant or timid support.

The AFL, which had achieved limited success with industrial organization, remained unconvinced that workers in modern mass production industries could organize. Industrial workers themselves had yet to be convinced that organization would work for them, for they recognized that, with little or no skill required in their work, they were easily replaced. Only by organizing entire plants or industries into a union could they hope to succeed, and the history of mass unions did not offer an encouraging prospect. Division of these workers into even smaller groups, which was required of them by the AFL, would only further weaken them. Convinced that inherent weakness prevented organization of the unskilled, the AFL made unenthusiastic attempts to organize them.

The issue had divided the union movement for generations, of course. Conservative craft unionists viewed with alarm the radical posture of industrial organizers, and industrial workers found the craft unionists too cautious and skeptical for such desperate times. Although craft unionists counseled unskilled workers who approached them, and occasionally gave modest material support, the AFL could not solve their problems, so unskilled and semi-skilled workers gravitated to those who believed in large scale industrial unions, to individuals and organizations undiscouraged by the difficulties of mass organization. These industrial workers guarded a faith in unions and awaited only the means to effective organization. They wanted change and did not trouble themselves over labor's legal right to organize. They wanted jobs, adequate wages, and decent working conditions, and they were not satisfied to wait for them to "filter down." Uncertain how jobs would be created, they were certain that work ought to return a living wage under working conditions that protected each worker's dignity. They believed they could achieve these goals if, following an American tradition over a century old, they united and demanded them from employers. A union, they believed, could help; the problem lay in how to organize an effective industrial union.

This belief awaited only articulation and encouragement. Not surprisingly both came from politically able and committed people whose analysis of the status quo explained to workers the reasons for their powerlessness and proposed a program and tactics that would rescue them. Organizers found receptive audiences in workers who experienced daily the failure of the free market economy, and who readily discounted a speaker's affiliation with the Communist Party, the Socialist Party, the American Workers Party, the Socialist Workers Party, the Socialist Labor Party, or the American Labor Party. Whether William Z. Foster, Norman Thomas, A. J. Muste, James P. Cannon, Daniel DeLeon, Mother Jones, or Leon Trotsky addressed them had less significance than the program and experience the speaker brought to the problem of the Depression. This faith in unions marshaled human resources behind powerful and even explosive leaders. By the time Congress enacted and President Roosevelt signed the NIRA on June 16, 1933, dissenting voices had begun to gather into organizations eager to lead industrial workers in the quest for dignity and a decent standard of living. Often these organizations hoped that this quest, once begun, would lead well beyond immediate goals of improved wages and working conditions to revolution.

These organizations and leaders vied with each other for leadership; each rejoiced in its own victories, each tried to explain its own defeats. For example, in Toledo, Ohio, followers of A. J. Muste influenced the strike at the Electric Auto-Lite Company, declared it their victory, and froze out the Communist Party. In San Francisco the Communist Party exerted great influence on the longshoremen's struggle and so declared its ascendancy over other left parties. The Minneapolis Teamsters strike of 1934 remains the seminal achievement of the Socialist Workers Party which claimed Leon Trotsky as its ideological, tactical and spiritual head. The SWP emerged out of the dispute within the Communist party between Leon Trotsky and Joseph Stalin, who battled for leadership of the Communist Party in Russia after Nicolai Lenin's death in 1924.

On October 27, 1928, the Communist Party U.S.A. expelled leftist supporters of Leon Trotsky.[9] The split erupted from several causes, but chiefly from differences in tactics and strategy with respect to the international trade union movement. These expelled members established in the United States a newspaper called *The Militant* to broadcast and explain their policies. In May 1929, it published their platform, and at a Chicago convention that same month the group adopted the name "Communist League of America, Left Opposition of the Communist Party."[10] Though small, the group had dedicated leaders and, at least temporarily, a clear posture. The contingent from Minneapolis did not number more than "a couple of dozen,"[11] but it included in its ranks able leaders in Vincent R. Dunne and Carl Skoglund,[12] who played critical roles in the struggle for union recognition in Minneapolis. Most impressive to workers in Minneapolis, Dunne and Skoglund exuded confidence that they understood the worker's plight, the main currents of the trade union movement, the workings and weaknesses of capitalism, and the tactics that would achieve immediate goals of recognition, higher wages, and better working conditions. Workers themselves, they understood the feelings of desperation around them and could express those feelings in familiar terms. Confident in their analysis of the capitalist system and in their estimation of local circumstances, Dunne and Skoglund planned and acted with assurance and determination. They believed Section 7a of the NIRA might be useful, but they did not trust it. The organized worker, they argued, not capitalist government, or capitalist law, could determine future economic, social and political conditions.

Controversies that troubled Congressional debate over the NIRA continued even after its passage. Many doubted the NIRA's future. Whatever the NIRA's virtues, hardly a day passed when critical articles or editorials failed to appear in both national and local newspapers. Criticisms came from both left and right. Clarence Darrow spoke forcefully and dramatically in opposition to NIRA powers to cancel the anti-trust laws, even temporarily.[13] Of course major industrialists mourned not a whit at paralysis of the Sherman Anti-trust Act. The addition of Section 7a fueled the controversy more for it implied an employers' obligation to recognize unions. William Green, President of the AFL hailed Section 7a as labor's "charter of freedom."

Implementation of Section 7a rested initially with the National Recovery Administration, which quickly discovered a wide range of problems. Labor seldom had an effective voice in setting code wage scales or hours.[14] Employers evaded or ignored Section 7a by refusing to meet with employees or by dragging out meetings because they did not intend to reach agreements. To head off organization, employers facilitated or sponsored associations of workers. Industries did not establish codes as rapidly as Roosevelt expected.

In an attempt to stimulate drafting codes, on July 10, 1933, President Roosevelt offered employers a voluntary Re-employment Agreement that recommended minimum wages and maximum hours for all industrial and white-collar workers. Signatories were authorized to display the Blue Eagle which symbolized their support of President Roosevelt who encouraged the general public to patronize especially those firms displaying the emblem. By the end of July many more codes had been submitted. However, industries submitted codes requiring work weeks of 40 hours or longer, rather than 35 hours and few included a 10% wage increase as the President requested.[15]

Despite problems with implementation, the NIRA encouraged workers who interpreted Section 7a to sanction formation of unions.[16] Employers tried to evade Section 7a, and experience tended to confirm that the state could not enforce its provisions, so the wise realized that, Section 7a or no Section 7a, organization depended upon the strength of their union. Nothing was going to be handed workers without a struggle.

Membership in trade unions rose after passage of the NIRA,[17] but this increase was discouragingly matched by growth in the number and size of company unions. The National Industrial

Conference Board announced that their questionnaire of November 1933 distributed to

> all the 10,335 manufacturing and mining companies whose capitalization exceeded $500,000 brought replies from 3,314, whose employees totaled 27 percent of all those engaged in those industries. Of the 2,586,000 workers covered by the replies, 45.7 percent were reported to deal with their employer individually, 45 percent through company unions, and only 9.3 percent through outside unions.[18]

This same survey revealed increased membership in company unions 56 percent greater than the increase in independent union membership. Company unions were increasing at a greater rate than independent unions.

Strikes that swept the country in 1934 occurred in virtually all industries, and demonstrated a worker militancy and a level of violence that demanded federal measures. Pennsylvania mine owners confronted 30,000 striking miners; at the Kohler factory in Wisconsin, despite its company union, private company guards fired on strikers killing two and wounding more than 50; the Anaconda Copper Company of Montana and the textile industries in Alabama both faced determined workers demanding recognition.[19]

In San Francisco, vigilantes raided strike headquarters; at the Electric Auto-Lite Company in Toledo the National Guard fired on strikers killing one and wounding 200; and in the Minneapolis truck drivers' strike four died and over 200 suffered injuries.

> Legal and extra-legal violence was widely used in efforts to crush the revolts of labor. In 1934 more than 40 workers were killed on picket lines, and the number of injured ran into many hundreds. In the first year and a half under the NIRA upward of 40 injunctions were issued against labor, and in 16 states the troops were called out against strikers.[20]

In sum, the issues and events generating the Minneapolis teamster strike owe their origins in part to the time and circumstances that had developed nationally, but they also owe a great deal to their particular historical context, not the least of which derives from the state's political history.

These political, social, and economic circumstances enveloped the forces which came together in violent conflict during the spring and summer of 1934 in Minneapolis. They provide at once the context and the focus of the analysis which follows in this volume. Citizens of Minneapolis found themselves searching for a new consensus in this strike. They sought a new modus vivendi to restore dignity to a working class shattered by depression and the industrialization of work. They coalesced into groups of shifting composition and purpose in this search, and they succeeded. This is not a record of failure though there are failures to be found in the crisis. It is rather the record of struggle from which a new consensus emerged. The Citizens Alliance of Minneapolis and Minneapolis General Drivers and Helpers Union Local No. 574 of the United Brotherhood of Teamsters, Chauffeurs, Stablemen, and Helpers of America played central roles, and thus deserve individual attention.

The events in Minneapolis challenged local and state government, and drew the attention of an emerging regulatory system enacted by the federal government. Thus Minneapolis became a testing ground for practices and procedures that eventually guided implementation of the Wagner Act of 1935, which set national policy for resolving industrial disputes. The Conciliation Service of the Department of Labor, and the National Labor Board played important roles in settling the strike, and so they too receive special treatment in this book.

Most importantly, the people who led, who followed, and who witnessed these strikes deserve special treatment, for their testimony converts the musty records of another generation's struggles into a living memory for today.

Notes

1. U.S. Department of Commerce, *Historical Statistics of the United States: Colonial Times to 1970*, Part 1 (Washington D.C., 1975), 224.
2. Ibid., 126.
3. U.S. Department of Labor, *The Monthly Labor Review* 39, no. 1 (May 1934): 83.
4. Joseph G. Rayback, *A History of American Labor* (New York: The Macmillan Company, 1961), 275.

5. Ibid., 295.

6. Ibid., 312.

7. Steven Fraser, *Labor Will Rule: Sidney Hillman and the Rise of American Labor* (New York: The Free Press, 1991), 289.

8. U.S. Department of Commerce, *Historical Statistics of the United States*, 177.

9. James P. Cannon, *The History of American Trotskyism* (New York: Pioneer Publishers, 1944), 55.

10. Ibid., 77-79.

11. Ibid., 63.

12. Ibid., 71.

13. Fraser, *Labor Will Rule*, 310.

14. Ibid., 298.

15. Ibid., 300.

16. Ibid., 292.

17. Ibid., 293.

18. Maurice Goldbloom, *Strikes Under the New Deal* (New York: League for Industrial Democracy, 1935), 25.

19. Ibid.

20. Ibid., 29.

1 | The Citizens Alliance

FOUNDED IN 1903 BY a group of Minneapolis businessmen, the Citizens Alliance grew by 1934 to a membership of nearly 800. Membership rolls of 1934 read like a "Who's Who" of Minneapolis entrepreneurs. Although its name implied general civic interests, the organization's statements of purpose and its activities reveal modest commitment to the cultural, social, or spiritual life of Minneapolis. Little interested this Alliance beyond business matters, particularly employer/employee relations. From its inception the Citizens Alliance had a single purpose: to limit or defeat outright workers' attempts to form unions. The *sine quo non* of membership was commitment to the open shop.[1]

Before 1934, employers in Minneapolis, like employers nationally, had organized associations along specific industrial lines such as: building and contractors, implement dealers, coal dealers, printers. Not infrequently these associations had members in the Citizens Alliance, but no association approached the size or power of the Citizens Alliance. Despite its size and influence, the Alliance failed to attract the core of the social, cultural and political elite of Minneapolis. Wealthy though Alliance members might be, perhaps like Sinclair Lewis' George Babbitt, many never quite belonged. Alliance leaders were *nouveau riche*, self-made businessmen who either created their own businesses, married into a business, or took over and transformed a small business into a large one. Had they chosen to buy a summer home on Lake Minnetonka, they might have found acceptance, but they likely would not have received certain prized invitations. Horatio Alger's heroes would have felt at home among them.

The Citizens Alliance of Minneapolis joined a network of similar organizations around the country, initially seeking guidance on forms of organization and formats for statements of purpose. It requested copies of research on wage rates and productivity. The Citizens Alliance did not aspire, however, to become a study group; rather, it explored ways and means to defeat unionism and to maintain the open shop.[2] Within a decade of its founding, the Citizens Alliance successfully established the open shop in Minneapolis and subsequently defeated every major strike in Minneapolis from that time until 1934.[3]

The Citizens Alliance economic power derived from its members' common understanding of ethical business practice, and the members proven ability to manage affairs well enough to support the growth of the Minneapolis economy. Since bankers profited from growth, it is not surprising that the Citizens Alliance sought influence in banking policy and practice. It is more surprising to learn how quickly and effectively the Citizens Alliance came to influence the newspapers. On April 11, 1905, Lucian Swift, Manager of the Minneapolis *Journal* wrote a letter to George K. Belden of the Citizens Alliance:

> In accordance with my promise to you I had a talk with Mr. Barbour, our advertising manager, in regard to the article you ordered inserted in the Journal. As you stated to me, you ordered this article in, and agreed to pay for the same, so that as far as the Journal is concerned the transaction was in accordance with your orders at the time. I certainly think the Citizens Alliance a very desirable aid for the businessmen of Minneapolis and I am perfectly willing to subscribe on the part of the Journal for its share of the expenses; therefore, I will send you the bill for this article and you can credit the amount as a subscription paid by the Journal. I think it better that the Journal should subscribe its proportionate share for the benefit of this association and then when you have any article inserted it should be paid for the same as any advertisement. This leaves it much better for the Journal, for if it is known that this article is inserted as an advertisement it does not commit the Journal and also requires the other parties to pay for any answer or publication they may wish to make. With this understanding I think we will have no difficulty in the future.[4]

Understanding is the operative word, for the Alliance rested upon a set of understandings. The relationship between the Alliance and the *Journal* certainly became closer when Lucien Swift's daughter married A. W. Strong, a charter member and in 1934 the President of the Citizens Alliance.

Rob Cramer, Editor of the Minneapolis *Labor Review* recalled how understandings worked more directly. During labor difficulties with one of Minneapolis's major department stores, the Dayton Company (George Dayton was an Alliance member), a delegation from the Central Labor Union visited the manager of the *Tribune* to complain that the newspaper treated them unfairly. That they even bothered to complain suggests that they felt the *Tribune* offered a more sympathetic hearing than *Journal*. The *Tribune* manager informed the delegation that the Dayton Company inserted about one and one-half million dollars of advertising in the *Tribune's* pages annually and that, furthermore, he did not think the *Tribune* articles were hurting the union much.[5]

The Citizens Alliance through the three decades before the Teamsters' strike kept files on activists, whether native to Minnesota or passing through, who protested on behalf of workers. For example, it kept extensive newspaper clipping files on the Industrial Workers of the World and the Communist Party. In 1919 the Alliance wrote the San Francisco District Attorney requesting information on the Mooney case so they could counter union organizers using the Mooney case to persuade teachers in Minneapolis to form a union. In the same year it congratulated a prominent San Francisco businessman for effecting an open shop agreement. The Alliance gathered statistics from across the country to compare costs of public construction—schools, public buildings, etc.—under union agreements and under the open shop to prove that the cost of public construction was consistently lower under the open shop.[6]

Alliance leaders were too militant to limit themselves to writing letters and collecting newspaper clippings, however. They used a special mimeographed form, probably developed by Lloyd MacAloon, a detective hired early in the Alliance's history, titled "Special Service Reports (for private file only)," that carried the caveat that the information included was "received from reliable sources but not vouched for." One such report dated May 19, 1921 was titled "History of the Workers College of Minneapolis" and listed the officers and active members. It identified union members as well as Wobblies (I.W.W.), socialists, or communists. A report on a specific meeting on Monday, May 16, 1921, at 8:15 p.m., gave the address of the meeting, identified all speakers, and relayed information gathered by "No. 11."[7] Another report on the journeymen building laborers' and mechanics' organizations listed names and addresses of committees and officers. This system of operatives and spies continued through 1934. One report dated November 5, 1934, after the conclusion of the strikes, summarizes a meeting of the Communist League held November 1, 1934: "The Communist League Local Branch held a meeting at the Labor Lyceum, Sixth and Humboldt Avenue North Thursday evening, November 1st with eighteen active workers of the League present including Goldman, an active national figure in the League from New York. He acted as chairman of the meeting." It lists names of seven other members present, a number of whom were instrumental in the teamsters' strikes, and announced the League's merger with the A. J. Muste group.[8]

Labor leaders of the time confirm widespread use of labor spies whom they would uncover often accidentally when, for example, they found two or more membership cards to different unions in a spy's possession.[9] The existence of such spies proved effective even when reports offered little confidential or secret information, for they spread doubt and suspicion. How thoroughly such spies infiltrated labor organizations became known publicly two years after the strikes during the LaFollete Hearings which led Congress to ban such practices.

The Citizens Alliance engaged in practices we might find reprehensible, but they were widely used by businesses during that time. Clearly, the Alliance gained effective access to some labor organizations. The information they gathered was meant to be used; the Citizens Alliance did not intend to play a passive role in labor relations.

In 1922 a dynamite bomb exploded at a contractor's home in Minneapolis. In an attempt to implicate labor in the bombing, the Citizens Alliance hatched an elaborate plan to frame Dan Mahady, a former union official. Using a private detective named Gleason, the Alliance hoped that Mahady could be induced to blow up a safe. Gleason contacted a local minor underworld character named Fred

Myers and put him in touch with Mahady. At the last moment, Gleason became frightened and had the pair arrested for stealing dynamite. The following day he attempted to secure their release, but the case had already come to the attention of the Hennepin County Attorney, Floyd B. Olson. Questioning brought the story to the surface, implicating Gleason and O. P. Briggs, President of the Citizens Alliance. Since Myers and Mahady had not committed the crime, Olson decided not to press charges, but, he declared: "It was a dangerous and dastardy [sic] act on the part of Briggs and Gleason to incite these two irresponsible men to gain possession of explosives."[10] Olson issued an unmistakable challenge to the Citizens Alliance of Minneapolis:

> If private organizations, no matter what kind they may be, which undertake to enforce the law without cooperating with the duly constituted authorities, and in disregard of the police, are not wiped out, this country will soon reach a condition where faction and class violence will be the rule rather than the exception.[11]

Charles R. Walker, in *American City*, tried to understand the men who organized and led the Citizens Alliance through a biographical sketch of A. W. Strong, Alliance charter member. Many members, like Strong, had risen to their positions through personal initiative, willingness to take risks, loyalty to employers and loyalty to creditors; they perceived themselves as self-made men. Strong found employment in Minneapolis as a very young man. He rapidly became a supervisor and a valued, loyal employee. He obtained a loan on his word and name only to buy the business he had joined as a young man. He directed his business himself. When a union representative attempted to organize his employees, Strong talked with his employees and found no complaints over wages or working conditions, but found broad sentiment for a union. Strong refused the union representatives' demands and banded together with other employers to defeat the ensuing strike.[12]

Albert William Strong was born January 7, 1872, in Fondulac, Wisconsin, and in 1934 at age 62, served as President of Strong, Scott, and Company which manufactured flour milling equipment. He married Grace Swift, and was an Episcopalian and a member of the Minikahda and Lafayette Country Clubs. He was a strong family man. On September 3, 1926, when his son and a friend were injured in a car accident, he chartered a train that set a speed record from the Twin Cities to Two Harbors as he raced to his son's side.[13] He valued personal loyalty, and he determined that he would run *his* business as he saw fit, employing workers loyal to his leadership. He felt that he met his obligation to his workers by devotion to business, thus assuring business success, and so worker security.

When his workers banded together to improve their economic position, he saw it as disloyalty—a blow at the very foundation of social and business relationships that accounted for his personal success. Economic success, he believed, rested on individual initiative exercised within the context of a traditional employer-employee ethic that assumed open, direct, and manly communication between worker and employer. The employer was the boss, but he took his obligations to take care of his worker's best interests seriously. Unquestionably, he believed he recognized and protected that interest.

Unions, Strong believed, undermined a way of life. Each individual should be free to ascend as far as his abilities and desires would carry him. Each individual should be free to bargain with his employer and obtain the wage scale and working conditions commensurate with that individual's ability and desire. Unions would interfere with this personal relationship. Employers like Strong, then, perceived no contradiction in their assertions that they were not anti-labor, but just anti-union, for they felt like defenders of individual workers' rights to improve themselves. The employers had risen through their own efforts. Why should they deny this possibility to other workers?

Consistent with this faith in individual initiative, the Alliance early in its history established a trade school and a free employment agency. Primarily, the trade school taught the skills of building tradesmen. Skilled building craftsmen were in short supply in Minneapolis, so training craftsmen served not only the trainee, but the community as well. The building trades, however, were the most thoroughly unionized in Minneapolis, and increasing the number of trained workers would reduce craftsmen's bargaining power and increase employers' choices. An employer could sort through workers and hire only those he thought merited hiring.

The Alliance's free employment agency struck more directly at union activities, for it provided a clearing house for "safe" workers.

The Citizens Alliance encouraged its members to hire all employees through this agency.[14] However, the agency proved unable to meet the employment needs of Minneapolis, or even of Alliance members. One might infer that workers were reluctant to be identified with such an agency.

The Alliance tried to accommodate the times and workers' desires to organize by establishing rules for company unions. In June 1933 the Alliance's Employment Relations Department issued "Employment Relations Policies and Rules and Regulations Governing Employment."[15] It advised, "if employees choose to organize, it should be only for legitimate and lawful purposes."[16] It declared that individual initiative and ability should govern advancement and listed numerous offenses for which an employee could be discharged without further notice.

> The possession or exercise by any employee of any habits, demeanor, characteristics, action or course of action that make him objectionable to other employees, the public, or to management, or that make his retention in service disruptive of the spirit of harmony therein, or would cause other employees to leave the service; engaging in organization activities or any other activities outside of regularly assigned duties, during working hours; practicing or encouraging by conspiracy or force the lowering of personal efficiency, the limitation of output, or advocating, encouraging or participating in activities or action tending to create discord between employees or between management and employees.[17]

The Alliance justified a company union on the grounds that an employer might thus protect that "spirit of harmony" he had created in the work place. Preferable to a company union, the Alliance recommended that wages and working conditions be determined through direct negotiation between the worker and his employer, rather than with any group, even a company union. If the worker did not like the arrangements, he was free to seek employment elsewhere in June 1933.

Consistent with this company union plan, the Citizens Alliance fought the anti-injunction bill proposed in the State legislature in 1933, a bill that mirrored the federal Norris-LaGuardia Act of 1932 that outlawed yellow dog contracts and defined fair labor practices.

The *Special Weekly Bulletin* #739 of the Citizens Alliance, dated March 3, 1933, advised its members:

> This bill, identified as S. F. #1045, H. F. #1255, would make unenforceable individual contracts whereby an employee agrees with his employer that he will not join a union during the term of his contract, and the employer agrees with him that he will run an open or nonunion shop. The U. S. Supreme Court has upheld the validity of such contracts.
>
> Issuance of injunctions to restrain organization and maintenance of strikes for any and all purposes, however oppressive or criminal they may be, is forbidden under this proposed bill.
>
> *Please write, telephone, or see personally at once your representatives in the legislature and express your opposition to S. F. #1046, H. F. #1255.*[18]

In 1933 the Citizens Alliance attempted to defeat the state unemployment insurance bill on the grounds that times were bad and the additional tax would drive them out of business.[19] They could not ignore the high rate of unemployment, however, and during 1931 initiated and carried out a Job-A-Week Club. Members of the Citizens Alliance and friends of members agreed to provide one job per week such as lawn mowing or painting to an unemployed family man.[20] Although there were many contributors, this effort paled in the face of massive unemployment when thousands were on relief.

The period in which Alliance leaders rose to their positions as heads of businesses was a period of tremendous economic growth in Minneapolis. A. W. Strong's generation was the backbone of the Citizens Alliance. John G. McNutt, who became President and Treasurer of Ford-McNutt Glass Co. in 1920, was born in Glenwood, Minnesota, November 11, 1878. Charles Christopher Weber, grandson of John Deere, came to Minneapolis as a young man in 1881 and formed Deere & Webber in 1898 to manufacture farm implements. The experience of the late nineteenth century had shaped them. Men of little or no education struck out for themselves, bought existing businesses or created new ones and amassed fortunes. They had not depended on franchises or gifts of land to build their empires as had lumber, mining and railroad barons. They believed that they had risen through their own resources, through their abilities and personalities alone. No wonder these men felt allegiance to the ethic that encouraged and facilitated their success. Theirs was the success America had promised the thrifty, the honest, the energetic, the daring. What craftsman, what immigrant did not share that dream? Indeed, even today it has the power to lure thousands of young men and women into MBA programs to earn their ticket to ride.

Dreams do not always reflect reality, however, and the Depression did not lend itself to dreams, except on movie screens. The worker worried daily about survival. The rise of mass production requiring semi-skilled or unskilled workers encouraged young men to take jobs young, while administration of the same industry, due to its complexity, required more and more education. The requirement of increased capitalization to establish such businesses pushed them beyond the reach of personal loans based on a man's word. The American Dream that informed these businessmen's faith, had become increasingly difficult to realize. The Depression demarcated this change, but dreams are not overthrown in a day; tragically for Minneapolis, the leaders of the Citizens Alliance brought to their struggle with Local 574 a vision that no longer reflected the world in which they lived.

Notes

1. Early correspondence of the Citizen's Alliance, Citizens Alliance Papers, Minnesota Historical Society, St. Paul, Minnesota.
2. Ibid.
3. Charles R. Walker, *American City* (New York: Farrar & Rinehart, 1937), 87; V. R. Dunne, interview with the author, Minneapolis, September 1964.
4. Lucian Swift to George K. Belden, 11 April 1905, Citizens Alliance Papers, Minnesota Historical Society, St. Paul, Minnesota.
5. R. D. Cramer, interview with the author, Minneapolis, September 1964.
6. Construction Costs Survey, Citizens Alliance Papers, Minnesota Historical Society, St. Paul, Minnesota.
7. Governor Floyd B. Olson attacked the Alliance's use of spies in 1934. He challenged the Alliance to reveal who No. 11 was so he could examine him.

8. Special Service Reports, Citizens Alliance Papers, Minnesota Historical Society, St. Paul, Minnesota.

9. R. D. Cramer, interview with the author, Minneapolis, September 1964; V. R. Dunne, interview with the author, Minneapolis, September 1964.

10. A copy of Olson's statement is in the O. P. Briggs file, Local History Collection, Minneapolis Public Library.

11. Ibid.

12. Walker, *American City*, 185-92.

13. A. W. Strong, Local History Collection, Minneapolis Public Library.

14. "History of the free employment agency and the trade school," Citizens Alliance Papers, Minnesota Historical Society, St. Paul, Minnesota.

15. "Employee Representation Plan," Citizens Alliance Papers, Minnesota Historical Society, St. Paul, Minnesota.

16. Ibid.

17. Ibid.

18. Ibid.

19. Ibid.

20. Ibid.

2 | Teamster Local 574
Context and Leadership

GENERAL TRUCK DRIVERS' AND Helpers' Union Local No. 574 organized in the early 1920s and affiliated with the International Brotherhood of Teamsters, Chauffeurs, Stablemen, and Helpers of the American Federation of Labor. The membership of Local 574 rose to about 200 by the fall of 1933. Myrtle Harris, who represented garment workers on the Executive Board of the Minneapolis Central Labor Union in 1933, recalled that earlier that year: "I don't remember if it was forty-two or sixty-two, but that was all the members they had in the teamsters in Minneapolis at that time." Local 574 was small, cautious and conservative; it had succeeded in organizing one taxi company employing six drivers who owned their own cabs. In 1932 it listed nine coal yards out of some 62 as "union coal concerns."[1] Little about it suggested the dynamic, militant potential it would develop in 1934. Circumstances and creative, committed leaders transformed a conservative union into the voice of workers throughout Minneapolis.

In 1925 William Brown organized a picnic to kick off Local 574's organizing drive for that year.[2] Members called on him again in 1927 when they elected him President. Brown, a colorful, gregarious personality, had been a truck driver in Minneapolis since 1919[3] and had come to know many of the drivers in the coal industry. He recognized that truck drivers and laborers in the coal yards could be organized, but his union council only agreed to support picnics and other timid measures as organizing drives. He found more sympathy among more restless elements in rank and file, particularly among a group of leftists who had sought jobs in the coal yards because they perceived organizing possibilities there.

Relations between Brown and the council were delicate. Council members might demur at aggressive organization of the coal yards, but they had to deal with Brown's popularity among the rank and file. For his part, Brown appreciated the status of legitimacy that came with Local 574's affiliation with the International Brotherhood of Teamsters. However constrained the Council felt in dealing with Brown, it felt no obligation to accommodate other union members who pressed the case. When Carl Skoglund, a coal driver and Brown's friend, submitted a resolution calling for an aggressive campaign to organize all workers in coal yards, the union expelled him,[4] and authorized a timid campaign to urge union members in the city to patronize only the nine coal yards already organized.[5]

Council members rejected efforts to go further on two grounds. In the first place, they recognized, painfully, the union's weakness, and feared its complete destruction if the attempt failed. In their judgment, failure was certain. Local 574 did not have power to assert itself forcefully with the few employers they had already organized, let alone with new, hostile employers. In the second place, and much more problematical, Brown proposed that the union organize all workers in the coal yards as one group, regardless of their jobs. This proposal ignored traditional craft lines that Daniel Tobin, President of the International Teamsters' Union, was determined to defend in accordance with the policies of his union and of the American Federation of Labor. Seeing potential for growth, Brown swept these considerations aside, and declared: "Hell, if we lose, we're no worse off than we were. This is no union we've got now anyway, but if we win, it will be like a red flag to a bull."[6]

The craft autonomy policy of the AFL and its International Teamsters' Union made little sense to Brown and his supporters among coal yard workers, for, they argued, division along craft lines would only weaken them. It made no sense at all to socialists like Skoglund, and his friends Miles Grant and Vincent Dunne, who worked in the coal yards and urged union organization as a matter of economic and political philosophy. Committed to working class solidarity, they rejected Tobin's and the AFL's principle of craft differentiation, characterizing it as the "American Separation of Labor," as a tactical posture that offered a formula for failure. They accepted the craft union assertion that employers could readily replace unskilled and semi-skilled workers, but they rejected the conclusion that attempts to organize them were fruitless. They argued that these workers did possess inherent power, but it could only be tapped through mass organization and worker solidarity broadly felt within the community. Commitment and correct tactics could assure an organizing victory.

The tacticians behind the growth of Local 574, Carl Skoglund and Vince Dunne, worked in the coal yards and understood the men who worked there and the conditions they worked under. They offered coal yard workers a coherent explanation for the difficult conditions under which they struggled, and they communicated that explanation to other workers forcefully, credibly, and effectively. Most importantly, they knew and trusted each other. Clara Dunne, Grant Dunne's wife, recalled Carl Skoglund:

> Carl Skoglund was really the beginning of it and of course he got the Dunne brothers and Farrell Dobbs and Bill Brown. They had a very small Union before, just a handful and they never got very much vote.
>
> *Question:* So Skoglund really persuaded your husband and Ray Dunne and Miles Dunne to become active in it?
>
> Yes, he was a very good friend of all of ours. He lived with us for quite a few years. It was about in 1932. He lived with my mother and father-in-law before that and then they were getting so old they had to sell their house and he lived with Grant and I. Carl and Grant had a lot of things to discuss among themselves. Of course this was at home. If it was anything to settle they were all in on it. He was a big man; he was tall.
>
> I don't know exactly how I'd say it, but I had high regards for all of them. They all done their jobs and they liked to have fun along with business. They weren't afraid to laugh.[7]

Harry deBoer found work in the coal yards as a young man in 1932. Carl Skoglund made a lasting impression on him, convincing him to become active in the union:

> The Dunne brothers and Skoglund were all in the same yard. That's how I met them. We used to call Skoglund the old Swede although he was only about 40 years old. He was generous and a nice fellow and most of the fellas knew him.

Grant had a truck, Mickey Dunne had a truck. Ray Dunne was the weigh master and Carl Skoglund had a truck. There was another socialist Martin Soderberg—he had a truck. Due to the fact that these people were socialist, they had the interest of the working people at heart. So if they did have a helper, they tried to treat him fair.

Q: Were you a socialist when you went there?

Yes and no. I didn't belong to no party although I was sympathetic toward the socialist movement. My father was a Debs socialist, I remember. I was only a kid, but I remember an article in the paper when Debs was running for President. In our county he only got 4 votes, and that is my mother and my father and my two sisters that were old enough to vote. So I was sympathetic to the socialists at that time. I never did much reading on it until I got acquainted with Skoglund and the Dunnes and then we started to organize.[8]

Through his position as weighmaster, Vince Dunne came to know all the workers in his coal yard. Because the entire system of sales and distribution was determined by weight, a weighmaster played the crucial role of certifying, to coal yard manager and worker alike, that a load was precisely, accurately measured. Vince enjoyed the trust of both employers and workers.

Vince Dunne left school at age 14 when he went to work in the forests near his home in Little Falls, Minnesota, but his self-education continued his entire life.[9] He read continuously, and became politically active in his early youth. In the lumber fields in the Black Feet Mountains of Montana he encountered the Industrial Workers of the World,[10] which declared in the preamble to its constitution that "the employing class and the working class have nothing in common." He returned to Minnesota filled with ideas about class struggle and One Big Union:

The I.W.W. were primarily in the timber country, up north and further out west, building railroads, harvesting grain in North Dakota and Kansas and Oklahoma. That's what they were doing. When I came back here from the West Coast, I met Skoglund and he began to talk about these things after we got acquainted, but it was a long period of time before we had a chance to do anything. I was learning about the international struggle and the big mass revolutionary movement.

That's when I became a Marxist and an activist and finally I dropped out of the Wobblies and joined the Communist party.[11]

Vince joined his older brother William Dunne, already a Communist Party member working in Boise. He returned to Minnesota after World War I, when the Farmer-Labor Party in Minnesota offered voters a mixture of Non-Partisan League fire and Minnesota Federation of Labor organizing. Vince Dunne joined, became secretary of the Twelfth Ward Farmer Labor Club, and maintained his membership in the Communist Party of the United States. He served six years as secretary of the Twelfth Ward Farmer Labor Club, which then expelled him because of his Communist affiliation.[12] He continued his Communist Party affiliation until 1928 when James P. Cannon, a national figure in the Communist Party who had visited Russia and returned with some of Leon Trotsky's uncensored writings, and his followers were expelled from the party for supporting Leon Trotsky. At stake in the dispute between Trotsky and Stalin was power: the control of the Russian revolutionary movement. Which of Lenin's lieutenants could claim to be his heir? The issue came down to tactics: should the communist movement consolidate power in Russia, or should it devote its efforts to fomenting world revolution? Stalin wished to consolidate power; Trotsky advocated ongoing world revolution. This grand debate came down to a matter of party discipline in Minneapolis. The Minnesota Communist Party summoned its members to a meeting and demanded they endorse Cannon's expulsion and, in so doing, reject Leon Trotsky. A number of members refused, requesting more information to clarify the issues and to justify expulsion. Under Party discipline, their request could not be tolerated and it expelled the group, including Vince Dunne and Carl Skoglund. They joined Cannon to form the Communist League of America, Left Opposition of the Communist Party.[13] To the politically unsophisticated, confused by the nuances and distinctions of left-wing politics, and even to the relatively sophisticated, this dispute was at best puzzling. To Vince Dunne and Carl Skoglund, however, it was crystal clear, and of enormous moment.

One decision the Communist League made proved important for the trade union movement in Minneapolis: they decided to work within the trade union movement itself. They would not organize competing unions, nor emphasize political at the expense of union organization. The strike, they believed, offered an effective tactic to organize a union. Their premise that the holders of power would not freely give it up led them to adopt a skeptical attitude toward employers and government alike. Rights could not be given, they asserted, for those who gave had the power to take away. Rights must be exercised. Thus they established a consistent posture toward their opposition. This posture led them to anticipate a wide range of employer reactions to the militant appeal they issued to the workers of Minneapolis.

Confidence based on thorough planning rang in the Communist League leaders words. They knew their own minds, and they felt confident that the right would prevail. These leaders' confidence bred workers' confidence. Working conditions in the coal yards not only confirmed the organizers' analysis, but created a legacy of dissatisfaction and context of unrest which organizers could use. And there was work and thus employment in the coal yards.

Work in the coal yards in January, 1934 was available to workers fortunate enough to own their trucks, and to workers who had strong backs to help them. However, work depended on weather, particularly in 1934 when few customers had money to order an entire season's supply at once, and what work was available did not pay well. Harry deBoer worked as a helper, since he did not have his own truck:

> There wasn't no work outside of doing work in the coal yard. They'd hire anybody. At that time all you had to have was a strong back and they'd hire you to carry coal and shovel coal. If there was seniority, there would have been no work, but I walked in there and went to work. Of course I did mostly carrying. I was young. And for that I would get fifty cents a ton. If I was lucky, I'd get a load out that was two ton, and for that I'd make a dollar and a dollar was more than a lot of guys made working all day.
>
> People would have their house back from the street and you couldn't get in with the truck and it had to be carried in. I could carry a ton of coal in easy a half hour. Get a big basket, you could carry about 100 lbs. in the basket, if you was able to carry it. A lot of times some of the older guys would carry maybe 75 lbs. But then also, the drivers would want young guys like me cause they would get back quicker.

The only time you worked was when the weather was cold. If the weather was nice, you could hang around the "dog house," they would call the place where you could keep warm. Maybe sometimes you'd stay in the dog house and play cards or something 'til 4 or 5 o'clock at night then the weather would get cold. This was during the depression; the customers wouldn't order coal unless they needed it. The report would come that there was going to be serious weather coming, then they would order coal. Then you'd haul coal 'til twelve o'clock at night. Never got overtime.

The yard workers that unloaded the boxcars and loaded the trucks, they were working for 20, 25, 30 cents per hour and the only time they would work too was when the weather was severe. You'd come down early in the morning and actually some of the workers were hoping the weather would get cold so they would get work.

You'd only get paid while you worked. Maybe he'd call a couple of guys, they'd unload a boxcar, and if it took them three hours and there was no more, they'd send them back to the dog house and they would get three hours pay and maybe at night if a job came up, took an hour, then that meant they got four hours for that day. There was no guarantee or nothing; you'd just get paid from the time you worked.

Most of the drivers were working by the ton, rather than wage. The drivers had a peg system. They'd go according to the time they got there in the morning. If you'd get there first, your peg would go up, so you'd be the first driver out to haul the coal.

You'd come back and your peg would go up again. And then you'd be called according to your peg would keep moving down. So if the weather was cold, you'd probably be kept busy. If it wasn't, maybe you'd get one load that day, that's it. So if you hauled two tons of coal and it was a dollar a ton, you'd make two dollars. But you was paying for the gas and oil in your truck.

The driver, if he had two carries and two tons, he'd get $2.00 for his two ton and he'd get the dollar for the carry and then he'd give me the dollar.

Only the very big companies owned their own trucks, and those drivers were paid the same way. They got paid when they worked and if they got five hours of work, two in the morning let's say and three in the afternoon, then they got five hours of pay.

Many drivers owned their own trucks, often old Fords with an extra transmission that enabled them to carry two tons of coal. Workers who did not report to the coal yards each day and wait for a delivery, missed their turn when deliveries were available.[14]

The organizing cadre had experienced these conditions and recognized the rising wave of union sentiment among workers. Vince Dunne often asserted that organizers had not been guessing in 1934; they knew they could win. Doubtless, they had complete confidence in their success.

The council of Local 574, however, did not share their confidence. Despite Brown's efforts, the council rejected resolutions calling for an organizing campaign in the coal yards, so organizing took place outside the union, with the council's knowledge, but not under its aegis. Brown himself selected the Dunnes and Skoglund to do the organizing. They kept to the task, talking, persuading, explaining as they walked home with a friend. Their clear vision of the right thing to do proved infectious; their militancy increased, but they kept it under control. Their effectiveness is apparent in the recollection of Chris Moe.

> I don't know how I got the job in the coal yard. That was in '33. I had my own truck. I had a car and I traded that in and bought the truck. It was an old beat-up one; I worked the whole summer and rebuilt it—a little '28 Chevrolet. It was all by hand. Shovel it on and shovel it off.
>
> The company had their own trucks that got the gravy. We got the singles, and the carries. You went in there and sat in the doghouse all day and maybe you got a ton to haul and maybe you didn't. Sit there the whole week and maybe get a ton or two. When the weather got bad, you got real busy.
>
> I think it was Harry deBoer, or Carl Skoglund told me about the union, and I went to the meetings. We had to meet at houses on the Q.T. If they found out you had anything to do with the union, they'd just let you go. You couldn't even talk to the boss. If you wanted to suck hole or something like that he might give you something. I never did that.

Many coal companies distributed coal from yards located to speed delivery through Minneapolis. Some yards were quite large, and several coal companies distributed from them offering distinct advantages to organizers. Harry deBoer pointed out:

> It was easy to talk to workers because the DeLaittre-Dixon was a coal yard where the Dunnes worked and Ray was weighmaster with an old Company. A lot of the small companies, DeLaittre-Dixon, Reeves, oh, there was 10 or 15 small companies that hauled out of this big yard. Ford Motor Company had something to do with Fuel Distributors and by hauling out of this yard, they didn't have to have their own yard with the weigh scales and all this you see. They used the Fuel Distributors yard and scales and they paid so much a ton. It became the biggest yard in this area because there were so many independent companies.
>
> Plus an ice hauler, in the winter time he had his truck. In the summer time he'd haul ice; he had his customers. Well, he could consider himself a little company, and he'd haul coal out of there for his customers. So there was hundreds of these little guys hauling out of there too. So it was an opportunity to talk to all of the drivers about getting into a union. That's what helped get the coal drivers organized.

The nature of work in the coal yards created a context in which organizers could make effective appeals, despite the complex working relationships they found there. Not everyone worked for hourly wages paid by a single employer. Many workers owned trucks that they had modified for coal delivery, and, in a measure, they acted as independent contractors, seeking deliveries for which they would hire a carrier. These workers developed a system of sharing that reinforced the sense that they were all in it together, and that overcame difficulties inherent in such work relationships. As Harry deBoer described it:

> The last year I worked, we kinda worked together. He owned the truck, but then we kinda worked on a 50-50 basis and I bought a certain amount of gas and helped with the maintenance. He was a nice guy to work with, pleasant. Ordinarily you could pick up anybody; well then maybe the guy would be a good worker, maybe he wouldn't be and you'd have to stand there and wait for him to come back in cold weather.

In sum, coal workers hoped to gain better wages and working conditions, and some control over their working lives. By November 1933 socialists, communists, former "Wobblies" had assumed leadership in the coal yards. They proposed a revitalized union movement, not immediate revolution; the rank and file saw their commitment to building a strong union, and responded to the organizing drive announced publicly in November 1933. Because employers could easily replaced these semi-skilled and unskilled workers, union leaders needed careful timing and well developed tactics to maintain unity, but they never doubted that it would come to a strike.

Across the picket line, confirming the socialist analysis union leaders offered workers, the Citizens Alliance, which appeared to workers as the symbol and real expression of the arrogance of capitalism, entered the dispute. The Citizens Alliance's militant opposition to unions, ironically, added credibility to organizers' assertions that they were engaged in class warfare. The Citizens Alliance might have rejected the assertion, but it would not blush at the charge that it represented general employers' interests.

The public had an interest in this confrontation as well, so we will turn now to the institutions the community had created to deal with disputes between employers and their employees.

Notes

1. Minneapolis *Labor Review*, 30 September 1932.
2. Flyer, Citizens Alliance Papers, Minnesota Historical Society, St. Paul, Minnesota.
3. V. R. Dunne, interview with the author, Minneapolis, September 1964.
4. Ibid.
5. Minneapolis *Labor Review*, 30 September 1932.
6. Charles R. Walker, *American City* (New York: Farrar & Rinehart, 1937), 89.
7. Clara Dunne, interview, Minneapolis, 3 July 1974.
8. Harry deBoer, interview, Minneapolis, 31 July 1974.
9. Walker, *American City*, 193.
10. Ibid., 194.
11. Vincent R. Dunne Sr., interview with George Tselos, Minneapolis.

12. V. R. Dunne, interview with the author, Minneapolis, September 1964.

13. James P. Cannon, *The History of American Trotskyism* (New York: Pioneer Publishers, 1944), 57, 79.

14. V. R. Dunne, interview with the author, Minneapolis, September 1964.

3 | The Community Agencies

PUBLIC SEARCHES FOR resolution of industrial disputes arose historically within the context and traditions of community social control,
for the contending parties were integral parts of society itself and
helped define its shape and purposes. American culture committed
itself formally to the defense of individualism in the context of liberty. The culture thus generated unresolved tensions between community obligations and individual freedom. As often as not the
community was looked upon with suspicion. Indeed, cooperative
endeavors, with the exception of a church, raised eyebrows, and
sometimes one wasn't sure about the church. Leaders, consequently,
often found it difficult to generate a community spirit that would
support intervention in disputes between individual employers and
their workers. Only when those disputes spilled into the streets of
the community or disrupted normal life would the community
intervene. Even today the institutions created to address industrial
disputes stand upon the premise that collective bargaining will produce economic stability. These institutions, then, are designed to
measure good faith and assure fair play, but the essential resolution
of the dispute remains where the nineteenth century placed it:
between employers and their workers. This tension will became virtually palpable in Minneapolis.

Disputes, could and did turn violent, creating legacies of suspicion, distrust, even hatred to eat at the heart of a community.
Memories of such disputes run long and deep. The community
sought through its public institutions ways to control or end these
disputes and early tried to find ways to prevent or settle them. In the
nineteenth century the United States tried to decide where the public

35

interest lay, wandering in the process through a maze of confusing and conflicting concerns. Who articulated the public interest? Was it economic leaders who promised and achieved growth? Was it craftsmen who banded together to protect or advance their craft? Was it the mass of mankind who worked for wages, at times even as vassals to an employer's bidding? To whom should the community listen? And on what grounds could the community assert its right to intervene? Indeed, who was the community? Did not the entrepreneur have the Constitutional right to operate his enterprise freely? Did not the worker have the right to contract freely for his hire? When hundreds, thousands of citizens were used by these entrepreneurs to create great personal wealth, where was the public interest? Were not these thousands the public itself? Who, indeed, was the public? Where did special interest end and the public interest begin? These general questions cried out from strikes in the coal fields of Pennsylvania in 1873-74, from the great railroad strikes of 1877, from Haymarket, Homestead, and Pullman, and from thousands of less famous struggles conducted in the fields and streets of the country.

We should temper criticisms of nineteenth-century community leaders who found themselves unable to resolve these complex questions; indeed, such questions trouble us today as they did citizens of Minneapolis in 1934. In a measure, then, the struggle to define the roles of employer, worker, and the public, to distinguish between private and public interest, shapes the Minneapolis Teamsters strike of 1934. It is appropriate then to examine the institutions that attempted to assert themselves on behalf of the public interest in order to prevent, then to mediate, and finally to end the strike. The Minneapolis Teamsters strike of 1934 engaged the Governor of Minnesota, the city of Minneapolis, and the federal government, including the President of the United States. Analysis of their actions and inaction helps us understand the special role time, circumstance and personality played in the creation of a national regulatory posture. There we can find precedents that inform regulatory processes today. We will also find a case study of a community's search for a new consensus. This search established parameters for ethical behavior between employers and employees in Minneapolis, and began the process of creating institutions to monitor and enforce that ethic. We will begin with the changing political climate in Minnesota.

Minnesota's Governor Floyd B. Olson, elected in 1930 as leader of the Farmer Labor Party, found ample challenge to his principles and his political skill when he assumed office. He headed a loose but momentarily powerful coalition of home grown forces.

Minnesotans love to talk about the weather and politics, and both can be as stormy as a winter blizzard or as complacent as a warm August afternoon on the prairies. On those prairies agrarian reform movements germinated in the late nineteenth century; the Grange and the Populist movement found ready supporters among Minnesota farmers. The Non-Partisan League, founded in 1915 in North Dakota by ex-socialist A. C. Townley,[1] spread to the Red River Valley in Minnesota where, "convinced that the Twin City banks and terminal grain elevators, rather than the crumbling frontier economy, were principally responsible for his distress, the Red River wheat farmer enlisted."[2] The Non-Partisan League adopted this platform in 1916:

1) state ownership of terminal elevators, flour mills, packing houses, and cold storage plants;
2) state inspection of grain grading and dockage;
3) exemption of farm improvements from taxation;
4) state hail insurance on the acreage basis;
5) rural credit banks operated at cost.[3]

Minnesota forests and fields echoed with dissenting voices in the decade preceding World War I when lumberjacks, agricultural workers, and miners championed the Industrial Workers of the World, a militant industrial union organized in Chicago in 1905. Agricultural Workers' Union 400 maintained national headquarters in Minneapolis. Finding common ground in their radicalism, the Non-Partisan League and the I.W.W. even attempted to reach an agreement, despite the fact that one represented employing farmers, and one transient harvest hands. Arthur Le Sueur, counsel for the Non-Partisan League, expressed hope for an "understanding" at a convention of Agricultural Workers Industrial Union 400 he addressed.[4] World War I challenged both the League's nativism and the I.W.W.'s internationalism that concluded America should not intervene. Federal and state governments assailed the Non-Partisan League's opposition to World War I, imprisoning its organizers, and destroyed the I.W.W. through anti-syndicalist laws, trials, and imprisonment of leaders during World War I, but it failed to destroy the spirit which animated the movements.

In the gubernatorial primary election of 1918, the League backed Charles A. Lindbergh, Sr., for the Republican nomination, at least in part because of his opposition to United States entrance into World War I, but as surely for his progressive views concerning agriculture and labor. A lawyer from Little Falls, Lindbergh had been elected to Congress in 1906 where he created a reputation as a rugged individual and man of the land, who was noted for independent thinking. He asserted:

> The farmers must be organized exactly as every business is organized. There should be an adjustment between producers and consumers. Interest rates can and should be reduced to a reasonable scale. What the people pay for the service of transportation can be cut down. Uneconomic competition is an economic burden on all.

On Labor:

> In the past, labor has been figured as a commodity, treated as such and converted by many employers into great fortunes. Labor should not be competitive except in skill and quality. The day is near at hand when those who furnish the energy of the world's progress will govern.[5]

Both Lindbergh and the Non-Partisan League became targets for pro-war patriotic groups, and Lindbergh was soundly defeated in the primary by the incumbent Governor, J. A. A. Burnquist. Left with no senatorial candidate to support, delegates from the Non-Partisan League and the Minnesota State Federation of Labor met to nominate candidates for state offices.

> The final agreement on August 25 [1918] was much less than the third party advocates had hoped for. Within the MFL [Minnesota Federation of Labor President] H. G. Hall and [Secretary George] Lawson continued to resist fusion and third-partyism. When farmer delegates mixed in joint convention with some ninety union local representatives in St. Paul's Trade Union Hall, there was no agreement to sire a third party, nor were precautions taken to prevent its conception.

Rather, two committees met, one from the unions and the other from the NPL, and they negotiated a settlement on candidates. . . . This was but a beginning, a mere loose federation into which only part of the protest movement had been funneled. The hyphenated "Farmer-Labor" symbolized the separateness rather than the unity of its two branches.[6]

A. C. Townley agreed to include labor demands for the eight-hour day and for old-age pensions in the NPL program. Jointly the two forces selected nominees for the offices of governor and attorney general. "To satisfy legal requirements, both candidates filed as members of a Farmer-Labor party. The designation was adopted solely to get on the ballot; the party had no independent existence."[7]

The Republican party had controlled state government almost exclusively since the Civil War. Until the founding of the Farmer-Labor party, no alliance of progressive forces had entered the political fray effectively. The Empire Builders had exercised control over political fortunes, as well as their own, despite momentary lapses to the progressives. This new farmer-labor party promised to end that control, and sought alliances with radical groups. Socialists, ex-socialists, trade unionists and communists joined, though not always without controversy. Communists particularly occasioned controversy. An unsuccessful attempt in the Farmer Labor Association executive committee in 1924 to expel them succeeded in the committee in January 1925.[8] Despite that expulsion, Vincent R. Dunne, who still belonged to the Communist Party, was chosen as a delegate to the 1928 convention, and, finally, as a candidate for Congress on the Farmer-Labor ticket.[9]

Party cohesion rested on a perception that it had identified the true enemy of the common people in monopolies and money trusts. This coalition, like the Non-Partisan League, attacked the Minneapolis Chamber of Commerce and milling companies, and it excoriated the railroad and lumber Barons for charging excessive rates and denuding the land. Like the Minnesota Federation of Labor, it decried low wages and poor working conditions that buffeted the urban laborer. Both suspected bankers: the farmer trying to earn enough to pay off mortgages on his land, and the laborer who regarded them as allies of exploitative employers. Minneapolis bankers held the farmer's mortgage and extracted—the farmer would say extorted—exorbitant fees from the processing and sale of his produce. Both workers and farmers felt exploited, reduced to subsistence by those holders of capital who amassed fortunes. Both worker and farmer knew the enemy, but that enemy held power so formidable that only the strongest political forces could ever match it.

Minnesota's political traditions, then, included liberal, progressive, and radical elements. They had found common ground firm enough to institutionalize a political party that captured the governor's office in 1930 when Minneapolis attorney Floyd B. Olson earned the support of 57% of the electorate.[10]

Two federal institutions attempted to facilitate agreement and thus first to prevent, and finally to end the Minneapolis teamsters' strike of 1934: the National Labor Board established by Presidential order August 5, 1933, and the United States Conciliation Service, a division of the United States Department of Labor. NLB was first on the scene through its local organization, the Minneapolis-St. Paul Regional Labor Board, which entered the dispute between Local 574 and the coal yard dealers. The senior of these institutions, and thus a source of experience for subsequent governmental organizations, was the USCS.

Attempts to mediate industrial disputes in the nineteenth century tended to be ad hoc, creating panels or boards connected with a specific dispute. As a result, these bodies dissolved once the dispute was resolved, though they did provide through their experience and reports a body of tactics and ideas that subsequent mediators could draw on. The United States Conciliation Service began to operate in practice in 1913, and "in 1917, [it] . . . was formally organized as a subsidiary division of the Department of Labor, and the mediation work was concentrated in this division."[11] It was displaced by other mediation boards during World War I, but was re-established as a formal service in 1926. The authority for its operation rests on the act which created the United States Department of Labor and charged its director with responsibility to "act as a mediator and to appoint commissioners of conciliation in labor disputes whenever in his judgment the interests of industrial peace may require it to be done."[12] Its powers were limited. "While the Service was basically an agency for mediation, it could suggest arbitration, and it would name or help select an arbitrator."[13] This cautious approach reflected the emerging regulatory posture at the turn of the century which perceived government as, at best, an honest broker between contending forces. That posture, in turn, reflected an American tradition limiting government's powers in general and in economic life in particular. The economic health of the community, Americans believed, would be maintained by private decisions and private enterprise. The state might gently regulate the scope of those decisions, but it should never substitute its will for the will of a market economy. It might try to assure that fairness prevail in dealings between its citizens, but it should accept, finally, any free agreements those citizens reached. The U.S. Conciliation Service proved a perfect expression of limited government playing honest broker between its citizens. "It . . . has no specific statutory authority, and . . . its duties are not specifically prescribed by law. . . . In the language frequently used by the Commissioner of Conciliation, 'we have no law to enforce.'"[14]

With little power, the Service had to rely on persuasion. Although it might appeal to its authority for enforcement, in practice it depended on a reputation for honest, dispassionate, and fair judgment. It's credibility rested on credentials and performance. By 1934 the Conciliation Service had built a reputation that could carry weight in the Minneapolis Teamsters strike, once asked to intervene.

The United States Conciliation Service had gained respect through extensive work in industrial disputes. Even the very conservative economist Howard S. Kaltenborn, who had few words of comfort for workers who went on strike, could write in 1942 about the USCS:

> On the basis of contacts with a considerable number of commissioners of conciliation, the author is inclined to believe that the majority of the commissioners have had, at one time or another, union affiliations. However, with comparatively few exceptions, these men appeared to be conscientious public servants interested primarily in industrial peace rather than in fostering the aims of either employees or employers.[15]

When controversy arose over the settlement of the teamster's May strike, Henrik Shipstead, Farmer-Labor Senator from Minnesota requested USCS intervention, and on June 27, 1934, E. H. Dunnigan, an experienced conciliator, was assigned the case. The USCS entered the dispute after the Minneapolis-St. Paul Regional Labor Board had been active in the case for six months.

The National Labor Board had existed less than a year when it became involved in the Minneapolis Teamsters strike, and it had been a stormy year that brought to the surface issues that would have to be resolved to facilitate resolution of industrial disputes. The basis for creating the NLB and its regional associations was Section 7a of the National Industrial Recovery Act, submitted to Congress May 17, 1933, and signed into law an astonishingly short month later on June 16, 1933.[16] The speed with which the NIRA passed belies the controversy which surrounded Section 7a[17] The initial drafts of the NRA had not contained this provision. As James Gross and other historians of the National Labor Relations Board point out:

> Section 7a was actually an administration concession to the political strength which the AFL had demonstrated in its support of the Black thirty-hour bill. . . . [18]

This addition implied that the United States would rely on the process of collective bargaining to establish just and fair economic relationships between employer and employee. The government might facilitate the establishment of that process, but it would rely on a private system of collective bargaining to establish wages, hours, and conditions of employment. The vehicle establishing collective bargaining was the system of codes the NIRA envisioned. Each code was to contain the provisions and processes outlined in Section 7a, including the provision asserting that "employees shall have the right to organize and bargain collectively through representatives of their own choosing." Labor had seen such words before. How effective they would be,

> hinged upon how these provisions would be interpreted and enforced in the preparation and implementation of the National Recovery Administration's codes of fair competition. Section 7a, as industry was well aware, provided neither enforcement powers nor procedures to accomplish the selection of the employees' representative nor any indication of what specific employer actions would be prohibited. In addition, its wording was susceptible to interpretations that would

sanction company unions, proportional rather than exclusive representation, and individual rather than collective bargaining. It would
also permit an employer to avoid bargaining with a labor union
which represented his employees.[19]

Workers saw in it their industrial freedom; employers vigorously
resisted the provision. Workers organized by the thousands, and
employers refused to recognize unions that emerged.

> Since there was also no provision in the NIRA for either national or
> industry labor boards . . . , organized labor and organized employers
> relied on their political and economic power to pressure the New Deal
> administration to read into Section 7a the strongest endorsements of
> their own positions. Industry generally had the political power
> advantage as long as the New Deal recovery program remained an
> experiment in industrial self-government dependent upon employer
> cooperation rather than government control.[20]

The complexity and breadth of this struggle quickly revealed the
need for a system to resolve disputes.

> For workers, however, the meaning of Section 7a was plain:
> President Roosevelt wanted them to join unions. When they did and
> employers refused to recognize their unions or rushed to install com-
> pany-sponsored employee representation plans to forestall unioniza-
> tion, a strike wave followed. There were more strikes in 1933 than in
> any year since 1921, particularly in the second half of 1933 when "man
> days lost due to strikes which had not exceeded 603,000 in any month
> in the first half of 1933 spurted to 1,375,000 in July and to 2,378,000 in
> August." This increase in strike action was so severe that President
> Roosevelt issued a plea for industrial peace and, on August 5,1933,
> created the National Labor Board to "consider, adjust and settle dif-
> ferences and controversies that may arise through differing interpre-
> tations of the President's Re-Employment Agreement. . . . " The New
> Deal was being forced to piece together a labor policy on a
> crisis-by-crisis basis.[21]

Initially the President tied the NLB to his Re-Employment
Agreement which offered employers an interim general code to sign

in exchange for permission to display the Blue Eagle, which symbolized their cooperation in the recovery effort.

> This Board will consider, adjust and settle differences and contro-
> versies that may arise through differing interpretations of the
> President's Re-Employment Agreement [PRA] and will act with all
> possible dispatch in making known their findings. In return employers
> and employees are asked to take no disturbing action pending hear-
> ings and final decision. This Board will promptly proceed to establish
> such central and local organizations as it may require to settle on the
> ground, such differences as arise in various parts of the country.[22]

Inevitably, the National Labor Board assumed responsibility for
interpretation and implementation of Section 7a. Writing in
February 1934, Charles L. Dearing, on leave from the Brookings
Institution "to act as an assistant deputy administrator of the
NRA,"[23] tried to clarify the workings of the National Labor Board,
but he reflected the confusion and uncertainty about its administrative position and thus its powers.

> exact status of the board in relation to the National Recovery
> Administration is ill defined. It is an agency created under the
> Recovery Act, but it is not an integral part of the Recovery
> Administration. Its membership, except for the impartial chairmen,
> has been drawn from the Labor and Industrial Advisory Boards, but
> need not be. While it is not a part of the enforcement machinery of
> NRA, its work is in some degree complementary to that of the
> Compliance Division. Its permanent relation to the settlement of labor
> disputes is yet to be determined, but will presumably be much modi-
> fied if and when industrial relations boards are extensively set up
> under approved codes.[24]

The National Board was composed of five employer representatives, five labor representatives, and one neutral chairman. President
Roosevelt appointed Senator Robert Wagner to chair the Board. For
employers he appointed

S. Clay Williams, Vice president, Reynolds Tobacco Company
Walter C. Teagle, President, Standard Oil of New Jersey

Louis E. Kirstein, Manager, Wm. Filene's Sons, Boston
Pierre S. duPont, Chairman of the Board, duPont Company
Ernest Draper, Vice-president, Hills Brothers Company
Henry S. Dennison, President, Dennison Manufacturing Company.

For Labor:

Dr. Leon C. Marshall, Johns Hopkins University
Leo Wolman, Columbia University; Chairman, Labor Advisory
    Board of NRA
William Green, President, American Federation of Labor
John L. Lewis, President, United Mine Workers of America
George L. Berry, President, International Printing Pressmen's
    Union
Rev. Francis J. Haas, Director, National Catholic School of Social
    Service.[25]

In order to meet the demands for service pressing on the NLB, it
was authorized

> by the President's order to delegate to . . . regional boards such power
> and territorial jurisdiction as it deems necessary to the performance of
> their regional functions. . . .
>   The nature of the board's work, dealing in an intimate way with
> labor controversies in their local setting has necessitated the establish-
> ment of regional labor boards composed of employer and employee
> representatives and impartial chairmen.[26]

In his letter of appointment, President Roosevelt declared the NLB's
purpose: "to investigate and pass upon the merits of controversies
concerning or arising out of labor relations, which may operate to
impede the efforts of the government to effectuate the policy of the
[National Industrial Recovery] Act."[27] The NLB found ample work
for its twenty regional boards, handling over 1800 cases, involving
nearly a million workers in the first six months of its existence.[28]
A source of uncertainty over the authority of the NLB and its
regional offices stemmed from identification with the Presidents Re-
Employment Agreement (PRA), issued July 27, 1933, that Roosevelt
intended to bridge the interim between passage of the NIRA and the

establishment of its codes for every industry. As an immediate step, Roosevelt encouraged employers to sign an agreement that eliminated child labor, limited the work week to forty or fewer hours, fixed minimum wages, limited price increases, and encouraged doing business with other agreement signers. The NLB would mediate disputes concerning these labor provisions until a code was established, at which time the code machinery would police compliance. In fact, some codes written by major industries did temporarily establish their own labor relations boards. To handle the general run of cases, the NLB created regional boards to whom implementation of Section 7a fell whether a code had been signed or not. For Section 7a appeared to articulate national intent, if not effective law. Few entrepreneurs would risk open opposition to the recovery effort. The Minneapolis-St. Paul Regional Labor Board, which became involved in early 1934 in Local 574's attempts to organize the coal yards, was one of the twenty the NLB created.

Membership on the Minneapolis-St. Paul Regional Labor Board was offered to prominent men in the area. Not all those offered seats accepted them. C. MacFarlane, and Charles L. Pillsbury turned down appointments. Two others, James Ford Bell, and John S. Pillsbury considered the offer but declined.[29] In early 1934 the Board reflected the national board in composition with five members representing labor, five representing industry, and a neutral chairman.

Neil M Cronin, Minneapolis, Impartial Chairman
Hon P. J. Ryan, Vice Chairman, St. Paul
A. H. Harmon, Pres., Webb Publishing Co. St. Paul
Frank J. Anderson, Pres., Foley Bros. Inc., St. Paul
Frederick Power, Pres., St. Paul Foundry, St.Paul
J. A. Vaughan, Wyman Partridge Holding Co., Minneapolis
Geo. W. Lawson, Sec. State Federation of Labor, St. Paul
William Penn, [William Penn Stone Co.] Esq., Minneapolis
Emery C. Nelson, [Milk Drivers Union] 614 First Ave. No. Minneapolis
J. B. Boscoe, [Printing Pressmen's Union] 423 Daily Star ä Bldg. Minneapolis
Guy Alexander,[County Commissioner] 110 Court House, Mpls.
E. G. Hall, President, State Federation of Labor.[30]

The fifty-three-year-old bachelor, Neil M. Cronin, replaced Judge Thomas D. O'Brien of St. Paul when President Roosevelt appointed him October 26, 1933, "to represent the general public in mediation of labor controversies in your area."[31] Cronin had been elected City Attorney in 1921 and was re-elected until June 1933 when he resigned to enter private practice. More importantly, he had served as Chairman of the Democratic party's state convention in 1932. *Shopper's Guide* presented him to the public in a brief biography shortly after his appointment as impartial chairman.

> Mr. Cronin is a quiet, unassuming sort of person with a tendency toward baldness, a well modulated voice, a pair of twinkling eyes. He received his law degree from the University of Nebraska and began his private practice of law in Minneapolis in 1908. . . .
>
> His first entry into Minnesota politics came in 1914 when as a Democrat, he ran for attorney general. In 1916 he entered the race for Congress. In both of these ventures he was unsuccessful.
>
> In addition to his service as city attorney [to June 27, 1933] he has been a bulwark in the Democratic party, having served as a member of the state central committee, and delegate to two of its national conventions.[32]

Cronin served as Adjutant in the 350th Infantry, 88th Division in France during World War I. The year after he returned from the war he was interviewed about his experience.

> I learned to put up with the demands of army life, to take orders without question, to obey them immediately, to accept criticism of the way I did things, to do a lot of things that a man seldom invites willingly and to fit into the life of a vast organization working with a common purpose.
>
> Now that it is all over I can say that they were the happiest two years of my life.[33]

No salary accompanied the job of impartial chairman, and he again found himself part of a vast organization working with a common purpose. In early 1934 Cronin received another position that allowed him to continue his career of service but with pay.

Neil M. Cronin Minneapolis attorney and chairman of the regional labor board, Saturday was appointed by general Hugh S. Johnson head of the NRA, as labor compliance officer for Minnesota, according to word from Washington. He will continue as chairman of the labor board.[34]

In Minneapolis the distinction between the NIRA Compliance Division and the Regional Labor Board had thus become meaningless.

To Neil M. Cronin and his executive secretary W. W. Hughes, fell first responsibility for monitoring and mediating the initial dispute between Local 574 and the employers of Minneapolis. The Regional Board's involvement virtually ended when the National Labor Relations Board entered the dispute in July.

Rev. Francis Haas came to Minneapolis July 17, 1934 as a Special Mediator from the National Labor Relations Board. Born in Racine Wisconsin in 1889, Francis Haas was ordained a priest in his home rather than a church in 1913.[35] In 1919 he entered Catholic University of America in Washington, D.C., where he became a disciple of Father John A. Ryan. "Ryan's deep concern for the rights of workers, the just wage, and government responsibility for the welfare of all would be mirrored in Haas's later activities, and he never minimized the debt he owed to the man he affectionately called 'the great John A.'"[36] By 1922 Haas had earned a Ph.D. with a special interest in labor relations and social welfare issues and returned to academic life at St. Francis seminary from which he had graduated, and where he remained until 1931.[37] He came to the attention of newly appointed Secretary of Labor Frances Perkins during a conference she called for March 31, 1933 to address issues of unemployment and relief, and within days after passage of the National Industrial Recovery Act, she appointed him to its Labor Advisory Board. All other appointees had institutional ties to labor organizations.[38]

President Roosevelt responded to the rash of strikes that broke out in June 1933 by creating the bi-partisan National Labor Board to deal with them. He enlarged the Board October 6, 1933, naming Father Haas among the four new members. Haas became a primary trouble-shooter for the NLB. He came to Minneapolis July 17 fresh from facilitating settlement of the strike at Milwaukee Railway and Light Company on June 29.[39] He came as representative of the new National Labor Relations Board, which President Roosevelt appointed to replace the National Labor Board, but the continuity of his work was unbroken. The NLRB of 1934[40] became the fourth organization within one year to deal with issues related to labor relations in Minneapolis.

Senator Robert Wagner had become the vital force creating policy to govern industrial relations. He had introduced in March 1934 legislation to strengthen the government's powers in labor disputes, but it failed to pass Congress. On June 13 Roosevelt sought authorization from Congress to act on his own, and June 19 he received it. He appointed the NLRB to replace the NLB effective July 9. "Father Haas was recalled [from Racine] to serve as technical advisor to the National Labor Relations Board, which had replaced Senator Wagner's National Labor Board. Haas met with the new board members . . . from July 13 to 16, recommending appointments to the NLRB staff, suggesting procedures . . . and pointing out dangers."[41]

Father Francis J. Haas was an experienced, sophisticated mediator who understood the weaknesses of the regulatory system he was asked to enforce, but who also understood the forces contending in Minneapolis. The newly elected mayor of Minneapolis, A. G. Bainbridge, Jr. had no such experience and a very different understanding of those forces. His father, A. G. Bainbridge, Senior (1852-1925), organized the Painter, Paperhangers and Interior Decorators Union No. 186, and served as the local's business agent for seventeen years. He served as Director of the Minneapolis Board of Education during World War I, and became a foe of its opponents. He announced in September 1917 that all "disloyal" teachers would be asked to resign. He would consider membership in the Industrial Workers of the World as proof of disloyalty. He died tragically when a truck ran him down May 20, 1925 in an accident witnessed by police Sergeant Frank Forestal[42] who declared the accident "unavoidable."[43]

A. G. Bainbridge, Jr. found a life in show business attractive even in his youth when he ran away with the Adam Forepaugh-Sells Brothers circus. In 1934 he remained in show business as owner of the Shubert Theater. More importantly, Alexander Gilbert "Buzz" Bainbridge, Jr., entered the Minneapolis mayoral race Friday, May 13, 1933, won, and served as Mayor from 1933 to 1935. The Minneapolis *Journal* characterized "Buzz" as "a resourceful showman, as a service man, as a fraternal worker, as an unselfish citizen, as a man" and as "a confirmed Republican"[44] Bainbridge ran on a platform of improving the business climate by bringing conventions to Minneapolis, and he delivered: "he was instrumental in having Minneapolis selected as the 1934 national Shrine convention city."[45]

A retrospective article in *Civic Digest*, a Minneapolis magazine, captured Bainbridge's special qualities.

> Bainbridge is back in private life again, possibly thinking about returning to show business after one of the most amazing interludes in Minneapolis politics. Here was a man who never had attended a political meeting, never had made a speech, with the exception of an occasional brief announcement between acts at the old Shubert theater.
>
> "Buzz" Bainbridge ran for mayor two years ago, filing on Friday the Thirteenth of January and getting his picture, with an open umbrella and a black cat, [in the papers]. Everyone had a good laugh, gave "Buzz" credit for another piece of good showmanship.[46]

One of the more significant appointments "Buzz" made, had to be made thrice in the early months of his tenure as mayor.

> The third police chief in a period of six months, establishing a unique record in Minneapolis politics, was Michael J. Johannes, former Department of Justice agent and recently head of the police morals squad. He was literally deluged with letters advocating Johannes appointment, Bainbridge said. He estimated he must have received 200 communications from business men in support of the man who became the principal issue of the 1935 mayoralty campaign.[47]

Michael Johannes joined the Minneapolis police force in 1909. He left the police department in 1921 to become Chief Special Agent of the Bureau of Investigation, United States Department of Justice, but continued to work the Minnesota district. He returned to the Minneapolis police force in 1927, serving as a plain clothes lieutenant from September 1927 to his appointment as chief of police.[48]

Having identified the major parties to the disputes that erupted in Minneapolis in 1934, I can now turn to the events themselves to discuss how those parties interacted.

Notes

1. Philip A. Korth, "The Yeoman and a Market Economy," (Ph.D. diss., University of Minnesota, 1967), 136

2. George H. Mayer, *The Political Career of Floyd B. Olson* (Minneapolis: University of Minnesota Press, 1951), 18.

3. Ibid., 19.

4. Korth, "The Yeoman and a Market Economy," introduction; Charles R. Walker, *American City* (New York: Farrar & Rinehart, 1937), 50.

5. Ibid.

6. Millard L. Gieske, *Minnesota Farmer-Laborism: The Third-Party Alternative* (Minneapolis: University of Minnesota Press, 1979), 45.

7. Mayer, *Floyd B. Olson*, 31.

8. Gieske, *Minnesota Farmer-Laborism*, 97.

9. Ibid., 111-12, 115.

10. Ibid., 140.

11. Howard S. Kaltenborn, *Governmental Adjustment of Labor Disputes* (Chicago: The Foundation Press, Inc., 1943), 14.

12. Ibid.

13. R. W. Fleming, *The Labor Arbitration Process* (Urbana: University of Illinois Press, 1965), 11.

14. Kaltenborn, *Governmental Adjustment of Labor Disputes,* 15.

15. Ibid., 17.

16. Lewis L. Lorwin and Arthur Wubnig, *Labor Relations Boards: The Regulation of Collective Bargaining under the National Industrial Recovery Act* (Washington D.C.: The Brookings Institution, 1935), 26, 45.

17. Ibid. 5.

18. James A. Gross, *The Making of the National Labor Relations Board: A Study in Economics, Politics, and the Law,* vol. 1 (1933-1937) (Albany: New York State School of Industrial and Labor Relations Cornell University, State University of New York Press 1974), 11.

19. Ibid.

20. Ibid, 12.

21. Ibid, 14-15.

22. Lorwin and Wubnig, *Labor Relations Boards,* 93.

23. Charles L. Dearing, *The ABC of the NRA* (Washington, D.C.: The Brookings Institution, 1934), x.

24. Ibid., 52-53.

25. James Dysart Magee, *Collapse and Recovery* (New York: Harper and Brothers Publishers, 1934), 188.

26. Dearing, *The ABC of the NRA,* 54.

27. Gross, *The Making of the National Labor Relations Board*, 15.
28. Magee, *Collapse and Recovery*, 189.
29. Minneapolis *Journal*, 1 November 1933.
30. Letter Dated May 12, 1934 from Neil M. Cronin to Mrs. Mary Babcock Abbott, 645 Portland Ave., Minneapolis, RG 25, Box 387 File A, National Archives.
31. Minneapolis *Journal*, 26 October 1933.
32. *Shoppers Guide*, 8 September 1933, Neil Cronin file at Minneapolis Public Library.
33. Minneapolis *Journal*, 31 August 1919.
34. Minneapolis *Journal*, 11 February 1934.
35. Thomas E. Blantz, C.S.C., *A Priest in Public Service: Francis J. Haas and the New Deal* (Notre Dame: University of Notre Dame Press, 1982), 18.
36. Ibid., 23.
37. Ibid., 25.
38. Ibid., 71-72
39. Ibid., 102-4.
40. This board should not be confused with the current National Labor Relations Board created under the Wagner Act of 1935, which superseded Section 7a and all the labor boards of the NRA.
41. Blantz, *A Priest in Public Service*, 112.
42. Officer Forestal fought strikers in May 1934, and succeeded Michael Johannes as police chief in 1935.
43. A. G. Bainbridge file, Local History Collection, Minneapolis Public Library.
44. Minneapolis *Journal*, 14 June 1933.
45. *Civic Digest*, August 1935.
46. Ibid.
47. Ibid.
48. Michael Johannes file, Local History Division, Minneapolis Public Library.

4 | Organizing the Coalyards

The Coal Strike

THE COAL YARD ORGANIZERS and the organization they had built felt strong enough in early 1934 to press their employers for recognition. The legal atmosphere for organizing had changed with the passage of Roosevelt's National Industrial Recovery Act, Sec. 7a, that asserted workers' rights to form unions of their own choosing. Harry deBoer understood its importance. "In '32 Roosevelt was elected and one of the new deals was that workers would have a right to organize. One of the programs, Section 7a, was used in order to get the workers organized, 'cause here we've got a right to organize." Although Section 7a created a foundation of legitimacy for union organization that certainly encouraged workers and organizers alike, the strike was not entirely a spontaneous response to it. Carl Skoglund and the Dunne brothers had speculated about the possibility of organizing coal drivers, and had laid groundwork through planning and recruiting. Vince Dunne recalled:

> We had discussed when we were members of the Communist party, especially Skoglund, myself and 6 or 8 others, that we had the possibility of organizing and working the [coal yards]. I drove horses the first year and I drove trucks and quite a number of the others did the same. Sometimes they didn't have a truck, but they just had a little model A.
>
> They had the possibility of having the material that would aid them to getting a job there, that is, a second hand or a model A that they could turn into a truck that would haul two tons of coal. Sometimes

53

there would be two or three that would own one truck, take turns doing it. I had been already about six years in the coal yard and I knew the coal business very well. I was well known, to practically every person who delivered coal in this town, as a radical and as a Wobbly and as a Communist, and later on as a Trotskyist. And that was why I was the only worker in the entire coal industry who was taken in as a weigh master. They were usually "company men," and they knew that I was very definitely not that. I had been asked to run for office by the Communist Party, not by the Trotskyist. And I went through with that running for public office in 1928.[1]

Vince Dunne persistently and publicly supported left wing political movements, whether the Industrial Workers of the World, the Communist Party, the Farmer Labor Party, or the Trotskyist socialist movement; he left no doubt about his commitment to organizing workers. His public roles wrapped him in controversy, but they led him always to involvement.

The thing we wanted above all other things: be in the mass movement somewhere, doing something, organizing something, particularly in Minneapolis where they had company unions already. We had several people, my brother Miles was in the coal yard, and he and a couple of others had a battered up truck they used. And Carl Skoglund borrowed a truck one time. He was able to buy a truck. And from there it swelled out in several different places. In the yard we were in, I think it was seven to ten different people that were quite well known to myself. Some of them were members of the party, some were not. We didn't take only members of the party. We knew other people that were very willing to work with us. So it wasn't a simple thing of saying "now everybody get into the coal yard." That was very carefully handled. Three years went by before the strike; it took us three years to do it. I'm sure the employers knew it. They just laughed at it.[2]

Differences in tactics finally separated Vince Dunne from the Communist Party, which also sought to organize workers everywhere. Although he tried to follow directions from the Communist Party, Dunne judged their directions impractical, even romantic, and certainly uninformed by real experience in the world of work.

If we had remained in the Communist Party and not been expelled, we would have probably done the same thing under different auspices. They had very strange ways approaching this question of organizing; it had to be some production thing. People who couldn't get into the labor movement had sort of a stiff-neck. They wanted us to organize the flour mill, and there was nothing we could do at the flour mill. They didn't even have a company union there. The hired men were non-union workers who had been union workers. We had two or three of them that had been expelled from the union, very skilled men in the flour mill. Art Soderberg was a man then of about 65, 70 years old. He was a skilled man: he was a skilled engineer. He knew every movement of every wheel in every flour mill, knew the running of the machinery, and the power it took. He was working on the job, not a man that was part of the company, but he was working on the job doing the kind of things he was capable of doing. We understood him. To go into the flour mills, would have been one of the toughest things. We had to say, well, after all, it should be organized, but how have we got the possibility of organizing such a thing? We were not flour workers.

After we were expelled, the very fact that you were involved in mass work gave you a better chance to get people from the Communist Party. They have people in the unions too, you know, and they were saying we as Trotskyists were police agents, etc.

In contrast to the Communist Party's theoretical approach, the Dunne brothers relied on experience and a practical assessment of their possibilities.

Entering the coal yards was done very deliberately, because we didn't think we were going to have any opposition. We tried to get into 574. They didn't want us in there, because they had a couple of drivers and one coal yard: that's all they wanted. They said, come one at a time with your problems. We'll take care of them in the Union. You pay your dues. They weren't for organizing all the inside workers; [3] they were afraid of all of our people.[4]

Dunne and Skoglund could present themselves as workers just like anyone else, familiar with the work, and loyal to their fellow workers. They also made friends with workers already recognized as leaders.

Bill Brown was not involved in initial stages of planning. We were all underway. Mick Dunne was sent in to 574 three years at least prior to the strike. They let him stay there for a while, but then they just stopped taking his dues. They knew Skoglund as an organizer, too, because these people had known of him in the railroad shops in 1919 and 1922. Those strikes were crushed and he was the hero in the Twin Cities.

You see, Mick and Brown were, in a sense, a certain type. They loved a good time; they were very humorous people. They were very serious about the movement and all that and Mick began to know Brown because he was in the 574 longer than Skoglund and found out that Bill Brown was opposed to the executive committee of 574 who was opposed to taking us in. He hated them for that. He turned completely on this, and Mick saw this and began to talk to him about Skoglund, and me, and others. He had heard of Skoglund. He was very much younger than Skoglund; he hadn't been active when Skoglund was leading strikes here, but he knew of him.

Brown had a big standing there, and the milk wagon drivers were for us and that was the biggest union of the teamsters in the Twin Cities. They had fought Tobin in 1911 over inside workers.[5]

As early as the fall of 1933, coal drivers had called for a strike, but the organizers refused to attempt a confrontation with employers without firm and well established plans. Strong employer opposition, and intricate tactical problems seemed daunting to the 574 council and even the organizers. Caution tempered Local 574's organizing strategy in 1925, 1928 and even in 1932 when, on the pages of the *Minneapolis Labor Review*, it called upon friends of labor for support:

General Drivers' Union Local No. 574 is urging all members of organized labor and their friends to give their patronage to the following union coal concerns. All these concerns are employing only members of the General Drivers' Union and you are urged to patronize the:

> Hawthorne Fuel Co.
> Midwest Coal & Dock Co.
> Minnehaha Ice & Coal Co.
> Gartland Fuel & Transfer Co.
> Flour City Coal & Oil Co.

Cedar Lake Ice & Coal Co.
Hygenic Coal & Ice Co.
Robbinsdale Ice & Coal Co.
Hy-Art Coal & Ice Co.[6]

This approach had become, by early 1933, too timid for restless, impatient coal drivers. Bill Brown, who had been elected president of Local 574, had sought, after some debate with the Council, permission from the Teamsters' International Union to admit coal yard drivers formally to the local.[7] By November 1933 they had became the largest group of drivers in the union. They had won effective leadership of Local 574, and formally launched that month an organizing drive focused on the coal yards. Local 574 targeted sixty-two coal companies,[8] which were separated widely in the city. The traditions that governed the work itself and the relationships between workers in each coal yard, demanded careful and sensitive handling. Although most coal distributors owned some delivery trucks, they also relied on driver/owners to deliver coal. Drivers' families might invest all they owned in a truck, gambling their futures on the driver's ability to hustle up work. Thus a driver/owner acted much like a sub-contractor, hiring a man to carry. Some of the men they hired became members of the union later. Moreover, some coal yard workers did not go on deliveries; rather they unloaded railroad cars and loaded delivery trucks. Each type of work had a different status, a different feel about it, and the workers had distinct interests that could have undermined union bonds.

My own experience twenty years after the strike, speaks to this issue. I worked as both helper and inside man at beer distributor O.M. Droney Co., which was a union shop. Inside men arrived early in the morning, around four a.m., to load the delivery trucks. At that time unloading was done by hand; one man in the trailer unloaded and one at the end of a track, or conveyor stacked cases. By the time the driver came to work, we had loaded trucks according to their route. During the day we unloaded semi-trailers from the breweries, stacking cases of beer in the warehouse.

Truck drivers had significant autonomy in their deliveries, and could alter routes; no supervisor routinely followed them around checking on them. The helper assisted the driver in the actual delivery. At the end of the day, when delivery trucks returned, the inside men stacked the empty cases drivers and helpers unloaded. I recall the near fight that resulted between my driver, Preston, and the dock supervisor who ordered me to help stack empties in the warehouse. I was a helper on his truck, Preston insisted, not an inside worker, and should not be required to work in the warehouse.

It was much more attractive to me to work as a helper on a delivery truck, because I would invariably get in over-time, paid at time and one half, during those hot summer months. Inside men worked under constant supervision, had few breaks, and worked little overtime. It was heavy, draining work without letup, so the eight hour shift was physically demanding. Workers at Droney's recognized a status hierarchy of work, and the driver stood atop it, even though we were all in the same union. In fact, with a few notable exceptions, workers at Droney's tended to see work in the warehouse as mindless, as an initiation to becoming a helper, and eventually a driver.

There is no reason to believe that relations between yard workers and drivers differed in 1934; a proposal to include yard workers, then, created complex tensions within Local 574's council. Organizers made a challenging and complex decision, then, when they chose to include yard workers, a decision that assumed critical importance in the later strikes. On one hand, they brought inherent tensions into the union, for inside workers and drivers did not have precisely identical interests, although they had much in common. On the other hand, including inside workers avoided other problems, for it brought into the union one possible source of replacements for drivers on strike.

In 1934, few coal yard workers questioned the need to strike; the important tactical question concerned timing. A strike, they believed, offered the only way to bring about negotiations directly with employers in a collective bargaining setting. The newly appointed Regional Labor Board in October 1933 appeared to offer organizers a different avenue to negotiations. Accordingly Local 574 accepted the invitation of W. W. Hughes, Secretary of the Minneapolis-St. Paul Regional Labor Board, to discuss with him rumors he had heard at the beginning of January 1934 of an impending strike. Hughes feared that other union members would strike in sympathy with the coal drivers, so he invited union organizers and coal dock retailers to a meeting of the Regional Labor Board January

5th. Hughes summarized this meeting in a "confidential" report to the National Labor Board:

> This meeting was held and participated in by Messrs. Goldie, Brown, Dunne and Hall of the Drivers Union, and Messrs. Hopkins, Crail, and Kelly representing a portion of the coal dealers. The matters of union recognition, wage scales, natural gas competition, etc. were discussed, and it was agreed that Mr. Hopkins, Secretary, Twin City Coal Exchange would call a meeting of his members to discuss the situation and report back to Secretary Hughes.[9]

Hopkins was unable to bring about agreement among the employers in the Twin City Coal Exchange. Agreements, he advised Hughes, would have to be made between the Union and individual coal dock retailers. Hughes then invited over forty coal dock retailers in the Twin Cities—many of whom did not belong to the Twin Cities Coal Exchange—a representative of the Minnesota Federation of Labor (AFL), the conservative, established arm of organized labor in Minnesota, and Local 574 to meet January 16th with the Regional Labor Board to discuss the dispute between Local 574 and the coal dock retailers. He reported:

> This meeting was attended by approximately thirty dealers, Union officials, and Mr. T. E. Cunningham of the Minnesota State Federation of Labor. The Union's proposal was submitted merely as a working basis and was subject to change. The meeting adjourned with the understanding that dealers would conduct an investigation and submit a proposal.
>
> On January 23rd, Mr. Hopkins of the Twin City Coal Exchange, submitted a proposal for his group. Another group, dock dealers, apparently having no organization, but for whom J. B. Beardslee of the Pittsburgh Coal Company acts as spokesman, collected data and submitted a counter proposal. The wage scale recommended by the dock dealers was posted in their yards to be made effective February 1st. The dock dealers, however, refused to meet with members of the Union and would deal only with this office.[10]

Hughes offered to resolve the issue of legitimate representation through elections he would supervise in each coal yard, but the union rejected the plan. Hughes reported to Washington:

> Apparently the point at issue is recognition of the Union for the purpose of collective bargaining. This has been denied the workers by the dock retailers, their contention being they feel they have not been convinced that the leaders of the Truck Drivers Union have been duly authorized to represent the employees of the various dock dealers.
>
> A general meeting is to be held Friday, February 2nd, with the possibility this will result in a call for a strike.[11]

However confident the leadership and the rank and file, their decision to strike proved stressful and sobering. W. W. Hughes had concluded that the wage scale employers offered was satisfactory, and so might many coal yard workers. A wage increase, even when offered at the last minute, can weaken a worker's resolve; after all, it meets a major objective of a strike.

Harry deBoer remembers the night the strike was called.

> My God they were practically starving to death anyway. What did they have to lose, in a sense? I think what helped was the fact that they were working with men like Carl Skoglund. He was generous and a nice fellow and most of the fellas knew him and if he asked you to join a union, you pretty much had to. You knew he was serious about it. He understood what the workers would have to face.
>
> The night we were going to go strike, and we knew the members would vote strike because the leadership was going to recommend it, we decided we were going to leave all the trucks in the coal yard, which was fenced in. Even the dump trucks. Even the truck I was driving for Vince, and his truck. So we had to walk home. Carl Skoglund, personally, we walked over the Lyndale viaduct where he had got hurt when he came over from Sweden to the lumber camp, so he walked with a limp. So he had his arm over my shoulder. We was walking home and he was pointing out to me what to expect the next morning: how to conduct myself, etc. We went home to clean up and have supper, and then went to a meeting, and we voted to strike.

Weather influenced the timing of the strike, as it so often affects life in Minnesota. The winter had been unusually warm, so coal orders sagged throughout January. Late January seemed propitious, but a January thaw changed that date. Water ran in the streets. This unseasonable warm spell ended February 1, when the temperature dropped below zero. Coal orders increased, just as discussions with the Regional Labor Board reached impasse. The time looked right, so General Truck Drivers' and Helpers' Union, Local No. 574 on February 2 voted to strike February 7 unless their employers granted recognition.[12]

The employers rejected Union demands. In hopes of finding agreement, Hughes called a meeting February 3, but was unable to persuade the dock retailers to meet with Bill Brown, president of Local 574. Hughes reported the meeting to the NLB.

> Mr. J. B. Beardslee of the Pittsburgh Coal Company attended as spokesman for the dock retailers. About twenty coal companies were represented. Mr. Beardslee refused to meet with Mr. Brown of the Union saying "Mr. Brown means just exactly nothing to me." It was brought to Mr. Beardslee's attention that to come into this office and discuss the matter of an election with Mr. Brown would in no way constitute recognition of the Union. It was pointed out that the only purpose in conducting such a meeting would be to bring about a cancellation of the impending strike at least until such time as elections could be held. Mr. Beardslee refused under any consideration to talk to Mr. Brown.
>
> About half the representatives present expressed a desire to discuss the matter with Mr. Brown. The meeting ended without any progress being made toward a conference with strike representatives.
>
> Companies represented at this hearing were:

J. B. Beardslee	Pittsburgh Coal Company
A. J. Brand	The C. Reiss Coal Company
M. S. Hanson	The C. Reiss Coal Company
G. I. Crail	Crail Coal and Oil Company
Albert Johnson	Albert Johnson Coal Company
E. E. Swain	Swain Farmer Company
J. A. DeLaittre	DeLaittre Dixon Company
O. H. Olsen	Campbell Coal and Oil Company

Tom F. Danaher   Philadelphia and Reading Company
William Nelson   Great Lakes Coal and Dock Company
C. L. Swanson   Nels Swanson, Inc.
E. L. Larson   Hawthorne Fuel Company[13]

Beardslee's response joined the issue; Local 574 could either back down or strike. The only path to union recognition ran along the picket line, so the strike began on February 7, 1934, and immediately tied up the entire industry.

The strikers boasted that they had "the industry 95% organized" and that 700 workers had struck. The employers, disputed the numbers, claimed that only 150-200 men were out, and publicly questioned whether Local 574 really represented their employees. The Minneapolis-St. Paul Regional Labor Board attempted again to inject itself into the dispute. The union presented demands for improved working conditions, higher wage rates, and recognition of the union to the Board just as it had tried to present them to the coal yard operators. Coal yard operators cited the wage rates they had established February 1, and which they had posted in their yards. Nothing, they asserted, needed to be negotiated, for they had established a fair wage scale.

On February 9, William Brown met in an executive session of the Regional Labor Board. There he dropped all demands except the demand for recognition of the union and that demand he softened significantly. The Minneapolis *Tribune* reported:

> This demand did not include insistence that all men employed be members of the union, but meant that the union would be the agent for negotiations between its members at work on trucks or in the yards, and the employers.
>
> Workers not members of the union would be left free to make their own agreements.[14]

The coal dock retailers had hoped to create a public impression that they felt concern for employees' welfare and wished to pay a reasonable wage. They offered to discuss complaints with any individual employee who wished to present them. Their problem was that no employee had stepped forward with a complaint; instead, an outside group calling itself Local 574 purported to speak for their employees. Coal dock operators agreed that if their workers convinced them that this outside group legitimately spoke for them, they would confer with it. Under no circumstances, however, would they confer exclusively with the union; they would never agree to a closed shop. That, they asserted, would be unfair to their loyal employees.

The union cut the ground from under the employers when they reduced their demands, insisting only that the coal dock retailers recognize the union as representing its members. In the face of such a reasonable demand, the employers refusal created an image of recalcitrant, inflexible men. Local 574 succeeded in embarrassing the coal dock retailers, but the power to embarrass does not assure power to defeat. The Regional Labor Relations Board had revealed its powerlessness to the union as well, for it could not even persuade, let alone compel the employers to meet in the same room with the Union. If the Union hoped to succeed, it would have to find power within itself to prosecute its strike.

Strike strategists ruled out conventional picketing, for coal yards were located throughout the city. Could one picket a truck driving down the street? Perhaps. The union devised an unconventional method they called "flying squads" of three or four strikers who patrolled the various coal yards in cars or trucks. Each car or truck carried a driver experienced in the operation of coal trucks. Drivers' experience proved invaluable when a flying squad attempted to stop a truck on delivery; one of the strikers would leap on the running board, reach inside the cab and pull the emergency brake. While he talked to the scabbing driver, another striker would pull the dump lever and deposit the entire load in the street.[15] Strike leaders thus created a way to obstruct coal deliveries, but they also needed ways to facilitate communications, to control rumors, deflect public criticism, and keep striking workers together.

Organizers worked to sustain strikers' morale, which "was kept high by nightly meetings."[16] In one coal yard where orders for relief coal were filled (quarter-ton orders of coal paid for by local government to be delivered to people on relief), the union installed their own weighmasters, including Vince Dunne, and provided their own drivers to make the deliveries.[17]

The strike lasted three days. On Saturday morning, February 10th, the workers returned to their jobs and "business was proceeding as usual."[18] Recognition of the union was the only demand Local

574 believed it had won, but with recognition came an orderly means of resolving conflicts. Employers in the coal yards would have to negotiate work conditions and wages once they accepted recognition. Given the militant posture of the Citizens Alliance, one cannot but puzzle over its silence and the rapid conclusion of the strike, and over apparently granting recognition, something the Alliance had refused so adamantly to grant. Harry deBoer offered one reasonable explanation.

> One of the reasons, in my opinion, they finally agreed to settle the coal strike with a substantial raise and a contract is the coal industry was seasonal. This was already in February. March, the season is over and the workers go somewhere else. They felt, well, we aren't going to have to lose that much. Maybe we'll have to pay these wages for March and part of April, and next fall we won't hire any of these union men. But they failed to see that the rest of the drivers started to organize. We had a union; by then we had all of the drivers under contracts. If they had any idea that the coal strike would organize the rest of the drivers, they could have defeated us, a small group of workers in a seasonal industry. They did try to fire some of them, but the union was strong enough to put them back on the job. So that is one mistake they made.[19]

The issues of representation and recognition were to be resolved through elections. The Regional Labor Board, which entered the controversy early in the strike, arranged the elections after both the union and the employers notified the Board that they would accept the agreement. W. W. Hughes, executive secretary of the Minneapolis-St. Paul Regional Labor Board, set machinery in motion, "ordering" a certified list of the employees from the employers, so elections could be held within the week.[20] In the elections so ordered, and held February 14th and 15th, Local 574 won in nearly every yard.[21]

Some subtleties of the strike settlement foreshadowed continuing difficulties between Local 574 and employers. First, the employers refused to meet face to face with representatives of the union. They had considered the union demands, they noted, and had yielded on them. In their own minds, they could assert that they had not actually recognized the union, because they had not actually joined the union at the bargaining table. They had merely considered their

demands, accepted some, and rejected others. This symbolic aloof-
ness from the actual proceedings revealed a powerful determination
to refuse to recognize the Union. They had, in fact, only accepted
mediation by the Regional Labor Board and acquiesced to their
order. Second, although the Regional Labor Board "ordered" the
men to return to work, it waited until both employers and union
assured them they would comply. As subsequent events and attitudes prove, neither union nor employers harbored illusions as to
the board's strength. All three parties postured themselves in an
emerging ritual whose appearance implied more substance than was
really there. Both Union and employer played the role of yielding to
the Board's orders. Local 574 appeared simply to acquiesce; the
employers hoped to create a public impression of patriotic cooperation; despite their better judgment, they would yield to the state.
They could credibly assert that they did not enter the agreement of
their own free will, and thus they had not freely recognized Local
574; they yielded to the orders of the Regional Labor Board.

Employer recalcitrance emerges dramatically clear in the
"UNIFORM EMPLOYMENT RELATIONS POLICY OF COAL
DEALERS" dated February 19, 1934, which was apparently issued as
a guide for dealing with the union.[22] It declared: "It is agreed and
understood that, until otherwise agreed, we will be governed by the
following employment relations policies." The salient provisions are:

3.   No contract will be signed with any labor union or committee,
     whether or not the closed union shop is demanded.
4.   Supervision of the hiring and discharging of employes [sic] shall
     continue to be vested solely in the management and not to be
     subject to the approval of committee representing employes.
5.   Employes to be engaged, retained, or discharged, solely on the
     basis of merit.[23]

Recognition without a signed contract is empty. Vesting all rights
of employment in the hands of management eliminates the possibility of grievance review procedures, and resting employment on the
basis of merit rejects the seniority system Local 574 wished implemented. The strike had ended with employer recognition of Local
574, but the Uniform Policy suggests that the employers had only
acknowledged that Local 574 existed.

Sam Levy, a Citizens Alliance attorney, participated in the settlement.[24] The Citizens Alliance had surely been an interested observer from the outset, but Levy's appearance is the first clear proof that the coal employers' issues had not been isolated to the coal yards. The Citizens Alliance began to play an active role.

William Brown's prediction came true. The success of the coal strike brought members by the hundreds into the ranks of the union. At the Saturday night forums conducted by the union, new members would pay their dollar initiation fee and want to know when they could go on strike.[25] In April Local 574's forums had grown large enough to rent the Shubert Theater for $66 from its owner, Minneapolis Mayor A. G. Bainbridge.[26] Vince Day, Governor Floyd B. Olson's secretary and a "true friend of labor," attended the forum to read Governor Olson's letter in which he praised the union: "Out of assemblies such as yours come whatever benefits the working class is enjoying today." He sketched briefly the importance of cooperation, and lamented the terrible violence workers had faced historically, but over which workers had triumphed. He noted that "Vested interests have gone the limit in their attempt to defeat the union idea because they knew that complete unionism meant the end of their reign of exploitation of the working man and woman." He listed advantages of union membership, and concluded: "It is my counsel, if you wish to accept it, that you should follow the sensible course and band together for your own protection and welfare."[27] Such encouragement lent legitimacy to the movement. Within months the membership of Local 574 increased more than tenfold. "Two thousand drivers and helpers were sporting union buttons by the end of April, and nearly 7,000 by mid-Summer."[28] Encouraged by workers' support, the leaders of Local 574 planned a larger organizing effort.

To sum up, Local 574's victory occurred more swiftly, and with more dramatic increases in membership than organizers had dreamed. The rank and file of the union grew beyond the network of friends and acquaintances who knew and trusted Bill Brown, Carl Skoglund, and Mickey, Grant and Vince Dunne. These personal ties had initially bound coal drivers together. In addition, since drivers owned their own trucks and knew each other, replacing drivers was difficult; any scab would have to own a truck to replace a striking worker. Scabs, therefore, had to come from the ranks of the active drivers who were not in the union, and even if these drivers rejected a union, they would hesitate to scab on their friends. Replacing strikers, then, proved difficult. A common work experience, a common interest, and friendship undoubtedly account for the high percentage of workers who responded so enthusiastically to the union's appeal. As Chris Moe recalled:

> We took a vote and said "By God, we'll go out on strike!" We had 34 members, and we went out and tied up the town. I just got like a fanatic, like a religion. I didn't care what happened.

Strike leaders found ways to take tactical advantage of circumstances. The union timed the strike to coincide with a cold spell, held nightly strike meetings to sustain morale, and created innovative means of picketing by organizing "flying squads" of workers whom they could quickly transport to a place of conflict. By withdrawing all demands except recognition, the union weakened employers' justification for resistance. Employer claims that the union did not represent their employees had little credibility in the face of the union's ability to close down their operations.

Coal yard owners and managers refused to capitulate, however, and, risking public censure, they even refused to meet with the union. Why they decided to relent enough to end the strike cannot be determined from historical records. Harry deBoer's speculation that the employers gave in to protect their seasonal profits, confident that they could break a union at the outset of the next heating season by the simple expedient of refusing to use any union drivers, may be credible, but subsequent negotiations reveal that coal yard owners intended to accept only limited negotiations with Local 574, and then only for actual members of the union. They assumed the posture that the "committee" from Local 574 could speak for those who had voted for it. Employers would negotiate separately with those who had not, and thus they divided the workers. We might also speculate that the Citizens Alliance chose to confront the union later when chances to defeat it were better, when they could array broader powers against the emerging union.

However we might speculate about motives, this confrontation was undoubtedly about power. Chris Moe put it well: "The bosses had it, and we didn't have it. The strike is the only weapon the worker has."[29]

Notes

1. Harry deBoer, interview, 31 July 1974.
2. Vincent R. Dunne Sr., interview with George Tselos, Minneapolis.
3. The issue of "inside" workers as distinct from "drivers" loomed large in the later strikes.
4. Vincent R. Dunne Sr., interview with George Tselos, Minneapolis.
5. Ibid.
6. Minneapolis *Labor Review*, 30 September 1932.
7. Dale Kramer, "The Dunne Boys of Minneapolis," *Harpers*, March 1942.
8. Minneapolis *Star*, 10 February 1934.
9. Record Group 25, Box 384, Folder 2, Minneapolis-St. Paul Regional Labor Board, 1 February 1934 "Confidential" report submitted by W. H. Hughes, Executive Secretary.
10. Ibid.
11. Ibid.
12. V. R. Dunne, interview with the author, Minneapolis, September 1964.
13. Record Group 25, Box 384, Folder 2. Report of 3 February meeting apparently submitted by Hughes shortly after the meeting.
14. Minneapolis *Tribune*, 9 February 1934.
15. V. R. Dunne, interview with the author, Minneapolis, September 1964. Many similar accounts appeared in newspapers at the time.
16. George H. Mayer, *The Political Career of Floyd B. Olson* (Minneapolis: University of Minnesota Press 1951), 189.
17. V. R. Dunne, interview with the author, Minneapolis, September 1964.
18. Minneapolis *Star*, 10 February 1934.
19. Harry deBoer, interview, Minneapolis, 31 July 1974.
20. Minneapolis *Star*, 10 February 1934.
21. Geroge D. Tselos, "The Minneapolis Labor Movement in the 1930s," (Ph.D. diss., University of Minnesota, 1970), 212.
22. No author is identified. Its form suggests that the Citizens Alliance played a role in its drafting.
23. Citizens Alliance of Minneapolis Papers, Box 1, Correspondence & Misc. Paper, 29 Jan. 1929-28 Oct. 1953, Minnesota Historical Society, St. Paul, Minnesota.
24. Mayer, *Floyd B. Olson*, 189.
25. V. R. Dunne, interview with the author, Minneapolis, September 1964.

26. Teamsters Local 574, M494, Minnesota Historical Society, St. Paul, Minnesota.

27. Letter from Floyd B. Olson to William Brown, 13 April 1934, M494, Minnesota Historical Society, St. Paul, Minnesota.

28. Mayer, *Floyd B. Olson*, 189.

29. Chris Moe, interview, Minneapolis, 1 August 1974.

5 | Voices

Voices of the Coal Strike

A STRIKE IS A COMPLEX event experienced by participants and bystanders in a variety of discrete ways. No individual at the time could experience the entire event. The historian writing after the strike attempts to create an integrated picture of large dimension, and in so doing risks losing the immediacy, the particularity in which the event actually transpired. Through something akin to a scrap book, I will present in chapters titled "Voices" edited individual oral accounts in order to recapture that intimacy.

Chris Moe (striker)

I don't know how I got the job in the coal yard. That was in '33. I had my own truck. I had a car and I traded that in and bought the truck. It was an old beat-up one; I worked the whole summer and rebuilt it—a little '28 Chevrolet. It was all by hand. Shovel it on and shovel it off.

Harvey Boscoe (laundry driver)

I came here in 1927 when dad[1] was supposed to be here for three months on labor trouble and he never got out of here. He came back here in '28 to live. I finished high school in June of '28.

Minneapolis at that time was supposed to have been one of the lowest paying cities in the country as far as wages and scab work. There was no labor movement at all to assure better wages or anything. At that time dad was with just the printing trades because he was International Organizer, but as he got here and developed with the other groups in the city he got tied in with the entire city and some of the state organizations. So it turned out to be, in place of a three-month job, his lifetime work here eventually.

This architect I worked for folded up in '33 and I drove a truck those two years after that during the strike. The following year I went back into more or less architecture work, building these miniature buildings for the architect. Where the client couldn't read a blue-print, we'd build a small model with the trees and shrubs. We were doing that locally and then one month for *Better Homes and Gardens* magazine.

The office I worked in was on 10th and Nicollet in the Essex Building and Gross Brothers was right next door. The architect had to close his office because everything went to pot. Through the local cigar stand in the building where we all met from Gross Brothers and different ones, I heard that they needed workers over there and got in, first as a checker checking the drivers in. Then this one driver at Lake Minnetonka went bad, on collections etc., so they wanted me to take over for a while and I ended up with a job as a driver. I must have started driving on Lake Minnetonka route in the winter of '33. Then and I drove all of '34 and all of '35. Well, each driver was on more or less whatever he agreed to. I. D. Fink at that time was the manager of Gross Brothers and nobody knew whether there was a basic salary or not. In my case it was a guaranteed salary of $20 a week in the winter time and in the summer on, say over $200 a week gross sales, you would get a certain commission.

You had to get five more customers per week. You had to keep shuffling; besides the people you were dealing with, you had to call next door, trying to bring more people. You had a quota you had to meet every week and as I said each driver was more or less on his own basis with the management as to what salary he was getting. Nobody knew for sure what the other was getting and of course there was no union, no set wages, and no set hours. You worked until you got your truck empty or you just gave out for the day. In my case I had the $20 a week guarantee so that we could eat.

In the summer I was supposed to get my commission. In those years all the homes in Minnetonka were clapboard; they were summer places, so they moved in and out with the seasons. So in the summer all the customers moved way out there and business picked way up and come to find out my checks never got any bigger during the summer. I said why? They took me in and showed me the books, how much I went in the hole during the winter. They were holding what I hadn't made in the winter out of my summer commissions so I wound up practically at $20 per week. They didn't tell you that when you started. They were just being good to you, and give you a guaranteed salary, but they didn't tell you they would take it back out to make up the difference.

There was no recourse. If you hollered loud enough, you had no job either. There was no organization, and those who tried to organize, the company heard about it, they were out. Gradually enough of the drivers started to see the light on this whole thing and were going to form their own group. To counteract that, the company said "no, we will form the company union. You appoint your own men, and we will meet with you and settle all the differences." Of course they were trying to keep everything still in the company, and would dictate to you. While they were still down on 10th & Nicollet, Gross and different ones in the family called this meeting to start this company union to give the employees a better shake, but it was only a desperation move to keep the union out.

It seems to me that this was preliminary to the truck strike. I can't remember now. What makes me think so, I had talked to Dad about being in that low bracket end and he was with the Central Labor Union. But driving at Minnetonka, I got out and this last night when this was coming to a head with 574, the boys called a halt to all movement of the trucks. So all I could come was Oak Knolls: half way in from Wayzata, park the truck and come in by private car.

But it was surprising what you could buy for $5.00 in those days. You could buy a whole week's worth of groceries. We would go to Spring Park and with a coaster wagon and just load it full for the whole week for a five dollar bill. Even on a $20 a week guarantee, it wasn't too bad.

Harry deBoer (Executive Committee, Local 574)

I was born in Crookston, Minnesota in 1907. I done a little boxing when I was a kid. Started chasing around the country. I was a member of the IWW. When I was a member, they were sliding backwards already in a sense. Then I went to work in Missouri as a truck driver on a construction job in 1930 or '31. I finally worked up to be the traffic manager, and I got sick of it and started back towards the Twin Cities where my wife was already. Got here and there wasn't no work outside of doing work in the coal yard, which I went to work in the coal yard.

My father was a farmer. As a matter of fact he was a member of the Non-Partisan league. He was pretty well known in that area. He drove Governor Olson around and introduced him to various farmers, as I remember, during the campaign's early days. So I was sympathetic to the socialists at that time. I never did much reading on it until I got acquainted with Carl Skoglund and the Dunnes and then we started to organize.

Floyd Olson was governor. One of our organizational meetings we invited him to attend and he agreed to, but instead of coming he sent Day, his secretary and read a letter from him telling the workers to organize. We used that continually, telling what the governor said, and it helped organize the workers too of course.

I recall, and it was before I was actually familiar with what was going on, when we come to vote to accept the coal strike contract, I was one to get the members down to the hall to vote so I was one of the last ones to come to the hall because of that. Kelley Postal and I, we all really had agreed that we were going to accept this contract. It wasn't as good as expected, but we couldn't go no further. We'd probably lose support and probably lose the strike so we sat down and Bill Brown, who was the chairman of the Union and this hall was full and he said this meeting is going to be held for the coal workers and yard workers and all those who aren't members would leave. Well, there was at least 100 workers who left the hall. Kelley and I said what's going on? I found out later they were in there to vote against the contract. They weren't members of the Union; they were members of the Communist Party.

With the coal strike, there was I don't know how many yards and little yards and it was impossible to have a picket line big enough to stop trucks from moving. So a lot of times we just organized a "roving picket" we called it, with squads out, just looking around. We'd have one man in the yard, and he would call us if they were going to send a truck out and we would send a squad out and a car and a truck. If they got out on the street, we would dump their coal and send them back and tell them, now look we're fighting for these conditions, and you're a worker and you should be helping us rather than trying to defeat us.

In most cases, they went back and didn't come back. Of course, if they would have, they would have been dealt accordingly. We give them a chance and it worked out. That was true both in May and in the July strike. We had cruising pickets and they just cruised around, looking from one warehouse to another to see what was going on. If it looked like there was something stirring, they'd call and we'd probably send a crew down to investigate.

Harry Pfaff (driver)

I was in the coal drivers' strike. We were getting 90 cents a ton for hauling coal and we wanted a dollar. Before the strike they raised the price of coal to take care of the ten cents, fifty cents a ton. And after that strike they said they had to have another fifty cents a ton to take care of that ten cents a ton. They would give us that ten cents, so that's why we went out on strike. We didn't work by the hour. We worked by the ton. We owned our own trucks. If we made twelve dollars a day, we had a big day's work. The fact of the matter was we were working hard and starving to death.

Ed Ryan (Minneapolis policeman 1925-1947; Sheriff, Hennepin County, 1947-1967)

I didn't blame those men for striking. For many years a common laborer in this city was nothing better than a serf. Those who had a trade, like carpenters, or plumbers, they had a chance because they could organize, but the common laborer had no chance at all. I know something about that, because as a young lad, 1912, 1913, 1915, along in there, I drove a team of horses for one of the big transfer companies in Minneapolis. My father drove a team of horses for the same company. My father was a common laborer. He was born on a farm out here in what is now Edina. My ancestors were territorial pioneers in Minnesota, settled out in Edina around 1855-56. My father had no skill, no trade, but he knew horses, wagons. The best he could do when he came to the city was find a job as a common laborer.

We had to be at the barn at six o'clock in the morning. Be there at six, regardless of the weather. We rode in streetcars down there. We had to clean out the stables, water and feed the horses, harness them, hook them up to our wagon, and be out on the street at seven o'clock in the morning. All day long we hauled heavy freight. I think the pay was around ten, twelve dollars a week, and we were lucky to get that.

The owner of this company told me one day, "You know we like to have people like your father work for us. They have no skill and they have to work. They have large families."

So I never blamed these people, the Dunne brothers and the rest of them, for striking.

Office of the Minneapolis/St. Paul Regional Labor Board[2]
Meeting: Friday afternoon, February 23, 1934

J. B. Beardslee (spokesperson for coal yard operators): We understand there has been an election and a large number of our men want you, as a committee, to deal with us for them, and the Labor Board has called us together and we will be very glad to discuss the things that you represent with you. . . .

Clifford Hall (business agent for Local 574): . . . I would say that the first thing to do in my estimation, would be to consider our agreement, unless you people have a counter agreement to offer us. Did you people draw up a counter agreement of any kind?

Beardslee: I would say that the committee is empowered to perpetuate our present wage scale, including conditions of employment, and to agree in writing with the Labor Board to perpetuate that scale, until April 1, 1935. . . .

Hall: . . . In other words, you will go along with the Union under a verbal agreement. Is that the idea?

Beardslee: . . . I have already said we are willing to make an agreement with the Labor Board in writing. . . .

Hall: . . . I have an article here that we would like to have put in writing and signed by you people and it goes as follows: "All employees that have been employed previous to signing this agreement and who are eligible to membership, shall have seniority rights in yards that they previously worked at."

Beardslee: What do you mean by signing this agreement?

Hall: . . . You say you are going to sign an agreement with the Labor Board. . . .

Beardslee: Yes.

William Brown (president of Local 574): I claim that we represent a majority of the men, and not the Labor Board. It is just side stepping and getting away from the Union. . . .

Hall: . . . All of these men that work in your yards became members of this organization. You people were well aware of that. These people voted that we should represent the men, not the Labor Board, and my contention and idea is that you gentlemen should sign an official agreement with the local Union, not the Labor Board. . . . In so far as you gentlemen signing an agreement with the Labor Board, that is out of the question.

Beardslee: That we cannot do. We will sign an agreement with the Labor Board or with any Court, that we will perpetuate the present scale.

Hall: Then I don't see we have any reason to meet with you whatever. . . .

William Nelson (coal yard owner): Mr. Hall, I don't feel that because you and we disagree on one thing, that we throw it out entirely. I don't think that is fair to either side. We said that we would recognize a committee, and we don't agree on just one item.

Vincent R. Dunne: I would like to interject this thought: on this thing hinges the whole thing. A vote was taken at the yards and they have a ruling in the Labor Board that the majority has the rights. We didn't vote that the Regional Labor Board represent us. We voted for the General Drivers Union.

Beardslee: There is a difference of opinion between the Labor Board on the one hand and our legal advisers on the other, as to the interpretations of the N.I.R.A. law. Now you are, on your side, depending on the Labor Board's interpretation that you truly represent all of the workers in these yards. We, on the other hand, on advice of counsel, feel that you do not represent all of the men but we concede that you, as a committee, represent the men that voted for your committee. . . .

Hall: We are vitally interested in having an agreement signed with us and not with the Labor Board because if trouble arose, what would we do? The Labor Board would have to deal with us.

Nelson: We would meet with you now or next week. Are there any vital difficulties between the employees and the employers outside of the question of an open or closed shop?

Hall: We don't want a closed shop.

Nelson: Outside of the proposition that you are asking for a union agreement, what difficulties have we to thrash out?

Hall: Conditions in the yard and wages.

Nelson: Are you prepared to say what they are?

Hall: Yes but I can see no reason why we should continue unless we get the correct interpretation as to whether you will sign an agreement with us and our organization or whether you intend to sign with the Labor Board.

Nelson: This committee has not refused to work with you.

Dunne: What kind of an agreement would you care to sign and what have we to ensure us that it would be carried out?

Nelson: Past performance shows that we will carry out any agreement we make.

Notes

1. Harvey's father was J. B. Boscoe, Business Agent of the Printing Pressmen's Union, and in 1934 a member of the Minneapolis-St. Paul Regional Labor Board.
2. RG 25, Box 384, National Archives.

6 | The May Strike

THE COAL STRIKE, LOCAL 574 concluded, achieved qualified success. The meeting in late February between union representatives and coal dock retailers made it clear to the Union that real collective bargaining had not been achieved, but they were at least sitting at the same table and that might lead to talk about wages and working conditions. Objectively, a small number of workers had conducted a successful strike against a few employers. After all, coal drivers comprised only a small proportion of truck drivers, and so an even smaller part of the city labor force. It was not uncommon for local employers to respond to a successful union drive, as had the coal dealers, by increasing wages in order to blunt organizers' appeals. That did not happen widely in Minneapolis. Clearly Minneapolis employers had not been persuaded by Local 574's success in the coal yards to adjust their dealings with employees. The coal strike did not, then, improve working conditions and wages in the trucking industry, nor in the general labor community of Minneapolis. However, Local 574 had survived a strike, and wages for coal yard workers had improved.

This modest success had a powerful effect on Minneapolis drivers. Workers from all segments of the trucking industry flocked to union headquarters. Harry deBoer recalled,

We went back to work and news spread like wildfire. The workers, truck drivers mainly, went down to the coal yards. They wanted the leadership of the coal drivers to organize them, nobody else. They'd walk up to the Central Labor Union and the first thing they said was "Where's that union that organized the coal drivers?" That was proven that they had a leadership who knew what to do and wouldn't sell them out. Up to that point there was a lot of unions that went on strike and got sold out by the leaders and let down.

The resulting explosion of membership emboldened workers to organize, and organizers helped these workers recognize the pivotal position they held in the Minneapolis economy.

Minneapolis depended heavily on trucking to distribute goods brought in by rail. George Mayer, Floyd Olson's biographer, asserted that "The indispensable role of motor transportation in the commercial life of the city made the truck driver the obvious spearhead for any union drive." Some organizers certainly hoped for this role; certainly the coal strike's success improved chances for a successful general organizing drive. Without question, the coal drivers' success had special significance for Minneapolis workers. In contrast, shortly before the coal drivers signed their agreement, the upholsterers' union conducted a successful strike which undoubtedly encouraged workers, but did not lead to a broad organizing drive. Perhaps the mass of workers could not so readily identify with the upholsterers' narrower craft base; the skills employed in distributing coal were available to every worker. The average worker could easily see himself working in the coal yard, either driving or carrying.

Awareness that the truck drivers had power emerged from the coal strike itself. George Mayer declared that both employers and drivers began to recognize that "by walking off the job, [the driver] could virtually shut down industrial activity in Minnesota. Such a threat provided powerful leverage to pry union recognition from employers."[1] Few rank and file drivers aspired to disrupt the entire industrial system in Minnesota, and leaders of the organizing drive, whatever their ultimate aspirations, focused their attention on warehousing and distribution of perishable fruits and vegetables in the market district of Minneapolis, and most specifically on eleven major employers. Encouraged by the rapid increase in their ranks, and sensitive to the drivers' desire to strike, Local 574's leaders developed a strategy and opened their campaign. "On April 30, Local 574 . . . announced its demands: the closed shop, shorter hours, an average wage of $27.50 a week, and extra pay for overtime."[2]

Employers to whom the union sent demands called a meeting that same day at the West Hotel and formed a committee to meet with the Regional Labor Board. W. M. Hardin and Joseph Cochran conveyed information between the Regional Labor Board and committee members. They eventually came to act as spokespersons in subsequent negotiations and public statements purporting to represent the views of all trucking employers. Although only representatives of the eleven major trucking firms attended this first meeting, the group soon enlarged to include 166 firms.

Throughout negotiations Hardin and Cochran presented themselves as spokespersons for a "general employers' committee." From the outset they declared they had limited powers; they carried proposals back to the committee itself. Since they adopted no official title, I will refer to them as the General Advisory Committee (GAC), with the caution that such a title implies a more formal organization than initially existed.

When employers organized this group, however loose its structure, the strike escalated from a conflict between a fledgling union and the few employers it hoped to organize, to a broader confrontation between Minneapolis employers and workers of Minneapolis. The Citizens Alliance had begun to prepare for the organizing drive in March when it invited Minneapolis employers to a meeting to asked them to join its efforts to save Minneapolis from the Closed Shop and Communist revolution, a meeting which Farrel Dobbs, strike Committee member, infiltrated.[3] Although not all members of the GAC belonged to the Citizens Alliance, Joseph Cochran served as a Citizens Alliance Director. Formation of the General Advisory Committee was an impressive demonstration by the Citizens Alliance of its organizing power in the trucking industry. The conflict, thus, began to assume dimensions that eventually would involve nearly all segments of the Minneapolis community.

The General Advisory Committee charged that Local 574 did not represent employees of the 166 firms. That was, of course true. The GAC was, after all, formed by employers and was not designated by the Union as those firms to whom it directed its demands. One can readily see the strategies of the two groups even in these initial moves. The union targeted a limited number of larger employers in an effort to focus the strike, for that improved its ability to manage the situation and conduct a successful strike. To conduct a broader strike against large numbers of employers would have required sophisticated organization, extensive resources, and a large cadre of organizers. What was good for the union was bad for the targeted employers whose chances of defeating the union would be improved by stretching the union's resources as thin as possible. If the GAC could transform a dispute between a few employers and their workers into a broad struggle between respectable community leaders, who rose to defend their loyal workers against a disreputable, revolutionary cadre, then they might generate public support that would assure successful resistance. Ironically, the GAC strategy implied that the confrontation between eleven trucking firms and their workers was, in reality, an dialectical struggle between two classes, a struggle that might determine the form and quality of life in the entire community of Minneapolis.

The first face-to-face meeting between Local 574 and the General Advisory Committee took place May 1, 1934 in the office of W. W. Hughes, Secretary of the Minneapolis-St. Paul Regional Labor Board. The meeting was inconclusive because the Union and GAC wanted to discuss different matters. For example, the Union wanted to know specifically whom W. M. Hardin and Joseph Cochran represented. Hardin and Cochran refused to answer, but agreed to seek permission from the GAC to respond. In a letter dated May 3 they identified no specific firms but rather asserted that they represented "industrial and business groups employing truck drivers in the city of Minneapolis."[4] W. W. Hughes, Executive Secretary of the Regional Labor Board wrote to Hardin May 5: "Will you kindly advise us what companies are represented under . . . Wholesale Houses and Packing Houses?"[5] The GAC never met this request.

On May 7, the Union placed its demands before the Labor Board, including specific wages and working conditions. However, the Union asked the Labor Board not to forward these demands to the GAC until the closed shop question had been resolved. The Union also included a list of those workers whom the Union represented.[6] In a May 7 letter to W. W. Hughes, the General Advisory Committee refused to send representatives to meet with the Union, and declared its principled opposition to the closed shop. The GAC further established that its relationship with the Labor Board was based on "courtesy" rather than recognition of the Board's authority, and, revealing more anxiety than intended, the GAC protested that Local 574 had tried to intimidate its spokesmen.

1. The undersigned Committee does not recognize the General Drivers' Union Local #574 as truly representing the employees of the firms in the groups for whom we appear. No proof of any kind has ever been furnished by Local #574 or its committee or officers that it has any authority to represent any employees of the various firms represented in such groups.

2. This communication of May 7, 1934 [from the union] refers to an alleged agreement entered into in your office on May 1st between a committee representing a certain group of employers and a committee representing Local #574, claiming that by this agreement the committee of employers whom they represented would give them authority to negotiate with the committee of Local #574 for a settlement of all controversies.

   Such statement as to any agreement of May 1st, of this nature or character is not in accordance with the facts. On May 1, 1934, two members of our Committee were invited to your office for an informal discussion, with certain members of Local #574 as to what, if any, the demands were, and as to the threatened General Drivers' Strike. In courtesy to you as an official of the Minneapolis-St. Paul Regional Labor Board, these two members of our Committee appeared at your office.

   When they got there, they were met by a group of approximately 15 representatives of Local #574, accompanied by an attorney and a stenographer. At that time these representatives of Local #574 requested that the representatives of our committee furnish signatures of all employers whom they were representing, together with other written evidence of authority to negotiate for these employers. Our two representatives, Messrs. Hardin and Cochran, at that time declined to accede to such request, but they did state that they would submit this request to their full committee, which was done. There upon, under date of May 3, 1934, this full committee presented you with a written communication, stating the groups employing truck drivers in the City of Minneapolis whom they represented and also stating that there was no reason for any further meeting or negotiation with any committee representing Local #574 until specific grievances were presented or demands made upon employers represented in the foregoing groups. . . .

3. In the communication addressed to you under date of May 7, 1934, the General Drivers' Union states that it is submitting demands covering agreements for wages, working conditions and hours of work for the various groups named in that communication. However, the only thing submitted to our committee, through your office with respect to that communication is a copy of a proposed form of contract that the General Drivers' Union insists the employers must sign. That proposed contract is a typical, standard closed union shop contract which provides that no employer can employ anyone in connection with deliveries, transfer or trucking unless that employee shall be member in good standing of Local 574.

This proposed contract compels membership in Local #574 as a condition of employment and closes the door to all laborers who are not members of this local union.

Such proposed contract is strictly and directly in violation of the spirit and intent of Section 7a of the National Industrial Recovery Act, and the demand for such closed union shop agreement is hereby definitely rejected.

The firms we represent will not deny employment to any workman because of his affiliation or non-affiliation with any union or any other organization.[7]

GAC's attempts to drag out the negotiation failed, for the Union met each demand. It presented the Labor Board detailed proposals concerning wages and working conditions. Even the question of representation, the Union agreed, could be answered if the employers would negotiate on the demand for the closed shop. Faced with dissipation of these issues, the GAC retreated behind the closed shop issue and proclaimed it would defend the working man's right to work without requiring that he join a union. Because the Union demanded that they violate this high principle, they refused to meet with representatives of Local 574. They very pointedly assumed the Labor Board's lack of authority when they warned it that they had met with them only as a matter of "courtesy." By Wednesday, May 9, the situation deadlocked.

On May 10, the dispute moved to the front page of the local newspapers when the union issued its deadline,[8] and on May 12

Neil Cronin wired Washington requesting that a mediator be sent. Sunday, May 13, the union called a mass meeting for Monday night to decide whether to strike. Brown advised, "The closed shop is the big issue," and W. M. Hardin of the General GAC' Committee replied that there was no sense even to arbitrate on the closed shop issue. Wages and hours, he declared, could be arbitrated, but not the closed shop.[9]

The Citizens Alliance warned its members of the impending attempt at "starving the community into submission," and identified the headquarters of the GAC in Room 126 of the West Hotel where they should call for current information. Members were advised "not to send out any trucks" until they called this headquarters. Moreover, it warned, "Officers of the General Drivers' Union have frankly stated through the press *that their main objective is unionization of every truck driver in Minneapolis, and closed union shop control of all primary transportation.*"[10]

The Regional Labor Board appointed a sub-committee of two to investigate. William Penn and Guy Alexander were able to hold a conference immediately after the Board's morning session with Union representatives, but were not so successful with the GAC.

> Repeated efforts were made during the day to get in touch with the employers' representatives who held a session at the West Hotel Friday afternoon. Late last night [May eleven] a representative of the employers advised Mr. Penn that the Chairman of the employers' committee had left town Friday evening and therefore there could be no conference with the employers' representatives until Monday.[11]

Subsequent attempts by the Regional Labor Board to call the GAC to a hearing received a stinging rebuttal:

> We do not appear generally as consenting to nor admitting any jurisdiction on the part of your Board to, at this time, conduct any hearing on this matter; our appearance must therefore be noted as a special appearance, objecting, at all times, to the conduct of any hearing and refusing to concede or accede to any jurisdiction on the part of your Board with reference to any so-called hearing.
>
> We will, however, be pleased to enter into any informal discussion of this matter that may be necessary.[12]

In an informal meeting called by the Regional Labor Board and held at the Nicollet Hotel Monday morning, representatives from the GAC and officers of Local 574 met and discussed the issue of representation informally. The GAC refused to put anything in writing, particularly any statement that would guarantee no discrimination against union members, a practice with which Local 574 had had experience in the coal yards. William Brown addressed the GAC's Ivan Bowen who had declared that the employers would abide by Section 7a:

> There are members of this association [GAC] here who have told their men flatly that if they join a union they will fire them. Is that Section 7-A? If they do fire them what proof have we got that they were fired because they joined a union? I don't know what the employers' position is. I don't want a strike, but it appears to me that the employers want one.[13]

Ivan Bowen responded:

> For you to come in here and ask us to say that we are violating Section 7-A and therefore we are going to sign a new agreement, is putting the employer into a hole that no respectable man is concerned in getting into. You want us to admit in effect that we violated Section 7-A and in the future won't violate it.[14]

The GAC representatives returned again and again to the issue of the closed shop, which it refused to accept. No other controversy existed it declared. When the meeting adjourned and the Labor Board turned to an executive session, Chairman Neil Cronin lamented: "Somebody told me he understood the employers were agreeable."[15]

The GAC's position in this exchange with the Board, and in the conference that ensued was not a public matter. However, the GAC's public posture appealed for public support for upholding workers' basic freedom of choice. The dispute with Local 574, the GAC declared, would be fought out on the high plane of principle, rather than the base, perhaps confusing plane of money and profits.

In a surprise move on the afternoon of May 15, the Union undercut the GAC's high moral ground and shifted the dispute to a more mundane plane. In place of its demand for a closed shop, the Union substituted demands for a reaffirmation of Section 7a, for a priority rule in layoffs and rehiring, for a Board of arbitration and, most objectionable to the GAC, a demand that employers sign this agreement with the Union.[16] The GAC responded that "there is no requirement of law that any employer enter into any written agreement of any kind or nature with any organization, whether a labor union or otherwise."[17] The GAC refused to meet again with Local 574.

The Union's withdrawal of the closed shop demand created a public image of restraint and reflected an effort to recapture the high ground from employers. The GAC had no intention of yielding, but found difficulty in formulating a credible, powerful response equal to the principled position from which they had been unhorsed. They declared that they already had pledged to uphold Section 7a by signing their NIRA codes and that they would rather contract with the government than with a union. "Questions of priority," they advised, "can and should be settled by negotiations between employees of each concern and the management without intervention by unions."[18]

Ingenuously the GAC declared that no wage demands had been made by individual employees to any member of the General Advisory Committee. Since the Labor Board possessed these demands, the GAC's claim had little credibility. Although prepared to confront Local 574, the GAC found itself on the eve of the strike disadvantaged in a defensive position. Anyone following developments readily understood that the employers simply refused to recognize *any* union. Monday night May 14, at a scheduled mass meeting attended by approximately 2,500, workers rejected the Labor Board's call for delay and voted to begin the strike at midnight.

The GAC's campaign during the weeks leading up to the strike sought to enlist public sympathy. Clearly they perceived this struggle as a conflict that transcended the economic dispute between an employer and his organized employees. This search for approval led them to broaden the conflict, to attempt to marshal the entire community to the struggle, and to characterize the striking workers as social and political outsiders whose hidden agenda threatened the peace and tranquillity of Minneapolis. They tried to convince workers and businessmen of Minneapolis that to combat this menace the public welfare should safely remain in the hands of respected, responsible, businessmen.

Responding to this campaign, union leaders made their own public appeals. Since no employers would meet with them to negotiate a contract, indeed, since no employer would even recognize them, they had to accept the field the GAC chose. They too would struggle for the hearts and minds of the citizens of Minneapolis. They would attempt to convince Minneapolitans that the dispute could best be resolved by direct negotiations between union and employers, that the public welfare could best be served by such negotiations. Businessmen, they argued, represented only one interest within the community. Union leaders preferred a simpler, dialectic conflict with employers. After all, their ideological disposition led them to see in this organizing strike the seeds of social, political, and economic revolution; they did not refuse the broader arena, but they did measure their response carefully. They believed that in the struggle for the hearts and minds of the citizens of Minneapolis, they could not rely on the newspapers to tell their story accurately. Consequently they developed their own paper, *The Organizer*, which they distributed to the workers they hoped would support them.

On the eve of the strike one must be impressed by three facts about the union leaders' tactics. First, they controlled their vision of social, political and economic revolution, and focused their planning and practice on concrete principles of union organization. Second, they managed the broader arena very well indeed, capturing the high ground from the General Advisory Committee and its shadow cadre, the Citizens' Alliance. Third, they understood the importance of communicating with the workers of Minneapolis, for the Union's success depended on workers' support.

During the first few weeks of May, behind the scenes in the Minneapolis labor movement, a conflict arose that would prove troublesome for Local 574, uncomfortable for the rest of organized labor, and a source of hope and ammunition for GAC. When Local 574 requested permission to strike, the Teamsters' International Union denied it. The letter of denial from Dan Tobin, President of the International, also declared that Local 574 did not have the right to represent "inside workers" which the Union recruited.[19]

As a local of the International Teamsters, Local 574 had been a member of the Central Labor Union of Minneapolis since the

1920s. The leaders of Local 574, who had become widely popular in the Minneapolis labor movement, continued to send representatives to the CLU's meetings despite their difficulties with the Teamster Brotherhood. This information reached AFL headquarters, which sent a representative to the Minneapolis to advise the CLU to keep Local 574 out, or the AFL might pull the CLU charter. It was suggested from the floor that the representative be escorted out and down the stairs head first.[20] He left of his own accord, as did Local 574, leaving the issue of Local 574's participation still unresolved. CLU members certainly sympathized with Local 574, but the CLU dared not intervene officially for fear of losing its charter. This fear may account for the CLU's reticence during the May strike.

Dan Tobin's declaration that inside workers did not fall within the union's jurisdiction, and his suspension of Local 574, served GAC well, of course, but the real issue between Tobin and Local 574 arose from conflicting perceptions of union organization. Tobin attempted to direct attention away from philosophy by focusing on jurisdiction and by attacking the Local leaders' radicalism. Of course the two were related. Tobin's commitment to craft jurisdiction articulated a conservative tradition in union organizing theory that argued that only workers with a common skill were organizable. Like most craft union leaders, he rejected industrial forms of organization. Industrial unionists argued that modern production methods debased crafts, transforming workers into semi-skilled or unskilled machine tenders. Thus organizing workers in the same industry, regardless of specific work skills, offered their only realistic hope to regain modest worker control of their lives.

For example, in a trucking operation, one would find drivers, helpers who rode along with drivers, dock workers who loaded trucks, warehousemen who brought wares to the dock, checkers who made certain that dockmen loaded trucks correctly for a specific delivery route and that orders were filled accurately, clerks who distributed and processed orders, traffic managers who made certain that warehouses held the right quantity and type of goods. Where should the line of jurisdiction be drawn? Only drivers and helpers actually left companies to deliver. But a dock worker provided a service essential to deliveries, and not infrequently he might fill in as helper on a deliver route. Each operation required identifiable skills.

Should there be a union for each: one for drivers, one for helpers, one for dock workers, one for warehousemen, one for checkers.? Such a mode of organization, industrial unionists argued, weakened worker solidarity because it isolated workers who could then be readily replaced. One union should include all these workers, they argued, for only then could a union shut down an operation in a strike. Advocates of industrial unionism, then, tended to think in terms of large scale unions, and of broad social, political and economic implications to organizing. Not infrequently they joined or led radical political movements and thus strained the AFL policy of focusing on economic rather than political issues.

The suspension of Local 574 from the AFL had the potential of causing rifts within the Minneapolis labor movement and within Local 574 itself, which could destroy the union. However, rank and file members felt greater loyalty to local leaders than to Dan Tobin. Tobin's assertion that inside workers should be excluded from Local 574's jurisdiction did provide ammunition for GAC publicity and undermined with the public Local 574's insistence that they be included.

Despite these difficulties with the Teamster International and the AFL, the morning of May 16th found 5,000 workers, by union estimates, on strike. Union coal drivers were allowed to pass, as were union milk and beer truck drivers. The Minnesota Farm Holiday Association pledged to help provide food for strikers.[21]

The police were put on twelve hour shifts from 7:00 a.m. to 7:00 p.m. The police announced their intentions to protect the grocery and meat dealers in the market area while they loaded and unloaded their goods. Several market firms also announced that they had employed special guards whom the police would deputize.[22]

Union leaders applied lessons learned and methods developed during the brief February strike. A rented garage at 1900 Chicago Avenue became strike headquarters. From this center leaders mapped strategy and dispatched "flying squads" as roving pickets to enforce their ban on truck movement. The leadership kept in constant telephone contact with stationary pickets at key points throughout the city. "Picket captains were under instruction to phone every ten minutes from a known point, such as a friendly cigar store in their picket district, or a bar or a striker's home."[23]

Everyone remembers strike headquarters as electric with activity. It appeared efficient and orderly, inspired confidence, and maintained a high sense of solidarity even in the face of a determined opposition skilled at using the Minneapolis press. Nightly meetings to discuss strategy and plans allowed workers and their families to hear the latest news on strike developments and express their opinions about them. Thus they were kept informed and engaged. A Ladies' Auxiliary organized by Marvel Scholl and Clara Dunne staffed a cafeteria with strikers' wives, children, and friends who prepared food that the Minnesota Farm Holiday Association and other sympathetic farmers and businesses donated.[24]

The GAC, on the other hand, had been caught in an uncomfortable position. The closed shop issue, upon which it had based its greatest resistance, had been taken away from them. Its first responses seem uncertain. "Several of the major trucking companies kept their vehicles off the streets, apparently on the theory that an outraged public would demand the immediate restoration of normal traffic."[25] Although the GAC seemed confused about tactics, there was never any doubt that they would resist. During the first days of the strike George C. Jones, an insurance executive, stated that businesses would supply funds to pay for special deputies—citizen volunteers.[26] A less veiled threat of vigilante action came from Totton P. Heffelfinger who suggested that a "mass movement of citizens" might be necessary to halt the strike.[27] The GAC concurred.

After a council of war at the West Hotel on May 17, the Employers' Committee issued a sharp statement about the irresponsible group of men who "have seized the city and dictated how, where, and when we are to obtain the bare necessities of life." They called for police intervention to remedy the intolerable conditions.[28]

Police Chief Michael Johannes heeded the call and ordered anyone arrested who laid a hand on private autos or trucks. Over one hundred strikers were arrested in the first few days. Mayor A. G. Bainbridge authorized Chief Johannes to hire five hundred special police. The General Advisory Committee announced that trucks would move under police escort Saturday. The shipment was to be small, the GAC added ingenuously, because there was not much to ship.[29] That claim lacks credibility, for the strikers had prevented deliveries from warehouses. The warehouses, then, would contain everything that had been in stock when the strike began. We can infer that the GAC was unwilling to risk goods that might be damaged in the expected confrontation between strikers and police or special deputies. This public announcement of planned truck movements under police protection rang as loud as a bugle call to battle. Thus GAC and police issued the challenge that led to the first clash between strikers and police.

Violence started almost concurrently with picketing. The May 18 issue of the *Tribune* carried accounts of gas pumps pulled down, gas stations smashed, and attendants roughed up.[30] Strikers reportedly stopped automobiles carrying food stuffs, and turned over delivery trucks; some direct clashes with the police occurred, but those involved only a few police and small groups of strikers.

Other Minneapolis businessmen entered the dispute on behalf of "law and order" when C. C. Webber, grandson of John Deere and president of Deere-Webber, manufacturer of farm equipment, called a "mass meeting" of businessmen to meet at the West Hotel to determine how they should respond to the strike. The Minneapolis Civic and Commerce Association "guided the arrangements for the meeting in co-operation with the various employers' associations throughout the city."[31] This "citizens law and order committee" offered, in a resolution passed at the May 18 meeting, to raise money to pay additional policemen to restore law an order to the Minneapolis streets.[32]

Governor Olson called the GAC and the Union together Thursday evening, May 17, to attempt a settlement before these sporadic acts resulted in the major confrontation between strikers and police that nearly everyone anticipated and feared. He failed to persuade the GAC to recognize Local 574 and bargain with them directly. He asked the GAC to agree to a system of arbitration to handle disputes over wages and conditions. The GAC responded:

> We see no necessity for any arbitration of a wage scale for the firms we represent inasmuch as with respect to that scale there is nothing to arbitrate, as admittedly it is a fair scale.[33]

The GAC reiterated its position that they would bargain collectively with "any duly selected and accredited representatives, selected by the employes of the firm; provided, however, that we will not enter into any written agreement with any organizations of any kind or nature."[34] They would, however file a consent to any Regional Labor Board order with which they agreed. Further, they warned:

> We intend to and will start the flow of merchandise into its usual and customary channels forthwith and without any more delays. We ask you as the highest official of our state to aid and assist our business firms in the orderly conduct of their business. We cannot and will not permit or allow our city to be seized and its industry ruined by a group that admits it has no fault to find with us.[35]

Responding to the GAC rejection of his efforts, Governor Olson declared he was "grievously disappointed because of your refusal," but he offered again to facilitate agreement.[36] The public interest he represented demanded it. He advised the GAC that "the union agreed this morning to withdraw its demand for a direct contract," and he suggested that the employers respond in kind and agree to set up a Board of Arbitration. He observed: "It seems inconsistent to me for you to state in one sentence that you will agree to bargain collectively with your employees, and in the following sentence to state that you refuse to sign a written agreement with them. One who is willing to make a bargain is usually willing to bind it by written contract." Nonetheless, he would acquiesce in the trade-off of a signed contract for an arbitration board.

Governor Olson noted with alarm that

> You have undertaken to pay the salary and expenses of some 500 special city police officers who are, to my best information, being selected very indiscriminately. That these forces will clash is inevitable, if the strike continues. That serious physical injury will result to these persons is probable. That injury may result to persons having no connection with the controversy is possible.[37]

Olson concluded with a warning:

> In the event that local government cannot preserve law and order, it will be my duty to use the military force of the government. If that

becomes necessary, the military department will take complete charge of the distribution of commodities which the citizens of Minneapolis desire to purchase; and will commandeer such equipment and conscript such man power as is necessary to bring about that distribution and to maintain law and order. If these steps do not accomplish the end desired, further steps, consistent with military occupation of the city will be taken.[38]

Olson's information about the special police was accurate. The additional police hired for strike duty at the rate of $4.68 a day included salesmen, meat cutters, clerks, musicians, teachers, lathers, and electricians. Only a few had police experience.[39]

In their first clash on Saturday May 19, police defeated the strikers who gathered at First Avenue North and Sixth Street to meet the planned truck movement. Unarmed and in small numbers, the strikers believed that the police would not fight them, but their optimism quickly shattered. Police laid billy clubs across heads, on elbows, hands, and ankles, and routed the strikers completely. The workers returned to strike headquarters to nurse broken noses, arms, fingers, ankles, and their anger. In a letter to Governor Olson drafted at a meeting held as injured strikers returned to Union headquarters, Local 574 declared, "the cops were brutally breaking the heads of our workers with the use of clubs, black jacks, and lead pipes. We have twelve men seriously and maybe fatally injured in the hospital." Withdrawing its delegates from the conference Olson had called to facilitate a settlement, they warned: "We will throw out a general call for every worker in Minneapolis and vicinity to assist us in protecting our rights and our lives."[40]

Although special police had been hired to augment their ranks, the regular police had done the beating that Saturday morning. The "Committee of 25" led by Totton P Heffelfinger recruited at $5.00 per day an additional fifty Special Deputy Sheriffs, who pledged to uphold law and order. Volunteers included salesmen, clerks, laborers, lawyers, and college students.[41] CBS commentator Eric Severeid, then a journalism student at the University of Minnesota, recalled:

> Some of the boys from the Greek fraternities on the campus joined the police and Citizens' Alliance forces with baseball bats on their shoulders, in defense of what they regarded as law and order. Some

of my little crowd joined the strikers, in non-combative functions. Most of us, be it confessed, were not of the type that is willing to fight for its beliefs with brickbat or club. Fellow Jacobin Dick Scammon, son of the medical dean, was different; he was of the stuff from which true leaders are made. He was six feet four, weighed two hundred and sixty pounds, ate, drank, and sang with rabelaisian gusto, and belonged to thirteen political organizations before he could vote. . . . Dick could swing a club, if he were convinced there was no other resort. We were all morally courageous, but he had physical courage. The whole city divided in its sympathies.[42]

Most of Saturday and all of Sunday volunteers gathered at 1328 Hennepin Avenue, headquarters of Heffelfinger's Committee of 25, where they were armed with clubs and organized into groups. Whether they sought to uphold law and order, or to protect food for the city, they surely knew that their function was to break the truck strike. However, few volunteers realized the extent and intensity of the battle to come.

Sunday no clashes occurred, but the day was filled with activity as the two groups prepared their forces for the battle to come Monday. The *Tribune* reported from strike headquarters:

> In addition to the belief that picketing would be useless Sunday, union leaders said frankly they were saving their men for Monday. The rank and file of the strikers are tired from their activities of the past three days, and Monday will be another long busy day if truck owners go ahead with their plans to move trucks on a big scale, the union men agreed.[43]

From Saturday night through Sunday strikers gathered at headquarters to saw lengths of pipe, or to shape wooden clubs. Newspaper was stuffed inside of hats for padding.[44] Strikers were not going to be unprepared Monday.

The General Advisory Committee attempted Sunday to regain public backing for its resistance to union demands. Although W. M. Hardin had professed employers' readiness to arbitrate wages and hours in his reply to Union demands for a closed shop on May 14, the GAC reversed itself. May 20, in the first of many full-page advertisements in local newspapers, the GAC made public the declarations it had made in its letter to Governor Olson. It declared that 50 cents per hour and higher was being paid in the trucking industry. The Committee refused to arbitrate this wage scale as it was "admittedly fair," but agreed to bargain collectively so long as it did not have to sign a written agreement.

Their claim was suspect. Some employees of some firms undoubtedly received 50 cents per hour or more, but a Citizens' Alliance survey of the sash and door industry dated May eleven, 1934, showed truck drivers' rates as $42^1/2$ cents, 35 cents, and 40 cents per hour, while helpers received 30 cents, 40 cents, and 35 cents per hour.[45] Since the Citizens Alliance had joined the GAC, if, indeed, it had not organized it, this information should have been available to it. At best, the advertisement misled about wages paid in the industry. The GAC purportedly had raised the rate to fifty cents an hour at the beginning of the strike, but the GAC would not include that rate as a provision in a contract. Clearly the GAC had a special interpretation of collective bargaining: it could not lead to a contract with a union.

Sunday also witnessed a meeting in support of the strike from a quarter that strike leaders viewed with mixed feelings.

> The Communist Party, the Unemployed Council, and the International Labor Defense injected themselves into the truck drivers' strike.
>
> Under the auspices of these three organizations some 700 men and women gathered at Block 20 Sunday afternoon and raised their hands in a pledge to join the picket lines early Monday morning. . . .
>
> Sam K. Davis [head of the local Communist party] recited efforts to persuade the strike committee to accept help from members of his organization, told of rejection of those efforts, and of permission finally given to him to address the mass meeting of strikers at 1900 Chicago Avenue Sunday before the Block 20 session. Despite "this attitude," he declared, the International Labor Defense was going to mobilize its forces for cooperation. He declared that the "trouble with this strike is that the rank and file has no adequate leadership."
>
> "Now," he continued, "we're going in to help."[46]

Strike leaders generally welcomed support from any group, but Davis himself received a mixed reception. Vince Dunne recalled that when Davis entered strike headquarters and began to berate the strike leadership, strikers would attack him. On more than one occasion, strike leaders had to rescue him.[47]

During the strike's early days, organized labor was strangely quiet. Although union members undoubtedly sympathized with the strikers, little by way of official endorsement of the strike came from presidents of union locals in the city. Early in the strike, William Brown invited their support and declared that a general strike might be necessary to uphold the principle of collective bargaining.[48] St. Paul truckers struck, but settled in one day, and Minneapolis taxi drivers staged a one day sympathy strike. Although no general strike occurred, when strikers stopped the movement of all trucks in Minneapolis, they brought much of the city's commerce to a virtual standstill. When thousands of workers gathered in the Market district, they demonstrated that Local 574 enjoyed the broad support of Minneapolis workers. Years of poor pay, difficult working conditions, and insecure employment had made the market district a symbol for workers of their exploitation.

Re-enforcing GAC claims, leading members of the citizens' law and order committee sent a telegram Sunday to Senator Robert Wagner, Chairman of the National Labor Board, describing destruction and injuries resulting from the strike. The signatories asked for immediate action and petitioned the National Labor Board to instruct the "Local Regional Labor Board to assume jurisdiction and settle this strike at once."[49] On Monday, this committee directed its petition to the Minneapolis-St. Paul Regional Labor Board requesting that they "assume jurisdiction" and order hearings.[50]

Monday in a tense Market district, police and special deputies cordoned off the area in preparation for truck movement. Strikers gathered in the Central Labor Union building on Eighth Street.[51] A reserve of nine hundred gathered at strike headquarters.[52] Only a few strikers patrolled the market area itself. Loading delivery trucks in the market began the confrontation.

> In the predawn light a battalion of pickets 600 strong, armed for the most part with clubs, marched four abreast to the market place. Their sober discipline and military precision terrified the waiting citizens' army, which broke into headlong flight with hardly a scuffle.[53]

The police did not run, but formed a circle and repelled all attempts by strikers to break through. For a time police stood with their guns drawn facing in a stalemate the ranks of the strikers. A truck bearing a sign "Spring the trap and rid the city of rats"[54] roared around a corner and broke through police ranks.

> That was the signal for the battle. The strikers in the truck, armed with clubs, jumped out. Other strikers joined in the rush. Swinging clubs, gas pipes and hurling rocks, the strikers charged and drove police back for force of numbers.
> The fighting continued most of the morning and it required massing of nearly all police in the entire loop district. Scores were injured on both sides in the battle.[55]

Thirty-seven people, mostly police, were injured seriously enough to be treated at hospitals. The battle ended when police produced shotguns as they tightened their lines.[56] Both sides claimed victory; each side had learned that the other was determined to do their duty as they saw it. Strikers had prevented the planned movement of trucks.

Monday evening, May 21, at 8:15 p.m. the American Legion Fifth District met in Pioneer Hall of the Lumber Exchange Building to determine its response to the strike and to the day's battle. Given the American Legion's origins in the anti-Communist hysteria following World War I and its anti-union record, it is likely that it had been approached as a source of special police. Recruiters were disappointed by the resolution the Legion published in the *Tribune* and other Minneapolis newspapers. After declaring that Legion membership did not incur a special obligation beyond that incumbent upon any citizen to assist police agencies, the resolution asserted: "In any dispute between capital and labor [the] interest of the Legion is confined to maintenance of law and order and without taking part in either side."[57]

The Regional Labor Board continued its efforts at conciliation until the early hours of Tuesday morning, but failed to effect an agreement. Neil M. Cronin, chairman, reported that no differences over actual terms of an agreement remained, but that the question of a written agreement between the parties continued to hold up settlement. The GAC agreed to stipulate everything with the Board, but not in a contract with the union. The union insisted on a written agreement. Cronin speculated that the employers refused to agree because they saw any written agreement inevitably leading to the closed shop.[58]

The GAC's determination to move trucks did not flag. Tuesday morning May 22, the return match found thousands participating and thousands more watching. Twenty thousand people showed up at the market area. Radio station KSTP announcers and others at the scene reported an aura like a grand "sporting match,"[59] perhaps influenced by polo outfits some special deputies wore. The issue at stake and the arms brought to the market suggested no such sportive intent. The strikers were in dead earnest. The GAC had declared that the trucks would move; the strikers had warned that they would not. If the GAC succeeded, the strike could be broken. If the trucks did not move, the union could claim victory.

Strikers milled around, seemingly unwilling to start the battle until someone threw a crate of tomatoes through a window. The *Tribune* reported: "At no time was there any real clash between regular police and strikers, who stepped back when asked to by regulars."[60] Strikers focused their attack on the special deputies whom they regarded as strike breakers. These special deputies wore no uniforms, but wore badges and carried standard night sticks to mark them. The battle lasted less than an hour and resulted in a complete rout of the deputies and police who were chased from the battlefield. The market district was under complete control of the strikers who prevented looting and further destruction.[61] When the battle subsided, two Special Deputy Sheriffs lay fatally injured: one of them Arthur Lyman, vice-president of the American Ball Company and member of the Citizens Alliance.

The effect on public opinion is always difficult to gauge in such circumstances, but thousands of workers had supported the strikers in this battle. After clashes with police and the death of so prominent a citizen, GAC charges that the strikers were little more than a lawless mob gained credibility among citizens less directly involved, but the responsibility for this violence could fall upon the GAC as well as the Union. Without doubt, Minneapolis citizens not directly engaged in the struggle were shocked. Those who felt particular responsibility sought intervention from the federal government and even President Roosevelt. Keith Merrill, Executive Assistant to

Assistant Secretary, Department of State, who was born and raised in Minneapolis, provided the President the following "facts" that he had received from Rufus Rand, prominent Minneapolis business-man, who was apparently one of the special deputies:

> Governor Olson called a meeting of the striking truck drivers at the theater and told them to tighten their belts, arm themselves and take what they wanted.
>
> At any rate, yesterday when a mob of 5,000 gathered they depu-tized 1,000 special policemen to augment the regular force of 319. This 1,319 squad of law officers then approached the mob of 5,000. . . . The regular police officers led the advance and when they saw the temper of the crowd, ordered the special policemen to take off their coats with badges, put them on the pavement and also lay down their clubs.[62]
>
> As soon as the mob saw this they charged through the regular policemen and, splitting up into small squads, each squad of six riot-ers would jump a single special policeman. . . .
>
> The deputies apparently were the cream of the ex-service men who had volunteered during the war. Rufus Rand was a member of the Lafayette Esquadrille. . . .
>
> There is nothing young or hysterical about the character of any of these deputies. They were not looking for a fight but they volunteered for ordinary police duty on the same basis that they volunteered for the war. . . .
>
> All of this young crowd, I believe, turned to [President Roosevelt] in the last election. The typical representative was the president of the Young Mens Republican Club, Totten [sic.] Heffelfinger, who came out bluntly with a statement that Mr. Hoover should not even be nominated.[63]

That afternoon Merrill telephoned again to advise that there was no disorder in Minneapolis at that time, but warned that they expected disorder the next day because:

> The Communists have imported some 1,500 people from Chicago who are hopped up with cocaine and are really professional strikers— they are the type who killed Arthur Lyman the other day. . . . They [Rufus Rand's group] urge that the provision of a new law be taken

advantage of (in which all troops are put in the hands of the President for industrial purposes). All they want is for General Stone (regular Army General in command of Fort Snelling) to be put in charge of the militia.[64]

Not all responses were so exaggerated. On Wednesday, the Regional Labor Board ordered an end to the strike, granting essentially all the Union's demands, and including in paragraph B-4 the statement: "When agreements are arrived at in accordance with this stipulation between representatives of employees and any employer or groups of employers, the board recommends that such agreement be reduced to writing."[65]

Such a recommendation was exactly what the GAC refused to accept, but, sensing the drift of public opinion toward its camp, the GAC decided to re-open negotiations and encourage that shift. They refused, however, to meet with representatives of Local 574. The two groups sat in different rooms while representatives of the Labor Board served as messengers. Negotiations continued to falter over the issue of a written contract, arbitration, and Local 574's right to represent inside workers.

Governor Floyd B. Olson, responding to pressure to declare martial law after the battle in the Market area, mobilized 3700 National Guardsmen, whom he held in readiness to disarm both strikers and special police. Olson was reluctant to declare martial law because he understood the nature of the conflict, and recognized the complex political situation he was in. Much of his support came from labor. He did not want to break the strike, but was bound to prevent violence and protect lives. That the Regional Labor Board was ineffective did not escape him, so he supported a request that the National Labor Board intervene. Olson announced:

I believe that the intervention of the National Labor Board would increase the possibilities of settlement because as I understand the law, the National Labor Board has authority to enforce its orders whereas the regional labor board has no such authority. You will recall that one of the main desires of the strikers' committee was that any board which undertook to arbitrate the differences of the two groups would have authority to enforce its orders and thereby guarantee members of the striking union that they would be protected in the future.[66]

The National Labor Board response proved tepid indeed. Essentially deflecting appeals directed toward it, the NLB declared its confidence in the Regional Labor Board, and vested it with authority to assume jurisdiction in the National Labor Board's name.

Olson secured a forty-eight hour truce after the Tuesday clash, ostensibly to give this "new" board a chance to re-open negotiations. Grocery and produce trucks were allowed to operate under the truce, thereby placating the growing resentment of local truck farmers. The parties agreed to a twenty-four hour extension of the truce, but failed to agree on the definition of "inside workers."

No agreement on this issue seemed possible; either the union or the GAC rejected attempts by the Regional Labor Board to rework the agreement. To demonstrate solidarity with the striking truckers the Electrical Workers Local 292, the Roofer and Asbestos Workers Union, the Carpenters Union, and the Bridge, Structural and Ornamental Iron workers Local 19 all voted to strike May 24.[67] Sen. Robert Wagner, Chairman of the NLB, called Daniel Tobin, President of the International Brotherhood of Teamsters to ask him to encourage Local 574 to settle. Tobin wired John Geary, Fourth International vice-president with responsibility for the Minneapolis-St. Paul area:

> I fully realize that the open shop in most instances means the closed shop against union men. . . . However, I believe if they can now sign an agreement putting all men back at work establishing decent wages and obtaining an agreement giving the preference to union men that at the end of one year they will be able to sign a strictly union shop agreement. . . . Advise leaders in conference that it is my judgment that they should bring the matter to a settlement as soon as possible otherwise the federal government now deeply interested may interfere to the detriment of the strikers.[68]

Indefatigably, Governor Olson conferred with the GAC and the Union and persuaded the Union to settle for employer recognition of the Union as representing its members and for arbitration. Paragraph 3 of the final agreement, reached on Friday May 25, read: "All members of the General Drivers and Helpers Union Local No. 574 in dealing with employers may be represented by the officers of such Union." Paragraph 8, however, stated ambiguously: "The terms `employees' as used herein shall include truck drivers and helpers, and such other persons as are ordinarily engaged in the trucking operations of the business of the individual employer."[69]

The ambiguity shifted attention from the definition of "inside workers" to the definition of ordinary trucking operations. Did the warehouse worker who moved produce up to the loading dock engage in ordinary trucking operations? The Union thought so, and Union negotiators had proven too astute not to have recognized the ambiguity. Why would they sign an agreement that failed to resolve such a key issue? The answer, found in Paragraph 6, called for arbitration boards whenever agreement could not be reached, and thus established a mechanism that brought together representatives of the employers and of the union to resolve disputed provisions of the contract. Recognition, then, created a system for handling disputes; it established the first and essential step to normal collective bargaining.

Union leaders also placed great trust in the Governor. At a hearing called to review the meaning of the disputed phrase as it applied in the case of five workers, Farrel Dobbs represented Local 574 and argued that Section 8 of the settlement gave them the right to represent these five men at Jordan-Stevens Company. The company disagreed.

Mr. Dobbs: The Governor assured us [Section 8] would be interpreted to give us jurisdiction over these people.

Mr. Power: If he gave you that assurance there, why didn't he write it in?

Mr. Cunningham: He gave you assurance?

Mr. Dobbs: Yes, it was our understanding.

Mr. Power: The Governor agreed with your interpretation: something different than what is written?

Mr. Dobbs: No, it was not different from what is written. . . .

Mr. Power: Why didn't the Governor put it in?

Mr. Dobbs: You are asking me to read the Governor's mind.

Mr. Harmon: He didn't tell you how we would interpret it?

Mr. Dobbs: He said it would be the legal and logical interpretation. . . . We considered the Governor had a good legal mind and accepted his advice.[70]

Complicating the settlement further was the nominal dissolution of the GAC's bargaining committee. Although the General Advisory Committee spoke during negotiations for 166 trucking firms, it refused to guarantee the agreement. The agreement was "subject to the ratification of the individual employers who may be affected by the order."[71] After the Committee accepted the agreement, Local 574 had to negotiate separately with each of the firms employing its members, an ominous signal with respect to the arbitration provision of the settlement.

Despite these difficulties the strikers accepted the agreement and returned to work, hoping that concessions they had secured would establish handling of their concerns in a systematic and forthright manner. Although ambiguity about inside workers remained, none remained about drivers and helpers, they believed. After all, the Union believed, the issue of inside workers could be resolved through the Arbitration Board Governor Olson had proposed. To the GAC, however, arbitration meant something quite different. In a newsletter "Special Weekly Bulletin," the Citizens Alliance advised its subscribers:

> Under the final order terminating this strike, there is no closed shop nor is there any signed agreement with the union. It provides for arbitration under machinery to be set up by the Regional Labor Board in each case when complaints are filed in respect to any employer who was a party to the arrangement.[72]

The key phrase is "in each case." The employers would not agree to establishing a general Board of Arbitration; rather, each complaint over violation of the agreement would call for its own, separate and individual board.

In a sense, the Union had secured no agreement at all, for in practice the ambiguous definition of employees meant that the union had not gained recognition of its right to represent its members. Even if a board were formed, arbitration machinery would prove cumbersome and therefore ineffective. Employers refused to set up any Boards, and some failed to pay the agreed wage virtually at the signing of the order.

Peace spread over Minneapolis like a cheap veneer, thinly masking both workers' dissatisfaction and suspicion, and employers' determination never to bargain with the Union. The conflict between 166 trucking firms and Local 574 appeared to be over; in fact it had reached only a truce. Local 574 was strengthened by what appeared to be an agreement with the employers, but, like any agreement that fails to generate the commitment to see it last or the good will to work through its concrete application, it only papered over the conflict.

Governor Olson had taken much upon his shoulders. He hoped that the agreement, however imprecise, would take on a life of its own and *de facto* lead to negotiations between Local 574 and their employers. Local 574, probably following his lead in this matter, agreed to give it a chance. The Citizens Alliance, however, had no intention of cooperating with his search for the middle ground of conciliation.

Notes

1. George H. Mayer, *The Political Career of Floyd B. Olson* (Minneapolis: University of Minnesota Press 1951), 187.
2. Ibid., 190.
3. Farrell Dobbs, *Teamster Rebellion* (New York: Monad Press, 1972), 66.
4. RG 25, Box 384, File 6, National Archives.
5. Ibid.
6. Minneapolis *Tribune*, 8 May 1934.
7. General Advisory Committee Letter dated 7 May 1934 to W. W. Hughes. Citizens Alliance Papers, Minnesota Historical Society, St. Paul, Minnesota.
8. Minneapolis *Tribune*, 10 May 1934.
9. Minneapolis *Tribune*, 14 May 1934.
10. *Special Weekly Bulletin* #802, dated May eleven, 1934, Citizens Alliance Papers, Minnesota Historical Society, St. Paul, Minnesota.
11. RG 25, Box 388, National Archives.
12. Letter dated 14 May 1934 from GAC to Regional Labor Board, RG 25, Box 384 Folder 6, National Archives.
13. Minutes of Meeting 14 May 1934, RG 25, Box 388 Folder 1, National Archives.
14. Ibid.
15. Ibid.

16. Statement by the Minneapolis-St. Paul Regional Labor Board 15 May 1934, 4:30 p.m., RG 25, Box 384, File 6.
17. Letter dated 16 May 1934 from GAC to Minneapolis-St. Paul Regional Labor Board, RG 25 Box 384 File 6.
18. Ibid.
19. V. R. Dunne, interview with the author, Minneapolis, September 1964. This is also consistent with later published statements Tobin made. "Inside workers" became the focus of latter negotiations.
20. Ibid.; R. D. Cramer, interview with the author, Minneapolis, September 1964.
21. John Bosch, (president, Minnesota Farm Holiday Association), interview, Minneapolis, 9 July 1974; Dobbs, *Teamster Rebellion*, 68.
22. Minneapolis *Tribune*, 16 May 1934.
23. Charles R. Walker, *American City* (New York: Farrar & Rinehart, 1937), 99.
24. Dobbs, *Teamster Rebellion*, 69; Elizabeth Faue, *Community of Suffering & Struggle: Women, Men, and the Labor Movement in Minneapolis, 1915-1945* (Chapel Hill: The University of North Carolina Press, 1991), 11.
25. Mayer, *Floyd B. Olson*, 195.
26. Minneapolis *Tribune*, 19 May 1934.
27. Ibid.
28. Mayer, *Floyd B. Olson*, 197.
29. Minneapolis *Tribune*, 19 May 1934.
30. Minneapolis *Tribune*, 18 May 1934.
31. Ibid.
32. Minneapolis *Tribune*, 19 May 1934.
33. Letter to Honorable Floyd B. Olson from W. M. Hardin, dated May 19, 1934, RG 25 Box 384 File 6, National Archives.
34. Ibid.
35. Ibid.
36. Letter to W. M. Hardin, Chairman Employers' Committee from Governor Floyd B. Olson, dated 19 May 1934, RG 25 Box 384 File 6, National Archives.
37. Ibid.
38. Ibid.
39. List of "Additional Police for Strike Duty from May 19, 20, 21, 22, 1934," Minnesota Historical Society, St. Paul, Minnesota, M494.
40. Letter from Local 574 to Governor Floyd B. Olson, dated 19 May 1934, Minnesota Historical Society, St. Paul, Minnesota, M494.
41. List of Special Deputy Sheriffs, Minnesota Historical Society, St. Paul, Minnesota, M494.

42. Eric Severeid, *Not So Wild a Dream* (New York: A. A. Knopf, 1946), 58.

43. Minneapolis *Tribune*, 21 May 1934.

44. Walker, *American City*, 108.

45. Citizens Alliance Papers, Minnesota Historical Society, St. Paul, Minnesota.

46. Minneapolis *Tribune*, 21 May 1934.

47. V. R. Dunne, interview with the author, Minneapolis, September 1964.

48. Minneapolis *Tribune*, 18 May 1934.

49. Wire to NLB from W. C. Helm [Russel-Miller Milling Co.], John M. Harrison [Marsh-McClellan Insurance Agency and captain of the 1898 Minnesota football team], C. C. Bovey, George N. Dayton [Dayton's Department Store], Edwin Lindell, George C. Jones, Dr. Kenneth Bulkley, Thomas Vennum, George Dickson, Mrs. George Fahr, J. C. Wyman, J. S. Clapper [2nd vice President, Citizens Alliance], dated 20 May 1934, RG 25 Box 384 File 6, National Archives.

50. Letter to Minneapolis-St. Paul Regional Labor Board from W. C. Helm, et al., dated 21 May 1934, RG 25 Box 384 File 6, National Archives.

51. Walker, *American City*, 113.

52. Dobbs, *Teamster Rebellion*, 83.

53. Mayer, *Floyd B. Olson*, 198.

54. Minneapolis *Tribune*, 22 May 1934.

55. Ibid.

56. There are photographs of this clash on page 8 of the Minneapolis *Tribune*, 22 May 1934.

57. Minneapolis *Tribune*, 22 May 1934.

58. Memo from Benedict Wolfe summarizing conversation with Neil Cronin dated 22 May 1934, RG 25, Box 384, File 6, National Archives.

59. Mayer, *Floyd B. Olson*, 198.

60. Minneapolis *Tribune*, 23 May 1934.

61. Mayer, *Floyd B. Olson*, 198.

62. No other account of the clash reports this command.

63. Memo to Mr. Early for President Roosevelt from Keith Merrill dated 23 May 1934, RG 25, Box 384 File 6, National Archives.

64. Ibid.

65. Minneapolis *Tribune*, 23 May 1934.

66. Minneapolis *Tribune*, 22 May 1934.

67. Minneapolis *Tribune*, 24 May 1934.
68. Telegram to Geary from Tobin dated 24 May 1934, RG 25, Box 384, National Archives.
69. See appended final agreement dated 25 May 1934.
70. Hearing in behalf: General Drivers and Helpers Union Local No. 574, [June, 1934], RG 25, Box 384, Folder 6, National Archives.
71. See appended final agreement dated 25 May 1934.
72. Special Weekly Bulletin #804, dated 1 June 1934, Minnesota Historical Society, St. Paul, Minnesota, M494.

7 | Voices

Orrie W. Norton (driver)

I knew Bill Brown. He had drove for Swiller Transfer, and I knew George Frosig [Vice President of Local 574], he was also a driver in town. I knew Jack Severson: worked for Cameron Transfer, it was right down there near Murphy's and I used to talk to Jack. Right across the street was Hemple Transfer. I knew some of the fellows there. I knew two of the Hemple boys: Les Hemple was one. And I knew their father who owned Hemple Transfer.

Bill Brown was aware of Section 7a. Now where he had found out about it, where he had gotten his information, I don't know.

The first time that an organizer came up there on the docks at Murphy Transfer, that was at 900 North First Street, Bill Brown came up there, and of course they called the police to get him out of there. Bill left, and the police came. I met Bill after that. It got me more interested. Ted Rogers and I talked it over, on the principles of organization. Ted was for affiliating with the organization. I don't believe Ted had ever belonged to any organization before. Ted was one of the youngest veterans of World War I; he was 15 years old when he went to France. He was the nephew of Ed Rogers, the State's Attorney from Cass County, who was part Indian, and I think he was part colored, but that shouldn't matter because he was all man. He was very influential with the men. He was hard working, principles good. He and myself and another man, three of us went down and joined the union at once. Later on we went in there with 60 and joined the union.

Personally I was not in too bad 'o shape; I was single, although I had obligations, due to the fact that my sister and I had bought a house.

It happened to me in St. Cloud A & P Store. I remember the manager's name and everything. I went in there early in the morning. I had to back up in the alley. I had a full truck for him. I was unloading. They had all commodities. I'll never forget it. A carton of Sir Walter Raleigh smoking tobacco fell down and broke open. I repacked it, and I didn't pay no attention to the coupons on the floor. I guess I picked them up and put them in my pocket after I got it unloaded. I set on the tailgate, and the manager came out and he helped me pick up this carton, and he said, "I got to have some tobacco." I said, "go ahead."

He takes it in the store. I guess it cost about five or six dollars at that time. He checked over these and I'm a carton short. They watch you like a hawk, so you learn to watch them.

It turned out that when he checked over his invoice, which I didn't have—I just had the pieces—he was a carton of Sir Walter Raleigh smoking tobacco short. If it hadn't fell down and broke open, I'd never know I had it on the load. You just don't remember that. So he said you got to sign a short slip. So I signed a short slip, and I went up and seen the vice president of Murphy's, and just as honest as I am sitting here, I told him the full story of this thing. And he said, "what the hell do you expect me to do, cry about it?" I said, "No sir, I'll take care of it myself." It don't build your morale up any when you know you're right and they make a dummy of you that you are wrong. It gets into you and you don't forget it.

You had to pay for everything you were short. If you broke something, you paid for it. I thought about Magnussen. He dropped a washing machine and he had $150 damages on that damn thing! He had six kids, and as long as I worked there he never got a full pay day. They deducted for damages. He couldn't do anything about it. He just walked around in a daze trying to figure out how to get a quart of milk or something like that for them kids.

The union looked like a better way. I had never encountered it before. You see, we are not born radical or anything else like that, but when you see things like that it pretty near makes you radical. I don't classify myself as radical, but you look over the hardships, it is just unbelievable that this country could go into anything like the Depression. If you see something that is going to help the majority of people, you will get into it too.

Everybody was an organizer—everybody!

Iver Swanson (policeman)

I was born on a farm forty miles north of here in 1897 and was on the farm for twenty-nine years and moved to Minneapolis in 1928. I was married at that time, had one child.

The conditions on the farm weren't good in those days. It was all work and no play and we decided to cast our lot with the city dwellers for some reason or another. I don't know why exactly, but that's where we ended up. It took me about five or six weeks to get a job. We came here in November and the week before Christmas that year I got a job in the factory in Northeast Minneapolis, Electric Machinery, in the shipping department, more or less as a carpenter, making crates and shipping boxes. I was there for four years.

August 1930, I left there. When I left I was in the receiving department and stock room. In my quest for a job around the city, I had made application many places and also had left my application with the civil service commission as a patrolman and at that time they weren't hiring very many men because they only had a force of about probably 300 policemen. As the examinations came up, I thought well, I'd gone that far, I'd go through and take it. So I took the written examination and first we had a physical and there was some 1,200 or 1,300 that took the physical examination and 800 of those qualified physically.

Jobs weren't plentiful in those days. This was before '30. I had had my application since about in '27. This took so long for it to develop, my note didn't come up until '28 as I recall, and I taken my physical and after a certain number had been eliminated by the physical then the written examination came up and there were 800 that took this written examination and by a stroke of good luck somewhere, or another, I had a standing of number eight out of the 800. Of course this even surprised me, because I was more or less a hick from the country. I hadn't had any experience of writing examinations. So anyway they weren't doing any hiring, but I got my standing as number eight.

Meanwhile I was working at Electric Machinery and then come 1930 things were beginning to look pretty bad over there. They were laying off people and I had been one of the newer men in my department and so I knew that I would be one of the first ones to go, so in July of that year of 1930 I got a notice from the police department that my number was up. Well first they used to draw people from the eligible list for Park Police and City, also so I got a notice that I could go on the Park Police, but that didn't appeal to me, so I passed that up in spite of dire circumstances that we were in. It just didn't appeal to me that's all.

From the eight below me, there were four taken for the police department. At that time they had a veteran's preference policy of taking one veteran and one non-veteran and I was a non-veteran due to the fact that I was born at the wrong time I guess you might call it. World War I had just ended. I was the only one left at home with an invalid father and my mother to take care of the farm. That's how I didn't get into the service. If it had lasted another three months, I would have been in because they were scraping the bottom of the barrel for men at that time. My next older brother was in France at that time. I had a standing of number two on the civil service list for about eight months and they weren't putting anybody on. Finally I got a notice that they were going to appoint a couple of more patrolmen and there was three new men put on and two reinstated that had been suspended for insulting. We got the notice in the latter part of July to report to work the first of August. I don't actually know the number of men in the department at that time, but I would say that there was between 300 and 400.

For training police officers, you got your appointment and they called you in and you had an interview with a captain or the chief and they told you what your requirements were and what you need to do and they give you a cap, a badge and a stick and told you to go out and do your stuff. That's the training you got.

There would be two men assigned to this particular beat and you would work one hour on that corner and he would work one hour on that corner and then you patrol the area the rest of the time and you would get smatterings of information. If you got a good partner, then you were lucky. If you got one that resented new men, then you didn't get any information. I worked as a patrolman from August to about the first of November and then I went from the beat patrolman to the traffic department which was handled practically entirely by the men stationed on the corner. I worked there for quite some time. In fact I was the relief man on the traffic department for about the next year and you used to stand out in the street and flag the cars by. You had a certain area to patrol on your hour off, that you didn't have to stand on the corner. You were assigned an area that you checked the motor vehicles and checked them for overtime parking and stuff like that. Then I went back on as a beat patrolman. In 1933 is when the labor trouble started.

In 1934 we had the truck drivers strike. That was the larger one and naturally having been a factory worker before that, working for forty cents an hour, your sympathies had to be with the working man. I knew of truck drivers that drive semi-trucks that drove for $17 a week. Then in '34 the Dunne brothers came to town, and while they were not the most reputable and probably were pretty radical element, they did organize the labor movement.

Business had always had the upper hand until then. There was no question but what if you wanted a job you took what they offered to pay, and there was no ifs, ands about it. They had what they called Citizens Alliance at that time and most of the big businesses at that time belonged to it and they did everything in their power to squash the union, but they were unsuccessful. I can remember that even Dayton's belonged to this Citizens Alliance group and they donated a considerable amount of money to break the strike.

The union and the strikers were able to tie up the business enough so that the businessmen were beginning to hurt and they were going to try to break the strike by getting some of the trucks in town rolling. Down at the market in the produce area was the first place where an incident occurred. That's where I was involved the first time. In spite of the sentiment (I can't speak for the rest of them but for myself), your sentiment had to be with the workers because of the wages they were getting. That didn't make the procedure right, because they managed to tie up everything you know, and when the trucking industry tried to move merchandise out of the market, and the incident that started the thing off was Gamble-Robinson. That was a big produce house down on the market. That was the first incident of any consequence and there of course the confrontation was pretty rugged. I suppose that the strikers probably outnumbered the police officers who were assigned there twenty-five or thirty to one and a lot of the policemen got pretty well worked over.

In the melee that ensued down at the market, I don't know how many policemen were injured that day and sent to the hospital including myself. It was a free-for-all, I mean with anything from brick bats to iron pipes. I got beat over the head and got knocked out. The one incident that stands out: I had gotten hit several times and had a laceration on my forehead and had blood running down all over my face and they didn't seem to bother me much. Then somebody from behind clobbered me on the back of the head with a iron pipe. I passed out; I had a goose egg like half a walnut on the back of my head. I was laying on the street and I can hear and I could think, but I couldn't move. I thought I should put my hand over my face because somebody's going to step on me.

Then all of a sudden I heard "Get this man out of here" and somebody reached down and grabbed me by the hand, and the moment somebody moved me I came to and they got me on my feet. I was able to stagger off across the street and they rolled me into the patrol wagon and took me to the hospital.

Another thing, the Citizens Alliance had talked to a group of volunteers into being strike breakers to come down and assist the police, and in the second incident down in the market, I think that was about two or three days later, there was a man who led a bunch of volunteers down there. They were going to assist in breaking the strike. Of course the strikers concentrated on them more than they did the police because they knew the police were there under different conditions than the other people were, so they really routed them in a hurry. There were two volunteers that were killed in the incident, one from the Ball Manufacturing Company and then there was one a little later in the same area. I was down there, it was my territory. I was on Second Avenue North and fifth and Sixth Street.

I don't think the deputies were an asset. In the first place, they had no police training at all and they were resented so much more by the strikers, they were really a hazard.

There was no shooting at the first incident. That was hand-to-hand combat. Nobody used their guns. As things went on, the situation got more serious and finally of course it came to the point where the only way you could protect yourself or even enforce any kind of a regulation was with firearms, but there was none used in the first incident at all. I don't think that there was any shooting by the strikers when the three men got killed, but the two men that got killed in the market area from the volunteer group, they were clubbed to death. I wasn't there that day, that was about the Second or Third day. There was a picture in the paper of me being led

Pickets in an open truck intercept a truck convoyed by police in cars, 20 July 1934. (Minnesota Historical Society)

Police open fire on strikers who rammed truck guarded by police, 20 July 1934. (*Minneapolis Tribune,* Minnesota Historical Society)

Truck drivers strike, 1934. (Minnesota Historical Society)

Truck drivers strike, 1934. (Minnesota Historical Society)

Truck drivers strike,
21 May 1934.
(Minnesota
Historical Society)

Clash between striking truck
drivers and the citizen's army,
21 May 1934.
(Minnesota Historical Society)

Strikers clash with citizens' army "Battle of Deputies Run," 21 May 1934.
(Minnesota Historical Society)

Policeman and deputy sheriff George Hansen during truck driver's strike, 21 May 1934. (Minnesota Historical Society)

Minneapolis police on duty doing truckers' strike 1934. (Minnesota Historical Society)

Police intervene in clash between striking truckers and the citizens army, 21 May 1934.(Minnesota Historical Society)

Truck drivers strike
21 May 1934. (Minnesota
Historical Society)

National Guard marching on central labor headquarters 612 1st Avenue North, 1934. (Minnesota Historical Society)

Funeral of Henry Ness, striker slain in police fight, 1934. (Minnesota Historical Society)

Grant Dunne and attorney Albert Goldman met Miles Dunne, Vincent Dunne, and William Brown on their release from the military stockade at the fairgrounds, 2 August 1934. (Minnesota Historical Society)

Mediation leaders Father Francis J. Haas and Eugene H. Dunnigan shared handshakes with Governor Floyd B. Olson after the strike was settled 21 August 1934. (*Minneapolis Tribune*, Minnesota Historical Society)

across the street to the patrol wagon. I was kind of slumped over; they were dragging me along. I did have a clipping of that at one time, but I don't know what happened to it. There was four or five other guys that day that were sent to the hospital too. A fellow by the name of Percy Brock, he's in Arizona now, was in there. He was really beat up. He had a broken jaw and a broken arm. And there was another fellow by the name of Earl Richter, big tall guy, he was beaten unmercifully.

You were ordered to go in and try and keep order. Regardless of what your inner sympathies would be, you were still sworn to do your duty and that's what you'd better do. Either that or you probably would have gotten fired or taken off the job. I don't recall anyone that refused to go do their job.

Clara Dunne (Grant Dunne's wife)

Farrel Dobbs and I organized the lady's auxiliary. We didn't keep that very long after the strike. We thought we could help in some way. We made a march on the court house, I think Bainbridge was mayor at that time, told them that we wanted equal rights for the Teamsters. Some of them were making as low as $12 a week. Well, they didn't get their demands that they wanted in May, so that's the reason that they had the July strike.

Nineteenth and Chicago in a great big storage building, they brought in all these men that had been clubbed and beaten and if they needed medical attention they were sent to the hospital. We had our own doctor and a couple of women that were nurses. They took care of the ones that they could and what we had to work with. If they were too badly hurt, they went to the hospital.

There was a small office where they transacted business, but other than that there was nothing except they set up a place to eat sandwiches and coffee or something like that; we didn't serve cooked food: just sandwiches and coffee and maybe rolls and donuts, something like that. It was very active, like a beehive. People were coming and going all the time, all night, even, there was somebody there.

They would always have to have a meeting or two to see if the strikers wanted to accept their proposals. I never was a part of the drivers union. No one from the woman's auxiliary sat on the meetings of the main committee. It was "no women allowed." We did what they wanted us to do, if they wanted us to run errands.

Chris Moe (striker)

I joined the I.W.W. We was bummin' on the freights, and if you wasn't a Wobblie you better get the hell off. That's how I learnt what the hell it meant.

They treated you like animals out threshing. I would put up a tent near a straw pile, and that was it. You worked about twelve-thirteen hours a day. The pay wasn't too bad. I was a spike pitcher and I got about $7 a day. In about '27 that ended. The farmers bought their own rigs. A lot of time you couldn't get a job unless you belonged to the Wobblies, because the farmers didn't want nothing to happen.

At strike headquarters on Chicago Avenue we had a commissary; we fed them by the hundreds. I remember I went over to Feinberg's, and I hauled a whole truck load of wieners. Farm Holiday Association brought in pigs, cattle, chickens, and everything else. There was a spirit for union in them days.

They deputized some men and sent them down there to protect property. When the workers saw that, even women were there with big clubs on their wrist. Then it was a real riot. It was their way of putting us down.

Ed Ryan (Minneapolis policeman 1925-1947, Hennepin County Sheriff, 1947-1967)

Maybe like the French Revolution the strike was required to bring about the changes that had to be brought about. We had an organization in these cities known as the Citizens Alliance, an organization of businessmen. They were determined to keep Minneapolis an open city. They didn't want anybody unionized around here at all.

The Dunne brothers had a different idea. I knew them well: Vince. As a matter of fact a few years before the strike we had to escort one of them home, because his life was threatened. They were soft-spoken, gentlemanly little fellows, but tougher than hell! Boy!

The strike was beautifully organized. They had their own hospital. I think it was in a garage on Fourth Avenue around Twenty-fifth Street. They had their own canteen. They took care of their own wounded, fed their own people. Just a terrific job.

The Sheriff swore in a number of special deputies in the strike. I guess this badge [shows it to interviewer] was issued to them, according to what it says on there. Quite a souvenir.

I was down on the market place the day of the big blow-up. I was around Seventh Street and First or Second Avenue North, right in the Market area just as the thing was brewing, getting going. WCCO had microphones up there, and observers up there, they were giving a blow by blow account of the whole war right at Gamble Robinson and the other companies.

A big truck pulled up, loaded with bats and clubs and all sorts of weapons, and a big, husky character who I knew well, he was handing out these to the strikers.

It was said that they imported a number of tough characters from Chicago to participate in the strike, and these fellows wore caps down over their eyes so they couldn't be recognized by a photographer.

Now the police had orders not to draw any weapons. It was all right to be on the receiving end of baseball bats and as a matter of fact, a friend of mine with whom I worked on the East Side, had his jaw broken. He was in the hospital a long time, all wired up. His name was Percy Brock. He was knocked down, and that picture of him on his knees trying to fend off the blows, went round the world. He had a terrible beating, as did many others. Some of the police, I guess, never did come back to work because of the beatings. But they had orders not to draw their revolvers. I couldn't buy that at all. When I was down working there, I was in plain clothes. I was a plain clothes patrolman at that time. I had a revolver on my hip and I made up my mind that nobody was going to beat me up while I'm carrying this weapon.

Later on when I was sheriff, at mast meetings, I used to tell my deputies, you don't have to take a beating from any son of a bitch. Anybody who attacks you with a deadly weapon, to do you bodily harm, use any means at your disposal, with my blessing. Here these guys were taking all this beating. It wasn't their fault, the conditions. That was the fault of society, not the police. They took the beating.

The strikers drove the special deputies off Hennipen Avenue. They were throwing away badge, club. They just took over the town that day.

The sheriff in times like that signs up anyone they like.

When I was sheriff there wasn't anyone telling me what to do. I followed the law, and that was that. You can't stand by. You have a sworn duty to protect life and property. The Governor can remove you for nonfeasance, misfeasance, or malfeasance. So you better get in there and do what you can.

One day when the strikers were going to take over the Court House, I was standing on the Fourth Avenue side, near the Fourth Avenue entrance. Armored cars were all lined up, because these guys meant business. They were going to come in there and tell the judges, the mayor, and anybody else how to run the court house. There was an inspector name Frank Bleeg. Robust, phlegmatic Swede, and he had just as much guts as Sam Davis, or the rest of them ever thought of having. He was in charge of all the police operations there. So Sam Davis wanted to get up on the parapet there and give a speech. So Bleeg said, "Okay, I'll give you ten minutes, but remember, after ten minutes you're through. I don't have to let you talk at all, but since you're here, go ahead."

So he gets up and starts to dance up and down, do his act. He had a coat on like Hitler. So his ten minutes were up, so Bleeg says, "that's it." He wouldn't get down.

One of the police officers, I guess he got the wink from Bleeg, he got the gas gun with a long ranged shell in it. If he'd hit Sam Davis with that he'd have cut him in two. He grazed it right by him, and all the gas! I could see that shell bouncing down Fourth Avenue almost to Seventh Street, spewing gas all the way. Sam disappeared. I haven't seen him since.

The fact that the police could not draw their weapons and that they were taking all this beating, I didn't buy that. I will use a gun any time anyone attacks me with a weapon with intent to do me great bodily harm. I will kill him, just like that [snaps fingers], 'cause he'd kill me. Self-preservation is the first law of humanity. That's what I use to tell my deputies.

Harvey Boscoe (laundry driver)

In May everything was piling up in the laundry. One day they suggested we've got a big old Nash. I don't remember; it must have been a sedan. They said, "Now, we'll back it up to the plant in the alley." They had a little narrow driveway coming right back to the building. "We will take out all the seats and load it with laundry, load it flush, then put a blanket over it and you climb into it and sneak out of town with it." Once I get past Oak Knolls where my truck was I could deliver it. Well, evidently 574 had covered any sign of new movement around town. They had goon squads on the corners with four or five in a car, so I had no more pulled out of the alley of Gross Brothers and started down the street and I had the squad behind me, about five rough-necks. They caught me down at McPhail School of Music and they were going to turn the car over right there in the street. So I said, "I am just a kid working here. I don't know what they did. They told me to take this car out to Oak Knolls and meet somebody." So, then they argued back and forth and said, "Well, he's probably telling the truth. He's just doing what he was told." So they made me drive it back to Gross, back it up the alley and they stood there while we unloaded the whole thing. So I had the one thrill that time. But then they got so that Gross and some of the boys would load them at midnight—the same car—and I would come in at midnight and meet them at Oak Knolls and transfer it to my truck. That phase went on for quite a while, maybe a week or two.

Mrs. George Fahr (wife of University of Minnesota Medical School faculty member)

I was born in Pittsburgh and I am very proud of it. I'm a great girl to root for the home team. I have never really known the origin of the strike because at the time it occurred, I wasn't very old and I had small children and wasn't tremendously interested. But I had done a good deal in civic things and Mr. C. C. Weber felt that I could be of service on the employers' committee so I went. It was very interesting to me, because it was my first experience with trying to cope with a force that seemed almost impossible to master. I couldn't see really what they could do when the chips were down to stop this appalling strike. At first the other committee members were very patronizing. I always waited until they ran out of steam and when they stopped talking, I said how right they were, but,... and went on from there. They had quite a time with me, because I was so plain spoken. After all, that's why I was there. I was supposed to be a dissident voice and I certainly was.

I do remember how many meetings that they had. Taking it by and large now, the committee, when the chips were down, had a great regard for these strikers. They were not against them in a way that you felt was prejudicial. It was, when you boiled it down, a question of property rights. They felt their property was being infringed upon by people who had come from outside Minneapolis. The instigators came from Chicago, they came from Milwaukee, they came from various parts of the United States where they had very successful strikes. As I recollect, two brothers named Dunne, were the prime movers of the whole thing. I did meet them. They didn't know me—I mean they didn't know who on earth I was.

I made up my mind after that meeting, that if I were going to be on this committee, I was going to know something of what was going on down in the market. So I went down by myself. I wasn't very old—I was thirty-two at the time—but I did go down, and I had heard the stories from my husband, who was head of General Hospital, of the conditions that people were brought in to the General who were attacked by the strikers and how terribly beaten that they were. I thought: "I'm not interested anymore in hearsay; I want to see it." So I went down to the market and I was alone and one of the Dunnes, the older brother, came up to me and said "What are you here for lady?"

I said "I'm an interested citizen, and I have every right to be here."

He said "Are you on the strikers' committee?"

I said "No, I'm not. I am sorry to say I've never been clever enough to have a job so I have no eligibility for any union on the face of creation and I am simply here as a spectator. This is my city, and I want to know what's happening." He looked at me for a moment, and he went away. In about five minutes two men appeared—one on my left and one on my right. They stood on both sides of me, and one of them—they were talking over my head—

and they had come from Chicago and Milwaukee. I can't remember their names at this late date. They had been instigators of the strikes in those cities and they had come to help the Dunne Brothers. They looked down at me and they said, "Well lady, where do you come from?" And I said brightly, I'm a Pittsburgher. I come from Pittsburgh." I won't put on tape what they said about police and the state police and the state of Pennsylvania and the city of Pittsburgh, but I took it that they thought they were something. And I said, "Well, those strikes were long before my day, but I had heard of them and I realize that it was the Homestead strike that really began the union movement in this country."

They said yes it was and they asked me if I had known anybody. I didn't dare tell them that the only people I had known were Henry Clay Frick and Andrew Carnegie. I felt that that was not the time to mention them. We stood there and then I saw Arthur Lyman come, being pushed forward by the crowd and trying to push the strikers back. The floor of the market was cobblestone, and Arthur had worn mountaineering boots with metal cleats in them. It was just as though he was skating on a waxed floor or on ice. Nothing would have been more lethal than those boots were, and the strikers pressed upon him and he slipped and went down and they were on him like a pack of wolves. I've never seen anything like it in my life. No sooner had he gone down and there was a great shout and an ambulance came from the other side of Hennepin Avenue. They loaded him in, although they had great difficulty because the strikers tried to get into the ambulance with him. I suppose they didn't feel he really was dead. And they chased the ambulance almost to General Hospital from down on First Avenue North and Seventh Street in Minneapolis.

Well, by this time, my two friends were getting very edgy, so one of them said to the other "I think it's about time we and the lady got the hell out of here." And they said to me, "How do you feel about it."

I said "I couldn't agree with you more." So each one took me by an elbow and the next thing I knew I was on the other side of Nicollet Avenue. I don't think my feet touched the ground. We shook hands warmly at parting, and I thanked them very much for taking care of me, which they had done to the best of their ability, and that's the last I saw of them. I don't know, but I always thought that Grant Dunne had sent them over there to watch over me. After all I wasn't very old, and I wasn't obviously—it sounds rather snippy but I don't mean it to—but I wasn't the class of person that was down there. On the other hand I was enormously interested, because frankly anything that involves people is absorbing to me. Nothing to me is like "the proper study of mankind being man." And that is my most vivid recollection of the strike.

The men on the committee, I felt, were quite unrealistic. For instance, Al Ringley appeared in a polo helmet as a method of protection and was quite horrified when I suggested that if the strikers saw anybody on the other side with a polo helmet they would consider him a class enemy and it would do nothing but add fuel to the flame. And the men on our committee were armed with little wooden sticks about twelve to eighteen inches long. The strikers were armed with lengths of pipe with nuts screwed on the end, and believe me they were lethal weapons. I know, because I was in the market the day Arthur Lyman was killed and I was about as far from him as I am from you and they had absolutely no protection. They seem to have no realization of what they were up against. They seem to have left reason behind. These were entirely emotional reactions that they were experiencing. They weren't reasoning; they were simply reacting against something they considered most unjust.

We had a very stormy meeting of the employers' committee and I was quite amused because when they showed me what they had as defense against the strikers I really laughed out loud. They wouldn't have been any more good than blowing on them; they would have done nothing to protect themselves. Barney Clifford went home that night and said to his wife: "We have only one woman on the committee and she is the most blood thirsty of the lot. And she says we haven't adequate protection." So he says, "When I go down to the market tomorrow I'm taking a gun." Which he did, and it saved his life because he was cornered in one of the stalls in the old market and they would have beaten him to death as they did Arthur Lyman but he pulled his gun and they went away. The committee impressed me as being unrealistic.

It's been hard for me to understand, in a way. I realize that both sides had their points. It is still a marvel to me that people cannot sit down and talk their problems out and eliminate this ill-will. It still persists. I've been on several commissions in the City of Minneapolis and one of the men who is quite high up on the police hierarchy, when I said something about the double parking of trucks, he said to me. "Mrs. Fahr, since 1934 we don't question anything the Teamsters do." Now that was last year, and that's nearly forty years. He remembered hearing about the strike. His father was in the police force.

I think the police had a rugged time of it; I thought that the police showed remarkable self-control. I have always had great respect for them since my experience in that strike. They were much criticized, because people felt they should have just open fire and just mowed the strikers down and protected property, but they held their fire. They could have precipitated a major holocaust, but they held their fire and tried to handle it as best they could and believe me there were many of them very badly injured. They are human beings and make their mistakes, but on that occasion they showed great, remarkable self-control, because they were seeing their fellows badly beaten. Dr. Fahr brought home one night one of the weapons that had been left when Arthur Lyman was killed. One of the strikers left his weapon in the ambulance and Dr. Fahr brought it home to show to me. It could have killed anybody. With one good swing, they could have settled anybody's life for ever and a day. It was my first experience with brutal violence.

Arthur Lyman was a member of my church: St. Marks Cathedral. I knew him well. And he was a very fine man and the least combative person I think I have almost ever known. He was superintendent of the Sunday school at St. Marks and when it was a hot day and the Sunday school children were restless, he'd take the children out on the lawn and give them time to blow off steam. He was a very gentle, very kind, very nice man and it seemed a terrible thing that it should have been he who suffered so much. When it's all said and done he didn't hurt anybody. He was just there; it was his unfortunate footwork.

He was there because he was on this employers' committee.

The committee was the business community. It was from the presidents of companies, from the leaders of business, from the leaders in civic affairs. There was no representatives whatever from the truck drivers. It was entirely an employers committee.

I remember Joseph Cochran very vaguely. He was part of that committee. Of course I remember the people whom I knew personally and frankly whom I knew socially, because they were the people with whom I had contact. Mr. Webber was the chairman. Arthur Rogers who was a civic leader here, was on it. Joseph Chapman (I think he was President of the Northwestern Bank or First National Bank, I forgot which) and then he took over Donaldsons; you see he was again in the upper echelon in the business world. And Al Lindsey who supported his father's real estate; Parks and Lindsey owned a tremendous amount of real estate. Al never did much of anything but row on the crew at Yale. He was not interested in a business career, but he was interested in this, I think, for the adventure of it more than anything else. But those were most of the people. I remember Judge Larson very well. Now Mr. Webber was President of Deere-Webber, the implement business. Arthur Rogers had been mayor of Minneapolis and had some position in the Northwestern Bank. Al Lindsey was a gentlemen. Barney Clifford, you've heard of Cream-of-Wheat. That was his connection. But they were all of that caliber.

Mr. Webber of course inherited his business. And the men who worked in the banks, worked their way up in it. But all of them had influence before they started, and connections. It's just as true today: you get a job very often through pull, but you have to stay in it through your own push. And a great many of them inherited these positions through their family connections. Charlie Veelie, he was a cousin of Mr. Webbers' and his son, young Charlie Veelie is Veelie Motors. Charlie Veelie himself was in the Deere-Webber Company. He was a cousin of Mr. Webber's. You see they were all more or less tied up together, They had family connections. They were a close little group.

It was a small committee, about twenty-four, and it was quite frankly the leading businessmen of the city of Minneapolis. I was the Maverick. I was the only woman, and far and away the youngest. They were all distinguished in their line and they were all older men who had been successful.

I felt very badly, to be frank with you. I thought there should be somebody from the Teamsters on the committee, but again I was a voice crying in the wilderness. Nobody agreed with me at all. They didn't want a dissident voice. And heaven knows I was there more or less on sufferance and I was the only one that was dissident. I think there were times that they bitterly regretted I was amongst them. Well, after all, I was put on there for my opinion so why not give it? And I'm not Scotch-Irish for nothing.

The Citizen's Alliance were anathema to this group, were considered a little less than dust. They were really and truly very much attacked. A. W. Strong with the Citizen's Alliance was the one they ken to, but they felt when you got down beneath Mr. Strong you ran into an awful lot of odd-balls. But Mr. Strong worked with this committee and did a great deal. I knew his wife well. They were years older than I, but awfully nice to me when I came here. Many of these people I didn't know in any business connection at all. I knew them socially. It wasn't the rank and file of the Citizen's Alliance that they thought well of; it was the people at the top.

Judge Larson, I thought did a great deal on the committee; he was a quiet, very sound man, and unprejudiced person. I liked him very much. He was very steady. I felt he was the way a judge should be: very judicial, very steady, and unbiased. I really warmed to him.

Mrs. Beardsley took a great deal of interest in a great many civic things, but I was never close to her. Mr. Webber was old enough to be my grandfather, let alone my father. He was old at that time; they were old, but they were men to whom the City of Minneapolis meant a tremendous amount, and I think their great aim was to preserve the image of a great city.

Occasionally, the Citizens Alliance would send somebody over that didn't have exactly the point of view that the employers committee had and they found that difficult to understand because for their book there was only one point of view. Somebody, I don't know who it was, but he came over from the Citizen's Alliance and suggested a small group of two or three and possibly five talking to the Dunne brothers. That didn't seem to do at all. I was all for that, but I was informed that's because I was young.

I was a very modest house wife. I got a great many threats, because I was marked as being the only woman. They threatened to kidnap my little boy. We got all kinds of threatening phone calls, things like that. We had a detective in the house both day and night for two weeks because of my little boy, my youngest child. It was a horrifying experience. I had heard of the expression that people under strong emotion can be like wild beasts. I never expected to see it, but I did.

The National Guard was called out after Arthur was killed, They weren't called out at first. I think it's a good thing that they weren't, quite frankly At the time my reaction was that I didn't think they should be called out unless it was an absolute necessity. Something about calling out the National Guard seems to rouse people that hadn't been roused before. Public opinion was very divided, very divided. The University for instance was very strongly pro-striker, the faculty. The students in those days didn't get involved the way they do now, but believe me, the faculty took sides. Not in the graduate school; of course those are mostly the people I saw because of my husband being professor of medicine.

When the National Guard was called, they were relieved in a sense and deplored it. Men on that committee had helped to make Minneapolis, and they felt that this strike was a terrible thing for their city. I think that, aside from their protection of rights of property, which is very strong in most of us and quite understandable, they were men who had put their backs into making this committee something. They felt terribly disturbed about. I think they felt that if the National Guard really entered, it was a real battle, it was not just fun and games. I think they felt if the National Guard was too much involved that it would bring about a major cataclysm which would be very bad for the city of Minneapolis. They couldn't have avoided real bloodshed. As it was, I think Arthur was the only person that was killed. Many people were badly hurt, but as I recollect, Arthur was the only person that died, and he wasn't dead when they took him to General, but he was DOA.

My husband didn't like that I joined the committee. He didn't like it at all. Naturally if he didn't like it I didn't stay on. Before the settlement I retired. After Arthur was killed, I guess it had been within the week, George said to me, "Now, you've had enough." So I retired and all I heard after that was what Mr. Webber told me. I got so involved. But I felt if you're on a committee, you should see what you're being a committee for, and that's why I went down to the market several times. Of course, the market was right in the heart of Minneapolis. It was just over there on the other side of Hennepin Avenue and believe me it was right in your lap. It wasn't anything remote at all. It was right there.

The communists were supposed to be up to it to their necks. In fact the Dunnes were supposed to be communists and that was the great rallying cry for the employers. This is a fight against Communism. Their names were mentioned a great many times. And I suppose the Dunnes were communists. I never knew them well enough to inquire into their political thinking, but they certainly did have the reputation and admitted to be communists.

Better dead: you'd mention the name communists and they'd go off like sky rockets. You see their whole ideology was absolutely diametrically opposed to anything that the strikers were standing for. The committee felt that the strikers were motivated by communists that they were financed greatly by communists, and by fellow travelers and that's all they needed, let me tell you. That was the beginning of the terrific feeling against Communism in this part of the country. Politically, you know, Minnesota has been quite lively. What with the Farmer-Labor and all these various things. To me, who came from Pennsylvania where you were a Republican and you knew there were Democrats —you didn't know them personally, but you knew they were there—it was quite a shock to come out here where there was so much political free-wheeling. It had always entertained me very much.

I shocked my sponsor, Mr. Webber, on more than one occasion. And his language was frequent and painful and free and when Mr. Webber started off, let me tell you his expletives would sear your taste. But I was so fond of him, and he was basically extremely fond of me—he was godfather of my youngest child—we were very close. He was a darling, a wonderful man; they don't make that kind of person anymore, who just let everything go for his city. The things that those men did are forgotten so soon, so soon.

Arthur Hesle (policeman)

I was standing there watching and a guy sneaked up behind me and hit me. I never swung my club or anything. I had my uniform on. My ear was full of blood. I used to get dizzy spells. He must have socked me a good one, 'cause I didn't even feel it when he hit me. I just went out.

August Bartholomew (striker)

One thing I can say, never was on relief. I'd work doing anything, you know. During the strike I ate better than I'm doing right now to tell you the truth, because we had a strike headquarters up here at Nineteenth and Chicago. We had one up on Eighth Street, between Third and Second Avenue. Then we had one up on Glenwood and we'd go up there and they would have meals for us and we'd come home with butter, meat, bread, potatoes. One thing I'll give them, the outfits credit. The bakery drivers, the milk drivers and some of the meat drivers, they furnished all the bread and stuff.

They had chefs up there; it wasn't nothing fancy you know. Some guy thought he was a pretty good cook he'd go out there and cook up a good meal. Her and I used to walk up there and God oh Mighty, we'd come home with armsful of stuff, you know.

We had scouts out and they'd see a truck and they'd call into headquarters, then we'd jump in and go out and stop them. We had scouts running all the time, night and day. We'd all be around the headquarters. They would always manage to have enough cars around strike headquarters to take care of something like that.

There were special policemen, they called themselves. One come over and he was heading upstairs, and I lived downstairs. He come over with his big badge on. Boy he sure went out the door in a hurry. He didn't want to stay there very long. Alliance hired a bunch of them see, I don't know what they paid him.

I carried a rubber hose about that long and had lead in each end about that big and filled with sand and that was nice. Fifth Street and Second or Third Avenue, they pulled a truck out with just a little box on it see and they brought a couple van loads of these strikers or these strike workers down there and we was waiting for them. We waited until they got out of the van and then we took after them. The truck had the windows all barred, you know, screened and the windshield. We had the truck and the truck pulled: you probably seen the picture of it in the paper there, where he pulled up front and stopped. We chased them strike breakers. They scattered like rats when we got that truck.

Skoglund, I don't know what his first name was. He talked kind of broken, you know, and he was negotiating the contracts. Before he'd leave there he'd have the contract signed too. He wasn't rough but he'd get there and he'd hold them until they saw things his way. It's kind of hard to understand him so I think lots of times they didn't know what he was talking about. I think they call the Dunne brothers communists because they went out and fought for the men. They were right out there with you; they weren't hiding no place.

Governor Olson was more for the workers than I think he was for the big shots. You know, you gotta have something like that, if it gets out of hand you gotta do something.

Western Union

MISS DEWSON.

CHAIRMAN [DEMOCRATIC] NATIONAL COMMITTEE WASH DC TERRIBLE STRIKE HERE UTTERLY MISMANAGED ONE OF OUR FINEST YOUNG MEN JUST KILLED AND HIS BROTHER SERIOUSLY INJURED AND MANY OTHERS IN JEOPARDY SACRIFICING THEMSELVES AS DEPUTY SHERIFFS IN SUPPORTING POLICE AGAINST RIOTERS WOMEN OF MINNEAPOLIS FINDING NO SECURITY AFFORDED HERE BEG YOU TO USE YOUR INFLUENCE TO SECURE SOME IMMEDIATE FORM INTERVENTION BY NATIONAL ADMINISTRATION

MRS CHARLES S PILLSBURY MRS ELBERT CARPENTER

[Penciled note on telegram] (I have written Mrs. Pillsbury (the flour magnates) that I would give this to the President. It would be fine if it was answered by the White House. She is a strong Democrat. Molly Dewson)

Harry deBoer (Executive Committee, Local 574)

As a matter of fact one of the men killed was a Citizens Alliance lawyer. Lyman was a lawyer. We had two battles and the police didn't want no part of fighting the strikers so the Citizens Alliance organized the special deputies which consisted of mainly businessmen. The first run in we had with the police, they were outnumbered four to one of course. At that time, they had some relatives that were workers. Emile Hanson, for instance, one of our organizers, his brother was a cop. So you see, it was a little bit more of personal feeling. The cops then, of course, weren't getting very much wages either. Some of them were sympathetic, but they were under Mike Johannes, Chief of Police and they couldn't do nothing but go out and fight if they were told, although we heard stories where some of them quit their jobs.

The second day was called "the deputy run." We chased them clean out of town. They found out that the workers were going to remain on strike 'til they got a contract. The first day I don't think there was much of a battle. It was just a matter of them showing their force and us showing our force. and the second day was our fight with the police and the third was the deputies. That's the one day that stays fresh in my memory, and that's seeing them running and laying under cars and everything else. It wasn't very healthy to have them show up with them badges. There was badges all over the place. They wanted to get away from being identified as special deputy, I assure you. They were recognized as the enemy.

We had the whole town tied up with the teamsters union and warehouse workers. It was better to leave the others work and support us financially and morally than to pull them out too; then we'd have to support them too and we didn't need that kind of physical support. We needed finances and moral support. A lot of these workers would come voluntarily on the picket lines when they were off duty. We had speakers that spoke to every meeting, every union meeting that would be coming up. We done it purposely to inform the rank and file what was going on because we didn't exactly trust the bureaucrats what they would tell them.

At one particular time the employer done a pretty good job of organizing the farmers against us, but again through the leadership of Dunne and Skoggy that understood capitalist politics we were able to reach the Farmers Holiday Association, and through them we were able to get the farmers to understand that they were being used by the bosses. Any legitimate farmer that had any vegetables or whatever they were raising and they were a legitimate farmer they could come in and unload and sell their product. We allowed them to. We don't have any fight with the farmer and we didn't care if they brought in their own vegetables. Of course if it was some company using their farm as a front, that was a different story. So that took considerable pressure off and it also helped because it showed that we didn't want any fight with the farmer. Our fight was with these big truck owners.

We took the unemployed right into the Union and explained again through our revolutionary leadership who understood, we told the unemployed to come and support this strike. We were fighting to get down to a forty-eight hour week and by doing that they'll be more workers going to work and you'll be put on the payroll on the Union contract if you support the Union. There was a lot of unemployed workers that fought along with the Union workers on the picket line to the extent that we formed Federal Workers Section after the strike was settled to help these workers get relief.

At that time you had pride; you hated to ask for help. We pointed out that they were entitled to help and we helped them right up until the time we were convicted. Max Gilman and Palmquist were in charge of that Federal Workers Section and their job was to see that workers got due respect even to the extent of stopping the landlord from evicting them. If they didn't have no place to go, we'd see that the transport company wouldn't haul their furniture out until they found them a place to live.

We were serious about it, but joked among some of the members. At that time I believe it was the Warner Brothers picked chickens and sent them to Chicago and so the chicken pickers came in to the Union. Kind of far-fetched from the truck drivers, but that's how the workers came. We had the reputation we'd do something. We would start to take in a lot of these groups and we would get in a battle with the Central Labor Union so we agreed to organize them, but we said "you'll have to go to your respective union."

I recall, a good illustration, our headquarters was on Third and Plymouth. The Minneapolis Brewery is right between Plymouth and Broadway where the bridge crossed the river. There's only a matter of about four block walk. One afternoon about two o'clock five hundred or six hundred Brewery workers marched over the bridge. They just walked off the job and walked over and said here we are, we want to join your Union and get a contract. They were having trouble with the Brewery Workers Union.

The younger workers worked on a permit system. The old brewery workers, they belonged to the Union. They wouldn't take any other members in. They would have them work on a permit so if the work got scarce, the permit workers would get laid off. It was a job shop, so to speak. We got them in the Hall and explained to them that we were sympathetic with them, and they would have to change their union, but that we would support them. They should go back to their Union and put up some demands and if they went out on strike or anything that we would support them. They went back and got in their own Union and by this time these bureaucrats were scared that they would lose, so they loosened up. So this is an illustration of how workers would come to our Union.

It had to be handled pretty carefully, but that is one of the reasons why we really got power. We had all of the workers, regardless what union they were in. They knew we had supported them when they needed it, so they supported us when we were in trouble.

Marvel Dobbs and Clara Dunne were in charge of women's section. They handled problems and seen to it that there were no evictions. Everything was pretty tied up; it was hard for a transfer to go move you out. And they got food. As a matter of fact, some families were fed right at strike headquarters. There was a big kitchen. They fed all the strikers. That headquarters was a hospital and a kitchen. They took care of anybody that was hurt, anybody hungry. They were well organized. The cooks and the waiters would send down cooks and waiters to cook the meals.

We sent pickets out with cans you know and a lot of people donated quarters, dimes, just like the Salvation Army. They had a banner on soliciting for the strikers' union and the bars had cans. We got good support. As a matter of fact that's the only reason we won the strike.

I've got to give credit to the revolutionists, the Dunnes, warning the workers what to expect, that the police weren't our friends. The police tried to leave the impression "Well, we're working, we've got to do this and we're your friends," but they'll hit you over the head if you turn your back. So the workers were warned what to expect, which helped win the battle for us. After all the police represented the bosses.

Totton P. Heffelfinger

I was one of the originals that was asked by our Sheriff, who was John Wall, to organize a group of special deputies, which I did in May 1934.[1]

At that time there were very few trucks run by big organizations. Food was brought in by farmers. Our desire was to see that they got into town. The police were supposed to protect them once they got into town. The police didn't do it. They couldn't do it. There weren't enough of them.

The main problem was that there was a great thought that these strikers were going to shut off all food to the Twin Cities. The reason for organizing this group was to go out with other sheriff deputies, on to the highways to see that these trucks weren't stopped. These were not official trucks. These were trucks owned by farmers bringing stuff into town. We had a headquarters in Minneapolis, but our organization was to be picked up and taken out with other sheriffs to see that these trucks were not stopped by the strikers. That was the reason for the organization. We did that a good many times.

All of a sudden, we were organized also with the police department. Somehow we got fouled up between the police department and the sheriff department. Our people were called into the street of Minneapolis. The police called us out to help them out. We had a Headquarters on Hennepin Avenue. We had a number of fellows in there. We never took any arms out onto the streets. Except one day there was a great big truck that stopped out in front of this headquarters and there were five of us left in the headquarters and fortunately we had two shotguns. We ran out and stood there and the strikers left very rapidly. They came up to tear our headquarters apart. Two trucks came up and they were going to go in and beat up our headquarters and beat up any of us in there, but we did have something that I was smart enough to have there, after being in the service.

Whether it was the Citizens Alliance that got me or not, or the sheriff contacted me, I don't recall. The deputies were young men I knew. Some of them had been in the service: friends of mine, and several of them had friends and helped me get this group, I think there were sixteen or eighteen of us. I can't remember exactly.

The police didn't call this thing. A group of citizens, it probably was the Citizens Alliance, I was active in the Citizens Alliance, went to the sheriff to get something done. They were trying to get food into Minneapolis, to feed their families and the people of Minneapolis.

They killed one of our men, I know. He was a friend of mine.

Note

1. At the interview in 1974 Mr. Heffelfinger opened his wallet to show he still carried the Deputy Sheriff badge that had been issued to him in 1934.

8 | The July Strike

THE AGREEMENT OF May 31 actually crystallized the differences between Local 574 and the 166 firms arrayed against them, differences which led seven weeks later to a second strike in the trucking industry. On May 26, several issues over which Local 574 originally struck remained unresolved as the Union withdrew picket lines and drivers returned to work but the Union had gained much. Employers had been forced to sign an agreement, no matter how vehemently they denied it. Local 574 had carried out a successful strike in a city known for the Open Shop, demonstrating to workers impressive leadership ability and union power. Legally speaking, the trucking firms may not have recognized Local 574, but workers certainly recognized that an organization capable of matching the power of the Citizens Alliance emerged from the strike. Not surprisingly, drivers, helpers, and inside workers from across the city flocked to join Local 574. The Union even established a section for unemployed which grew, according to the Union, to a membership of almost five thousand. Howard Carlson, streetcar motorman, recalled:

> It radicalized people. They think differently. They read differently. When this broke out in 1934, this was something new in the labor movement. They had a leadership, that really knew what to do. They took possession. All of the tactics they could use to bring this thing into being, I learned as I went along. I was a dumb cluck, you know, but I could see they really knew what to do. Radio was a new thing at that time. They used new electronics. They had microphones and loud speakers at their headquarters. It wasn't a private affair. Everybody

came. Everybody was welcome. They didn't say that, but gee, the headquarters during the two strikes were always full, and they had big meetings down at the parade grounds just west of Hennepin.

Whenever I got the opportunity I went down. Whole families went down there. It was a perpetual picnic.

As membership increased during the remainder of May and June, the Union attempted to open negotiations with each of the firms against which the strike had been directed. Generally negotiations failed. No specific wage rates had been included in the settlement; they were to be determined by the National Recovery Administration codes and by negotiations. Although trucking firms increased wages before the conclusion of the strike, and promised to keep the rate in effect until April 1935, some reduced them to pre-strike levels. The Union charged employers with chiseling, i.e., chipping away agreed upon wage rates, and failing to comply with the terms of the Labor Board's order. Various forms of chiseling appeared. "In the market area, checks for higher wages were made payable at the payroll window only, where they were uniformly cashed for smaller amounts. Employers persistently refused to select their representatives for the arbitration boards."[1] The Regional Labor Board sat powerless to enforce the agreement.

On June 14, Local 574 sent a letter to the Labor Board complaining that employers' refused to comply with the agreement. A copy of the letter was forwarded by the Labor Board to Levy & Dretchko, the attorneys representing the employers. On June 16, they replied and demanded that the Labor Board enforce its order ending the May strike, claiming that they had "carried out to the fullest extent every provision of that order." In reference to the Union letter they advised, condescendingly,

> The communication of the General Drivers' union . . . mis-states the provisions of your order. This may be through lack of understanding of the terms of your order.
>
> We insist and demand that your Board immediately assert itself by notifying General Drivers' Union of the rights of the respective parties and by obviating and preventing any further misunderstanding or misinterpretation of what your order means.[2]

Union and employers understood "rights of the respective parties" differently. The crux of the differences lay in the arbitration
clause. Employers still refused to meet with representatives of Local
574, but understood by the arbitration clause that differences would
be submitted to the Regional Labor Board for arbitration.

> The communication of General Drivers' Union . . . claims that the
> employers have agreed to set up a Board of Arbitration with represen-
> tatives of Local #574, to arbitrate wage scale or other conditions of
> employment. Such is not the fact, has never been the fact and the
> Order of your Board is just the contrary.
>
> During the hearings before your Board and in the final conferences
> with the Governor and the attorney for General Drivers' Union, our
> Committee took the position, repeated it, re-stated it, reiterated it,
> insisted upon it, and based our written consent to you making an
> order upon the fact that many of our employers had no employees
> who were members of Local #574; that Local #574 did not represent
> their employees, that they would not set up an Arbitration Board for
> their employees with Local #574 as claiming to represent them. Hence
> our consent and your Order provided that if any employer cannot
> agree upon a wage scale or conditions of employment with his
> employees or their representatives, that employer will submit those
> subjects to *your Board for arbitration.* . . .
>
> But as just stated, so far no employer has been advised by his
> employees that there is any dispute or disagreement as to wage scale
> or as to conditions of employment.[3]

Undoubtedly, the employees had not advised their employers of
"any dispute or disagreement," but the Union had presented
demands directly to employers in the name of their employees.[4]
Attorney Sam Levy's fine distinction revealed an enormous difference; the 166 employers refused to negotiate with union representatives or participate in arbitration boards. The Regional Labor Board,
they asserted, would handle all arbitration when arbitration was
appropriate. It was inappropriate, however, where Local 574 did
not represent their employees. In such cases employers were justified refusing to meet with the Union's representatives. To substan-
tiate their claims that the Union represented very few workers, they
conducted

a survey which showed that in the 166 firms affected by the Regional Labor Board's Order of May 31st, which employed approximately 4,400 truck drivers, helpers, platform men, and such inside workers over which Local No. 574 claimed jurisdiction, there were actually only 309 men who were out on strike; that all others were either working or were available for work, when called, or were on the payroll. This survey also disclosed that in 120 of these firms there was actually no one out on strike.[5]

Given employer hostility toward unions, it is surprising that surveyors found in a telephone survey 309 men who would declare that they were on strike, for such a declaration certainly made them marked men. Recall that Local 574 originally struck only eleven firms. The survey attempted to reify the 166 firms employers, not the Union, had grouped together.

The Regional Labor Board was not really the audience for this survey, for it knew full well that elections would resolve the issue; certainly workers on strike were not the audience. Since a critical audience would question this survey's validity, if not relevancy, surveyors must have intended to rally trucking employers in the group of 166, or to reach the less informed Minneapolitans already predisposed toward them, and for whose support they contended with Local 574.

The Union's radical statements lent credibility to the employers' claim, for Local 574 did claim jurisdiction over general truck drivers in Minneapolis. It had struck only eleven companies, but no one doubted, particularly no workers doubted, that success with those eleven firms would emboldened the Union to reach out to organize others. Trucking employers simply anticipated the Union's next step, attempting to force their hand while they were yet weak.

The employers' refused to meet union representatives let alone arbitrate differences, and thus obstructed peaceful means to settle differences and correct the chiseling practiced by a few firms. The Labor Board, weak and ineffective, had no legal power to force compliance, even if it could have reached consensus. E. H. Dunnigan, the Commissioner of Conciliation who was sent to Minneapolis in early July, reviewed with Secretary W. W. Hughes the Board's handling of Local 574's arbitration request. He minced no words in his report:

The board took a vote on the question of appointing the arbitration board but the board was deadlocked on the question I inquired of [Hughes] how a board of 11 members could become deadlocked. He said the chairman of the board, Neil Cronin, declined to cast the deciding vote on the grounds that he thought the other members of the board ought to decide the question. I told him that, in my judgment, one of the main functions of an impartial chairman is to cast the deciding vote whenever the labor members and the industrial member on the board are equally divided on a question.

The representatives of the union are very much incensed over the position as taken by the chairman of the board. Personally, I think the chairman of the board is derelict in performing his duty as chairman of the board, particularly in a situation where the two groups are equally divided on a vote.[6]

Voluntary compliance, the basis upon which the Labor Board established its authority, had achieved little. Finding their workers' employers unwilling to bargain, Local 574 had no alternative but to prosecute another strike.

On June 28, Vince Day advised the Governor concerning developments in the Minneapolis situation. "Red Cramer [Editor of the *Labor Review*] of Minneapolis advises that the employers refuse to keep the terms of the strike settlement."[7] Olson's hopes that differences would be settled through arbitration dimmed.

On July 1, the battle for public support returned to the front page of Minneapolis newspapers which carried the views of the Employers' Advisory Committee. This organization was headed by Joseph R. Cochran, a Director of the Citizens Alliance, who had spoken for the 166 employers in May. As we shall see, this new formal identification reflected a more disciplined organization. The *Tribune* carried a letter signed by Ivan Bowen and Citizens Alliance attorney Sam J. Levy, charging that *Tribune* accounts of the difficulties were based largely on rumors that the employers were not living up to the agreement. They asserted that the May settlement order declared: "when the board is advised of the failure of the parties to reach an agreement, then and not until then is the board called upon to provide a board of arbitration."[8] They concluded that no basis for calling an arbitration board existed.

We can understand the logic of their position best this way: Local 574, employers declared, did not represent their workers. Because it did not represent their workers, employers refused to meet its representatives. Thus, there could be no negotiations with them. Accordingly, no one could inform the Board of a failure to reach agreement, since no agreement was being negotiated. Since no one could advise the board of a failure, no arbitration board could be called.

The dispute began to focus on which workers 574 represented, a dispute that, ironically, had alienated Dan Tobin, Teamster President, as well. Who rightly qualified for membership in Local 574? Who should determine these qualifications? Union leaders were predisposed to let the individual worker decide whether he or she wanted to join. If that worker joined, then the Union had an obligation to represent that worker. As we have seen, thousands flocked to join Local 574, and the Union attempted to steer these new members into appropriate craft unions. Throughout, Local 574 defined its jurisdiction broadly, but not as unlimited. For example, it referred brewery workers who came to them for help back to their craft union.[9] In the case of trucking and warehousing, the Union asserted a broad jurisdiction that extended from the driver's seat well into the warehouse itself to "inside workers"; it intended to negotiate for all its members within that jurisdiction, and refused to allow employers, or Dan Tobin for that matter, to define their jurisdiction unilaterally. These "inside workers" represented not only a significant part of Local 574's support, but an expression of industrial union philosophy. Certainly some workers must have been tempted to jettison inside workers or delay their organization in order to consolidate the gains of the May strike, but drivers and helpers proved willing to risk their gains to support inclusion of inside workers. Strike leaders prevented compromise on this issue from becoming a serious possibility.

Local 574 admitted into the Union workers whom employers refused to accept as qualified for Local 574 membership. Employers also had workers who opposed Local 574, and so could declare correctly that Local 574 did not represent all their workers. This defined an issue that might be resolved through bargaining, or through review of individual cases, but could not be resolved in the press.

Local 574 answered the Employers' Advisory Committee's paid advertisement in a letter to the *Tribune* that declared the real difference was which occupations the Union had the right to represent. The Union asserted it had the right to deal for all its members and further, that the EAC was aware that their employees were Union members. On the question of wage demands, the Union stated that such demands had not been submitted to the Labor Board, but had been presented directly to employers.[10]

The distance between Union and employers had not been lessened by this exchange. The Union claimed employers were not living up to the agreement, but the employers claimed they were. To support their claim, the EAC offered a $1,000 reward for proof that they had not lived up to the agreement. The Union "flatly refused to consider the reward offer"[11] as it diverted attention from the necessity for direct negotiations between the Union and the employers. Even in the unlikely event that the Hennepin County judges suggested as referees would ever find for the Union, even if information and records could be obtained, the Union had little interest in pursuing this challenge. Such a reward appealed to the Minneapolis citizenry, not union members; it attempted to conduct negotiations in the press rather than at the bargaining table. Local 574 called a mass meeting July 6 to rally support for a strike.

Following a huge parade, Roy Weir, President of the Central Labor Union, John Bosch, representing the Farm Holiday Association, Robert Fleming of St. Paul Teamsters Local 120, Rubin Lotz of the Laundry Workers Union, and Myrtle Harris of the Garment Workers Union, as well as Local 574 leaders, addressed the rally. Governor Olson did not appear, nor did he send an official representative, as he had in May, but Roy Wier of the Central Labor Union alluded to Olson when he claimed that labor's "ends are achieved through political action."[12]

Olson's political supporters included radicals and trade unionists alike, but many radicals had become disillusioned with him. After the May strike, the Communist Party attacked the leadership of Local 574 and Governor Olson, calling them traitors to the working class. They accurately charged that the May agreement did not specifically meet union demands. Strike leaders, they asserted, had "sold out" workers to employers. Curiously enough, one of the most outspoken and vituperative critics in the Communist Party was

William Dunne, brother of Vince, Miles, and Grant Dunne of Local 574.[13] This opposition had little affect, for workers endorsed a strike in a standing vote, and set a deadline of 7:00 p.m. Wednesday, July 11. A strike vote was to be taken at 8:00 p.m. that same day by all unions in sympathy with Local 574.

Union supporters received a jolt July 7 from the Labor Board's interpretation of the ambiguous Section 8 of the agreement.

> The Regional Labor Board interprets the meaning of `employees' as noted in Section 8 of the consent order of May 31, 1934 to mean truck drivers and helpers and any such other platform men as are directly engaged in loading and unloading trucks.
>
> However, the board recommends that all workers of the firms involved who were out on strike should be dealt with on the basis provided in the consent order . . . and be subject to all the terms and conditions of said order including arbitration provisions thereof.[14]

The EAC readily accepted this narrow interpretation because it accepted their assertion that only truck drivers and helpers were covered by the May agreement, but it chided the Labor Board for adding the recommendation.[15] The Union demanded that the recommendation be made part of the Board's definition because it properly accepted all members of the Union, including inside workers. The Board's equivocation satisfied no one. Hopes for preventing a strike faded.

On July 10 the EAC opened a two front attack on Local 574 through a series of advertisements in local newspapers, appealing to Minneapolitans, workers and ordinary citizens alike, from an angle not used extensively in Minneapolis during May: the strikers they charged, intended to foment a Communist revolution.[16] The EAC reasserted that the dispute had nothing to do with wages. The strike, the EAC declared, threatened civil, economic and political order in Minneapolis. The strike, they asserted, created social upheaval that the Communists would exploit to revolutionize Minnesota

Vince Dunne made no secret of his membership in the Communist League. Carlos Hudson, a member of the Communist League, served as editor of Local 574's *The Organizer*, which began publication on June 25[17] and became a daily at the beginning of the July strike. *The Organizer* offered inflamed rhetoric, and militant analysis of the strike as class warfare. The charge, then, had credibility. The EAC ignored distinctions between the Communist Party USA and the Communist League, and it did not identify rank and file strikers who were actually members of the Communist League. Rather, it focused on the leadership, on highly influential strike leaders like Vince Dunne, Grant Dunne, Miles Dunne, Farrell Dobbs, and Carl Skoglund, all of whom belonged to the Communist League.

The Communist League took pride in its involvement and trumpeted any success the Union achieved. It portrayed itself as an informed, objective organization that followed a rational plan based upon sound principles, accurate analysis, and precise tactics. *The Militant*, the official organ of the Communist League, declared that it had accurately predicted union sentiment, had consciously selected Minneapolis and the truckers as the vanguard of their national movement, and had perpetrated and led the whole strike.[18] It may have exaggerated its claims when it implied that the workers had been systematically educated to class conflict, systematically aroused, organized, and directed by the Communist League alone, but organizing and planning for the strikes rested largely in the hands of members of the Communist League. However, not even the Communist League claimed extensive membership from the union rank and file.

The EAC took advantage of the League's pride in its role, advertising its proclamations that the strike was an incipient revolution. Subtle differences between communism, socialism, and social democracy disappeared beneath the EAC's avalanche of anti-red propaganda. Almost daily, advertisements quoting *The Militant* appeared sounding the alarm about "Another Communist Strike."[19]

The EAC added a second and related front to red baiting by drawing a picture of Local 574 as an illegal union outside the AFL Dan Tobin, President of the International Brotherhood of Teamsters, and William Green, President of the AFL provided, through their criticism of Local 574, a ready arsenal for this attack. The issue between these labor leaders and Local 574 arose from differences in union philosophy. The AFL had declared against industrial unionism as early as 1901 in its Scranton Declaration[20] and compromised its doctrine of craft autonomy reluctantly. Local 574 accepted members from all phases of the trucking industry and thus became an industrial union. The AFL identified industrial unionism with radical, left wing or communist forces. In an attempt to further isolate the Union, the Employers' Advisory Committee quoted AFL and Dan Tobin attacks on the leadership of Local 574 in its advertisements, even though in fact it would not have negotiated with either.[21]

These advertisements placed the Minneapolis Central Labor Union in a very awkward position. Sympathetic to the attempts of Local 574 to win recognition, it found itself at odds with national leaders who attacked that union. Officially, the CLU felt it could do little, but city leaders could and did support Local 574 individually. Local interest and loyalty proved stronger than national associations and members of the AFL unions joined Local 574 on the picket lines.[22]

City newspapers attacked the threatened general strike directly. The *Tribune* declared in a front page editorial:

> The history of all labor conflict in the United States will not show one instance where a so-called general strike was effective. . . . Such a strike imposes more and greater hardships on the working class than it does on any other class.
>
> Losses are sustained to compensate for which further economies must be enforced.
>
> The *Tribune* can see no reason for either a general strike or a strike of the truck drivers. It does not appear that there is any general question as to wages, hours, or working conditions. . . .
>
> Every wage worker should ask themselves whether any attainable results would justify the price that must be paid.[23]

Despite this barrage of propaganda, the Union didn't waver. Wednesday, July 11, the deadline passed, but at the mass meeting held that night, a standing vote endorsed the strike to commence at midnight Monday, July 16. Time remained to negotiate; the Union hoped that employers would reconsider. However, the call for a general strike had not been welcomed by organized labor in Minneapolis; and St. Paul truckers voted at a poorly attended meeting not to strike. The July strike, just like the May strike, became a strike of Local 574 alone.

The cumulative effect of the employers' advertisements and the newspaper attacks raised doubts in some workers' minds. Sunday,

July 15 the *Tribune* announced a meeting at Wesley church for union members opposed to the leadership and the strike. The agenda included a call for a secret ballot on the strike and a demand that Brown and other leaders of the strike resign because negotiations had been improperly conducted.[24]

The meeting commenced with many strikers in attendance, but when the meeting was called to order, some strikers rose and called to those remaining to join them and walk out. Grant Dunne seems to have intervened to keep the meeting orderly and recalled the group who threatened to walk out. Bill Brown arose to declare that he didn't want to strike, but the employers forced the Union into one. He answered EAC charges, re-stated at the church meeting, that Local 574 was trying to build "One Big Union," a charge that might frighten employers, but troubled workers far less. Turning the charge around, he offered a worker's perspective. "The charge had been made that the leaders planned to build a union so large and powerful that it could control industry. That was precisely the intention, he said."[25]

Grant Dunne presented two resolutions to be voted on at the regular meeting Monday night July 16. They asked if the Union members wanted a change in leadership and if they wanted to take a secret ballot. In closing, Miles Dunne added that the Union had its own meeting place and did not need one provided by the employers.[26]

Whether the EAC actually arranged the meeting remains unclear, but the meeting hardly came off as its organizers planned. What started as a protest meeting against union leaders and the strike became a rally for the Union. At the Monday night meeting, Union members endorsed both the strike and the Union leadership. The strikers walked off the job at midnight Monday night.

Tuesday papers announced the Union's strike vote and the EAC's countermove: an offer by the 22 market firms to arbitrate wages with Local 574 for their "warehouse employees" on the basis of comparing payrolls and membership rolls. The proposal also stated, "Nothing contained in our offer to adjust the affairs of our group upon the above basis shall be deemed or considered any precedent affecting any other employer who accepted the Labor Board order of May 31 which order is still in full force and effect."[27] In May employers had augmented the strength of the eleven firms Local 574 originally targeted by rallying 155 other trucking firms to their defense. Now those additional 155 firms were party to the May settlement with Local 574. The EAC's offer apparently to separate these twenty-two firms implies a reconsideration of their general strategy.

The Union refused the offer. Why now negotiate with twenty-two firms rather than 166? The Union would undoubtedly lose in many of the 144 remaining firms, but any victories would provide a welcome if unanticipated accretion to their strength.

From city government, the Union heard warnings that the strike would meet opposition. Chief Michael Johannes presented his funding request for the Police Department, asking to double the 1934 police budget. The money would hire 400 additional men, increasing the force to 895, and purchase "$1,000 worth of machine guns, 800 rifles with bayonets, 800 steel helmets, 800 riot clubs, and outfit 26 motorcycle police."[28] It would also fund a police training school which would prevent recurrence of the May "disgrace." The equipment and the school were necessary, he testified, "for police must be trained just like an Army to handle riots."[29]

Similar to the May strike, the Union set up strike headquarters with beds, an infirmary and a cafeteria, on Eighth Street South. It contacted farmer organizations, for local truck farmers who had been unable to market their produce in May had brought pressure on Olson to declare martial law. To correct this error, Union leaders met with the Farm Holiday Association and the Market Gardeners' Association to work out plans for member farmers to set up and operate a free market to which individuals and retailers could come to purchase goods unmolested. In return, these farmer organizations contributed food to the Union.[30]

The first day of the strike Tuesday, July 17, Minneapolis was a peaceful though tense city. The strike was immediately and totally effective, for scarcely a truck moved. Mayor A. G. Bainbridge requested troops from Governor Olson to assist city police. As a precautionary measure, Olson mobilized one battalion of the 151st Field Artillery and assigned it to the armory. Olson would not accede to the Mayor's request, declaring, "I will not take sides. I will enforce law and order if necessary. I feel the strike could have been prevented."[31]

The new National Labor Board sent Father Francis J. Haas, Advisor to the Board, to Minneapolis. Father Haas flew into the city as the EAC announced plans to move trucks later in the week. Haas conferred with E. H. Dunnigan whom the Unites States Conciliation

Service had sent July 6 at the request of Minnesota Farmer-Labor Senator Henrik Shipstead[32] Thursday they met with both the Union and the EAC in the Nicollet Hotel, but failed to secure an agreement.

EAC advertisements continued to warn that this was not a strike, but "really a communist rebellion"[33] which threatened to set up a communist soviet on orders from Moscow. Not to be defeated by communists, nor intimidated by their tactics, the EAC conferred with the police over arrangements to convoy trucks under police protection.

Thursday afternoon, July 19, police escorted a truck bearing a sign reading: "Hospital Supplies," in a movement well covered by reporters and photographers. Friday's newspapers carried pictures of the truck surrounded by police captioned "Food supply for hospitals is escorted by heavily armed police."[34] The Union's permit system set up at the onset of the strike provided for deliveries to hospitals. Although it is unlikely that this truck had such a permit, no police escort had really been necessary. It is not impossible that this move was calculated to establish a favorable police image in preparation for Friday's move.

Chief Johannes evoked the beatings police had taken in May, and issued unmistakable instructions to the escorting police.

> We are going to start moving goods. Don't take a beating. You have shotguns and you know how to use them. When we are finished with this convoy, there will be other goods to move.
>
> The police department is going to get goods moving. Now get going, and do your duty.[35]

Alarmed by this declaration, Father Haas and Governor Olson appealed to Chief Johannes for a forty-eight hour truce. Both Haas and Olson believed that Johannes had agreed, but Johannes later denied an agreement, declaring he did not have the power to enter into one. In his statement of denial, Johannes acknowledged, "I agreed to take up the matter with the Employers' Advisory Committee and to see what action they wanted taken." Curiously, in the same statement Johannes declared, "I am not one of the parties involved in the strike."[36] Whether or not Johannes promised a truce, he learned from the EAC that they wanted trucks moved, and Friday he intended to carry out their wishes.

The scene for the confrontation was, as in May, the market district, specifically, the Slocum-Bergren Co. on Third Street North. Police with shotguns cordoned off the area and strikers gathered. License plates had been removed and all identifying markings had been painted over on a truck that backed up to the Slocum-Bergren Co. dock.[37] A few crates of merchandise were tossed into the truck and, after waiting a few minutes, the police climbed into their cars and the truck pulled out. The New York *Times* reported the event.

> During the morning two food trucks had moved out of the district under police guard and had made deliveries to retail stores without molestation from a growing crowd of pickets. By afternoon 150 patrolmen had been sent to the scene to keep the throng in check.
>
> Shortly after 2 P.M. a third food truck moved out from a wholesale house. It was followed by twelve squad cars each carrying four policemen, all armed with shotguns.
>
> The truck turned onto Third Street North; another truck loaded with strike pickets cut in ahead of it. Policemen quickly lined the street, but the strikers plowed through the cordon and drove directly into the front of the truck. Police rushed from the convoy cars and opened fire with shotguns on the pickets' truck. Two pickets fell off, wounded, but the truck continued up the street, being fired on from both sides of the street. . . .
>
> At this point four truckloads of National Guardsmen, who had been held in readiness at the armory, arrived at the scene. . . . Only four wounded strikers were picked up by the city General Hospital ambulances, however, the others had been rushed in private cars to an emergency hospital at strike headquarters, a vacant garage in the Loop district. . . .
>
> Thirty minutes later the district had been cleared of pickets and the food truck continued on its way to make deliveries.[38]

When reports from shotguns and pistols ceased and the smoke cleared 67 strikers were wounded. Two later died.

The truck movement Friday differed from Thursday's "hospital" truck movement in two ways: the truck carried no propagandistic signs, and the police escorted it in force. Strike headquarters had been warned by National Guard Commander General Ellard Walsh that the police were planning to move a truck and that they were armed,[39] although the Union undoubtedly already knew this. Newspaper reporters and photographers knew; as for previous truck movements, they stood ready on roof tops to get better pictures and report any confrontation. The movement Friday differed from previous escorts primarily because it was ostensibly a routine movement of goods on an ordinary delivery. Symbolically, it defined the issue. That the confrontation might turn violent deterred neither the EAC, the police, nor the strikers.

Initial accounts rushed into early editions of the newspapers reported that the strikers were unarmed and that many were shot in the back,[40] but subsequent accounts modified the story. Some accounts, particularly in the Minneapolis *Journal*, reported that strikers were told to disperse and refused, that many warning shots were fired into the air, but went unheeded. Only then, the *Journal* reported, did the police lower their guns and fire at the strikers obstructing the "food-laden" truck. When pickets rushed forward from Seventh Avenue North, the *Journal* state, warning shots were fired over their heads, but when they kept coming, police fired into the pavement and strikers began to run. "The police followed, firing downward as they ran." The *Tribune* reported: "In the abandoned strikers' truck lay two wounded men, unable to rise. . . . Dozens of others limped about the streets, suffering from leg wounds."[41]

The most widely published picture of the shooting makes a lie of such distortions. This picture was taken as the strikers' truck rammed the delivery truck. Strikers still filled the truck box and one of the policemen has his shotgun in firing position aimed directly at the strikers. The few crates in the back of the delivery truck are clearly visible. It was definitely not "food-laden."

Friday's shooting raised a storm of public protest, but Mayor A. G. "Buzz" Bainbridge felt he had nothing to explain. "Strikers had ample warning that the police were going to convoy trucks and that the police would be armed. . . . What do you think police carry guns for, ornaments?"[42] Governor Olson declared that much needed explaining and ordered an investigation. It found that "twenty-five strikers had been shot in the back while trying to run away and four others while aiding the wounded."[43] It concluded:

> Police took direct aim at the pickets and fired to kill; physical
> safety of police was at no time endangered; no weapons were in the

possession of the pickets in the truck; at no time did pickets attack the police, and it was obvious that pickets came unprepared for such an attack; the truck movement in question was not a serious attempt to move merchandise, but a `plant' arranged by the police.[44]

Saturday, Chief Johannes, at the request of Mayor Bainbridge ordered a temporary halt to convoying trucks. The EAC agreed. Haas and Dunnigan conferred with the EAC, Local 574, and Governor Olson all day, visiting the EAC in the morning, strikers at mid-afternoon and returning to talk with the EAC that evening, all to no avail. Sunday the EAC announced its intention to move additional trucks. Mayor Bainbridge advised that police would convoy the trucks which were to carry "food, fuel, and other necessaries."[45] The EAC intended to stay the course.

Strikers reacted to the shooting angrily, talking of arming themselves and going after the police. Strikers stormed to the Mayor's office and demanded that the police be withdrawn. The Central Labor Union demanded the ouster of Chief Johannes and circulated petitions calling for the impeachment of Mayor Bainbridge. These petitions gained some twenty thousand signatures within ten days.[46]

The strike leadership feared that strikers would arm themselves and go after the police, and spent the day and night disarming workers who came to headquarters with weapons.[47] The sight of bloody strikers stumbling back to strike headquarters frightened many, and rumors of a planned police raid on headquarters sprang up. Despite fear, workers were grimly determined to go on.[48] At a rally held to vent their anger, to calm workers, and city labor leaders, Farm Holiday Association members, and D. T. Boner, president of the Independent Grocers Association urged strikers to continue their struggle.[49] Strike leaders warned strikers that if they armed and attacked police, they would endanger the entire strike. Troops could be called out against them, and the strikers would lose everything.[50]

The EAC perpetrated the clash, and so with it rests major responsibility for the tragedy. However, convoying this single truck required so many police for protection that it could not have been done on a scale large enough to break the strike. Even ignoring the enormous expense, police did not have the manpower to convoy trucks on any significant scale. William Brown understood this the day before the clash when he observed that "a few trucks might get by under police escort, but there will be no general movement of trucks."[51] Strikers might have let the challenge pass. The fact is, however, that the parties to the conflict accepted this challenge to their determination.

Friday, July 20, 1934, left no room for compromise. Both parties rallied to unyielding and militant positions determined to outlast the other. Employers had even a stronger need to justify their course. The Union dare not betray those who had been sacrificed. Undaunted, Father Haas and E. H. Dunnigan continued efforts to effect a settlement. On Wednesday they announced a proposal, which, they declared, was "one of our own," neutral, fair and impartial. This proposal became known as the Haas-Dunnigan Plan. Essentially it met all Union demands, listing minimum wage rates and defining inside workers more precisely than the May 31 agreement. The plan met EAC claims that the Union did not represent their employees by providing for elections.[52]

Both the Union and the EAC published counter-proposals that differed from the Haas-Dunnigan plan. The Union included inside workers in the bargaining unit, and proposed higher wages retroactive to May 26. The difference between these two proposals was not marked, and they were precise. On Wednesday, July 25, the Union voted to accept the Haas-Dunnigan plan.[53]

The EAC recommended many changes and clarifications which the *Tribune* reported

On rehiring:

We need not rehire anyone guilty of violence. Alleged cases will be brought before the National Labor Board. Their decision will be final. We need not rehire while the decision is pending.

On representation:

Any person, persons, or organization claiming to represent the employees of any firm shall be required to furnish definite proof to that firm before that firm shall be required to deal or negotiate with them. This shall not be deemed any requirement on the part of any labor organization claiming to represent employees to disclose the names of those employees.

On wages:

> We dislike and think it unfair to arbitrate a wage starting from higher
> than at the outset of the strike and then arbitrate upward.[54]

Father Haas wrote a terse letter to the Employers' Advisory
Committee requesting they reconsider their response to the Haas-
Dunnigan Plan.

> The plan, as submitted to both sides, was a compromise and called
> upon both parties to make concessions which we felt they should make.
>   . . . We note that your reply requests certain clarifications and
> modifications. We consider this a rejection of the proposed settlement
> which we submitted.
>   It is not improper to advise you that Local 574 has accepted the
> plan as submitted by us.
>   We consider it not too late for your committee . . . to reconsider . . .
> and to accept the plan as outlined.[55]

The Employers' Advisory Committee responded that Local 574
was communist and that the employers refused to deal with communists. To answer the EAC demand for proof that Local 574 truly
represented their workers, Father Haas wired NLRB Chairman
Lloyd Garrision to confirm his interpretation that "Section Seven A
requires any representation chosen be dealt with" by employers.[56]
Garrison responded: "If an election is ordered the employer is
bound under Section Seven A to bargain collectively with the representatives elected by the majority of his employees."[57]

The Union staged a mass demonstration at the funeral of Henry
Ness, killed by police. The Union began to call the shooting "Bloody
Friday." The Minneapolis press carried only superficial accounts of
the funeral; the crowd that gathered and marched to the cemetery
was estimated at 40,000, over ten times the number of workers actually on strike. *The Organizer* presented Ness as a martyr in the workers struggle for dignity. Strike leaders eulogized Ness and recounted
his last words—a charge to the strikers not to let him down—to firm
up their commitment and determination.

In the face of this sympathetic demonstration, the EAC reiterated
its intention to move more trucks. Given the course of events in

May, police clearly risked a second confrontation should they load other trucks, and strikers would come to such a confrontation in greater numbers and better prepared than on "Bloody Friday."

On Thursday evening, July 26, Governor Olson declared martial law, swearing he would make Minneapolis "as quiet as a Sunday School picnic."[58] Olson was criticized by both disputants. The EAC cited the decreasing number of arrests to show that since peace had returned martial law was unnecessary. Strikers demanded he take the soldiers off the streets and leave the picketing to them.

Olson sent a letter to the EAC castigating them for rejecting the Haas-Dunnigan plan.

> I do not agree that the plea for a living wage by a family man receiving only $12.00 a week is answered by calling him a communist. Neither am I willing to join in the approval of the shooting of unarmed citizens of Minneapolis, strikers, and bystanders alike, in their backs in order to carry out the wishes of the Citizens' Alliance.
>
> . . . You are constantly speaking in writing about the duty of the Government toward you. You must not forget that you also have a duty to the Government. . . . The agencies of government do not belong to you. . . . They belong to all the people and I propose to use the government agencies under my jurisdiction, including the national guard, for the protection of all the people of the city of Minneapolis and all people outside the city, including farmers, who desire to do business within the city.[59]

The National Guard established a curfew, prohibited downtown parking, and banned liquor sales after 9:00 p.m., but the inconveniences already caused by the strike were not greatly compounded. To meet demands from small businesses not targeted by the strike, the National Guard created a system of permits, administered by Guard officers, allowing trucks carrying necessities to operate on the streets. This system proved troublesome.

Olson did not want to break the strike, yet the permit system threatened to do so. After all, trucks moved on the streets of Minneapolis; the Union had sworn that the strike would stop all truck movement. Although permits were to be issued only to transport necessities, they were issued more generously than the Union approved. No one had defined "necessity." National Guard officers, commonly middle class, respectable citizens in their communities, who probably did not share Olson's sympathies for strikers, supervised issue of permits. There is little evidence of concerted attempts to sabotage the permit system, but most of the Guard officers charged with distribution of permits understood employers' problems more readily than the Union's. At first only a few permits were issued, but exceptions soon expanded the number. Close decisions favored truck operations. By Sunday, July 29, some 4,000 permits had been issued, not including farmer owned-operated produce trucks, public utility trucks, newspaper trucks, and military vehicles. From the point of view of Local 574, too many trucks were moving so Union representatives went to see the Governor and demanded:

1. Strikers be allowed to meet at their headquarters unmolested;
2. Peaceful picketing be permitted with permission to stop trucks suspected of chiseling on permits and the strike;
3. The Governor withdraw the troops from the streets and leave the picketing solely in the hands of strikers;
4. Pending completion of arrangements for efficient picketing, the Governor shall stop all truck transportation for 48 hours effective immediately.[60]

Olson recognized that the permit system threatened to break the strike, but he feared that to withdraw the troops invited further violence. Olson advised the Union that: meetings in their headquarters building had been and would continue to be permitted; troops would not be withdrawn and trucking would not be halted; violations of permits should be reported to the guard.[61] Olson's response failed to satisfy the Union which then called a mass meeting at the Parade grounds.

The strike had reached stalemate; each party held firmly to principle. Strikers reiterated their right to represent all their members; the EAC declared themselves protectors of the American way of life, who refused to "sell out the city to the Communists."[62]

On Tuesday, July 31, Governor Olson, addressing the citizens of Minneapolis, explained the situation they faced, and identified the issue that divided the parties, which was, he declared: "the issue of a fair or unfair wage scale for persons employed."[63]

Olson supported the wage scale Father Haas and Mr. Dunnigan proposed and asked all employers moving merchandise by truck under the permit system to pay that wage. Acceptance of the wage scale, Olson said, would not commit the "employers to the entire Haas-Dunnigan proposal." Neither would it involve "abandonment by the Union" of the position it had taken.[64] No more permits were to be issued, because violations of the permit system showed lack of good faith and unwilling to cooperate.

The strikers vehemently attacked both Olson's proposal and his declaration of martial law. They argued that Olson had declared martial law because the EAC had not agreed to the Haas-Dunnigan proposal, and yet martial law operated exclusively in the interest of employers. They charged that

> Despite all his harsh words directed at the employers, Governor Olson directs all his harsh blows at the Union and the strike.
>
> Against this attempt to undermine and break the strike, Local 574 has but one alternative, to fight. In so doing, we intend to assert every one of our constitutional rights.[65]

The Union issued a call for a meeting of "every sympathizer and supporter in the labor movement"[66] at the Parade grounds for Tuesday evening, July 31. The Union declared that it would start to picket again, not by forming picket lines, but by patrolling cars. Pickets were requested to gather, in direct defiance of the Governor and the National Guard, at strike headquarters at 4:00 a.m. The Governor had other plans.

> The guardsmen struck quickly Wednesday morning in answer to the threat of the strike leaders to resume active picketing. Just before 4 a.m. . . . 800 guardsmen descended upon the headquarters.[67]

Surrounding the building and blocking escape, the guardsmen succeeded in capturing Bill Brown, Vince, and Miles Dunne whom they took to a stockade at the state fairgrounds. Grant Dunne and Farrell Dobbs escaped. Indignant at the raid, strikers roamed the city in small bands tipping over trucks, ripping out ignition wiring and roughing up drivers. The list of calls for the National Guard reported by the local newspapers, grew rapidly.

Wednesday evening, Dobbs and Grant Dunne went to see Olson to demand the release of Miles, Vince, and Bill Brown. They had been arrested, he told them, because the meeting Tuesday night had been held without a permit. Dobbs and Grant Dunne asserted that they had secured a permit. Olson asked to see the permit and wanted to know who issued it. Thursday Dobbs and Grant returned with the permit and the leaders were released.

In the meantime Father Haas continued to seek agreement, reporting to the NLRB in Washington that "on the surface it doesn't look good. Internally, however, it is very encouraging." He remained on call as the EAC conferred.[68]

Olson also raided the Citizens' Alliance headquarters. Carried out early Friday, the day after the release of the strike leaders, the catch was disappointing. The Guard confiscated ample evidence of plans to obstruct mediation, but "the Citizens' Alliance had been tipped off about the raid and had shipped out four files the preceding day."[69]

The two raids proved more symbolic than concrete steps toward resolution of the strike. The raid on strike headquarters and on the Citizens' Alliance asserted the National Guard's authority and power over strikers and employers alike. Olson appeared even handed in his treatment of the two groups, although the *Tribune* labeled Olson "Our Blunder-in-Chief"[70] and editorially assailed the raids.

A flurry of activity created hope for settlement Friday, August 3 when Joseph Cochran, chairman of the EAC submitted a revised proposal to Rev. Francis J. Haas.

> Our proposal, as now revised, is our conclusive offer of terms on which we expect the strike will be settled. In the alteration of wording as presented to you now, we have gone as far as we can go in helping you to make this proposal acceptable to the men on strike. We presume that you will now present this revised draft to the men.
>
> We need hardly remind you that the only alternative to acceptance of this proposal by the strikers is an election to determine representation.[71]

Haas presented the EAC's proposal to the Union; it could accept most of the revised proposal, but refused to accept the EAC determination not to "return to employment any man now out on strike who is definitely known to have been an active participant in unlawful acts during the present strike."[72] With respect to wages, the Union accepted a fifty cent minimum for drivers and a forty cent minimum for other workers, but it also demanded establishment of a Board of Arbitration.

Governor Olson declared in a public statement concerning the EAC proposal:

> I have carefully read the statements of the Employers' Committee with reference to the Haas-Dunnigan wage scales, and find nothing in those statements which in any way challenges the fairness of those scales. Any differences of opinion between the parties as to the entire proposal can readily be adjusted.[73]

If settlement was not reached immediately, Olson warned, he would revoke all truck permits except for milk, ice, and necessities.

After conferring with Local 574 concerning the EAC proposal, Rev. Haas and E. H. Dunnigan advised the EAC that the primary sticking point with the union was the "return of strikers to their former jobs." They opined that agreement to reinstate "all workers on the payrolls as of July 16," and agreement to arbitration would end the strike.[74]

That same Sunday, August 5, Governor Olson issued an executive order to General Walsh revoking all trucking permits and establishing the Haas-Dunnigan proposal as the basis for a new permit system. Effective August 6, only "vehicles owned and/or operated by employers who subscribe to and agree to be bound by the so-called Haas-Dunnigan Proposal" would receive permits.

Divisions within the EAC increased, but did not produce a settlement. None from the 166 members of the EAC were among over 100 employers who signed.[75] Pickets still patrolled the streets, stopping trucks, and although the number of calls for the National Guard diminished, they still kept busy. Members of the Citizens' Alliance took their anti-red campaign attacking the Union to the air waves in a series of broadcasts to the people of Minnesota.

The EAC sent wires and letters to the President asking him to intervene, and turned to the federal courts for relief. On August 6, they petitioned the United States District court for an injunction against martial law, claiming violation of the due process clause of the 14th Amendment. Under martial law, they asserted, they had been denied free use of the streets and had, therefore, been prevented from conducting legal business.[76]

Olson chose to present the defense in person. Ignoring the EAC charges, Olson contended that executive judgment as expressed in martial law was not subject to judicial review. In his closing charge to the judges Olson refused to accept any responsibility for consequences to citizens of Minneapolis, if the court found against his declaration of martial law. The court upheld his right to declare martial law, but censured his handling of the situation.[77] The court's decision did not discourage the EAC nor lead to the strike's conclusion.

President Roosevelt visited Rochester, Minnesota, on August 8 for dedication ceremonies honoring the Mayo brothers. Olson joined him there and certainly apprised him of the situation in Minneapolis. A delegation from the Central Labor Union also went to Rochester to seek the President's help. Unable to gain an audience, the delegation met with Louis Howe, Roosevelt's secretary, who lay ill in a Pullman car. The delegation, headed by Robley D. Cramer, at Howe's request typed a statement for the President.

Cramer's letter containing charges, leveled in a telegram Emory Nelson, Secretary of the CLU sent to Lloyd Garrison, Chairman of the National Labor Relations Board, July 28 that Minneapolis banks in general, and representatives of the Reconstruction Finance Corporation in particular, provided financial support for employer resistance.

> The issue, aside from wages and working conditions is the right of collective bargaining. If it is "red" to demand and struggle for collective bargaining then it was "red" to enact section 7A guaranteeing the right to organize and no one mentally competent will contend that this is so.
>
> While the Mediators represent the federal government, it is appointees of the federal government who through the control of credit are preventing a settlement of the strike. We refer to Joseph Chapman, manager Reconstruction Finance Corporation for the district; John W. Barton, chairman of committee on industrial loans for the Federal Reserve Bank and C.T. Jaffray in charge of liquidation of

assets of closed banks. These people are all reactionary Republicans, held over from the conservative Hoover regime.

John W. Barton, during the Hoover regime, at a convention of National Bankers, delivered an address declaring that the only way to combat the depression was to reduce the standard of living of American workers to that of European workers, This so incensed the conservative Mr. Hoover that he bitterly criticized Barton for his remarks when he later addressed the convention. . . .

One word from President Roosevelt to these appointees that they should use their influence to have employers accept government settlement proposal would end the strike.

Furthermore for the benefit of the community and of the administration we urge the dismissal of these three mentioned appointees. There will never be anything like permanent industrial peace in Minneapolis so long as they retain their positions and continue to carry out their old reactionary policies and union smashing tactics under the sanction of a New Deal administration.[78]

Roosevelt's visit to Rochester set in motion forces that ended the strike, for Jesse Jones, head of the RFC, phoned Father Haas from Detroit that very day, suggesting that Haas call "C. T. Jaffray, President of the Soo Lines and Vice President of the First National Bank of Minneapolis, and . . . Mr. Theodore Wold, North West Banc Corp. of Minneapolis," with whom Jones had already spoken.[79] Haas reported that Jaffray was "all powerful in the community and can probably get the [employers'] committee to do as he wishes." Haas and Dunnigan sent Jaffray a note identifying "the obstacles to settlement" so he could discuss them "in an effort to bring the recalcitrants into line."[80]

August 9 Haas and Dunnigan, with C. T. Jaffray and J. W. Barton who were "in charge of RFC loans to industry" met with a subcommittee of the EAC in Jaffray's office.

> During conference, Mr. Jesse Jones telephoned and spoke to Haas and Jaffray separately. At end of conference, 6 p.m. employers agreed to arbitrate existing wage scales but refused to specify minimum hourly rates from which arbitration would begin. Also, they refused to dismiss workers hired since date of strike, July 16th, perhaps 800.[81]

The meeting narrowed, but did not overcome obstacles to settlement.

Negotiations between Haas and Dunnigan and John Barton continued, and C. T. Jaffray held further meetings with the EAC. The morning of August 11 Jaffray secured employer approval of options to be presented to the Union. "The employers would do one of two things—(a) dismiss new workers hired since strike but not include arbitration, (b) not dismiss workers hired since day of strike but include arbitration."[82] That evening, after the Governor's right to declare martial law was upheld, the EAC agreed to dismiss workers hired since the strike began, and "to arbitrate wages without specifying minimum amounts."[83]

Two days later, after the Union negotiating team rejected the EAC proposal, the mediators took the EAC proposal, without endorsing it, to a dramatic meeting with the Committee of 100, the Union's steering committee. The Committee admitted both mediators into their meeting and granted them permission to speak. The Committee of 100 endorsed the Negotiations Committee's rejection adding "we stand firmly on the original Haas-Dunnigan Plan."[84] Father Haas reported: "The Union objects to the question of arbitration without a fixed minimum wage and separate arbitration for each employer."[85] The *Tribune* carried banner headlines: "OWNERS, MEDIATORS AGREE ON PEACE PLAN; STRIKE LEADERS TURN IT DOWN."[86] Interestingly, no such headlines had announced the EAC's rejection of the original Haas-Dunnigan proposal.

On August 14 Haas and Dunnigan secured permission from both the Union and the EAC to attempt to draw up a strike settlement proposal. If approved by both parties, this proposal would be issued as an Order made by the two mediators. Haas noted that the only changes from the previous agreement "are that the violence clauses will be left out and a flat rate will be put in to avoid the necessity for arbitration."[87] The Union tentatively accepted the proposal, but the EAC rejected it. Father Haas reported:

> At the close of conference with employers committee, employers demanded an election. They agree to provide payrolls in each of the 166 firms affected. This is the first time that unqualified offer to cooperate in the election was made by the employer committee.[88]

The EAC wired the National Labor Relations Board demanding elections, a call made in similar wires to President Roosevelt from A. W. Strong, President of the Citizens Alliance, and Isaac Engstrom, business agent for the American Building Trades Association. C. T. Jaffray wired his personal request for elections to President Roosevelt, suggesting as well that a new mediator be sent in to resolve the "present impasse."[89] Father Haas added his formal request for elections in a wire to Lloyd Garrison. That all these requests came at once suggests coordination.

On August 17, one month after the strike had begun, P. A. Donoghue flew into Minneapolis to conduct elections, but the Union refused to participate, demanding instead that the strike be called off and strikers reinstated without discrimination before elections. The EAC must agree that wherever Local 574 won an election, the affected employer would accept the original Haas-Dunnigan proposal. The EAC insisted on elections first; they would only agree to bargain with representatives so chosen. They would commit to no proposal. They would "under no circumstances . . . meet with the Union Committee unless as elections were held they happened to be chosen in some way."[90]

Father Haas and E. H. Dunnigan remained in Minneapolis, although apparently removed from the case. Saturday evening August 18, at 6:00 p.m. Jesse Jones called Father Haas asking about points of difference. "Dr. Haas advised that union insisted (a) elimination of 'violence' clause [it allowed employers not to rehire any worker convicted of violence during the strike] and (b) inclusion of specific hourly rates as a starting point for arbitration."[91] Three hours later "Mr. Albert Strong, employers' spokesman, phoned to Mr. Donoghue saying that he wished to see Donoghue on the following day at 2:30. Strong had been called by Mr. Barton who in turn had been called by Mr. Jones."[92] A that meeting the next day the EAC agreed to drop the "violence" clause and to start arbitration from hourly rates named in the agreement. Monday, August 20, 1934, Union negotiators agreed, and on Tuesday, August 21, the EAC voted 155 for, 3 against the settlement, and the Union, at a mass meeting that evening ratified it.

Wednesday morning, August 22, 1934, Jesse Jones wired triumphantly to Roosevelt who was speeding across the country by train:

GLAD TO REPORT MINNEAPOLIS STRIKE SETTLED MEN AT
WORK THIS MORNING ALL REINSTATED ON MINIMUM WAGE
FORTY AND FIFTY CENTS AN HOUR ARBITRATION FOR
INCREASES STOP EMPLOYERS HAVE MADE SUBSTANTIAL
CONCESSIONS IN THE GENERAL INTEREST.[93]

The settlement surprised the public and Union alike. William
Brown and Miles Dunne were out of town, attending the State
Federation of Labor Convention, seeking support for Local 574's
strike. They hurried back to the city, however, and joined in the cele-
bration. The agreement conceded almost the whole of the Haas-
Dunnigan plan. The EAC accepted a wage rate of 52-1/2 cents per
hour for truck drivers and 42-1/2 cents per hour for helpers and
inside workers. The settlement defined salesmen as those spending
60 percent of their time selling, and declared them ineligible to vote
in the elections. In all other respects, the final agreement and the
Haas-Dunnigan plan were identical.[94] In the final analysis, the
Union secured a minimum wage, recognition, and the right to represent all of its members. It won everything.

The matter of elections remained, however, and both Union and
EAC looked to them for vindication. Elections in the 166 firms represented by the Employers' Advisory Committee, produced results
that both parties could use to vindicate their stance.

Won by 574	62 firms	724 votes
Tied 15 firms	102 votes	
Won by employers	68 firms	536 votes
No vote	21 firms	
Total	166 firms	1,362 votes

Only at Dayton Company and the Colonial Warehouse of the major
firms, and Hatch package delivery, Ferrin Transfer, and LaBelle
Safety Storage Co of the medium size, did workers not select Local
574.[95]

The EAC interpreted these figures to mean that workers had
rejected the Union in most firms. That assertion was clearly true.
The Union was less concerned about the number of firms than its
right to represent its membership. Local 574 had originally struck

eleven firms; it had no members in 21 of the 166 firms the Employers' Advisory Committee had organized to fight it. This Committee was a child of the employers and not of the Union. Of workers voting, however, the Union won the right to represent 724 workers—53 per cent. If one recalls that this organizing drive began in May by targeting eleven firms, then victory in sixty-two firms is indeed impressive.

The strike ended and the men returned to work, but all difficulties did not end. Some employers still chiseled on wages, but employers on the whole had had their fill of labor difficulties. The Citizens Alliance stepped from the shadows during final negotiations when its president, A. W. Strong, emerged as a central figure in discussions between banking leaders and the EAC. His power in the end to discipline the Employers Advisory Committee and to secure their agreement confirms an intimate role for the Citizens Alliance throughout the strike. Unquestionably the Citizens Alliance intended to play a continuing role in Minneapolis's economic life. However, the Governor's charge against the Citizens Alliance made during the strike had gone home. He had asked,

> You have repeatedly informed me that a contributing cause of strikes is the low wages paid by the so-called `chiseler' employer. These `chiselers' are members of the Citizens' Alliance. Have you ever attempted to hold them up to public scorn and contempt? Have you ever interceded in behalf of these low-paid employees? Your answer to these questions must be in the negative.[96]

The Citizens' Alliance hired Austin, Coward & Co., C.P.A., to conduct a payroll investigation of the Minneapolis Fruit Association firms, which included the twenty-two market firms that had become the locus of organizing in May and July. Their report, dated May 17, 1935, indicated that during the period September 15, 1934 to March 31, 1935, thirteen companies investigated were in accord with the terms of the strike settlement, but that eighteen firms had wage shortages due to violation of the strike settlement. The report further indicated that shortages resulted from slowness to raise wages, or not paying according to the overtime amounts, such shortages usually falling short by only a few cents. It was further advised that the discrepancies were due to the "vague wording of the strike agreement."[97]

The analysis was certainly charitable, for the final agreement had not been vague. The attempt to discount the discrepancies as small was of little merit, for at issue in the strike were only a few cents per hour. No matter the size of discrepancies, the Citizens' Alliance contacted all firms who were short and urged them to pay back wages due workers and to live up to the agreement. In those firms where no audit could be taken due to incomplete records, the Citizens' Alliance issued forms to workers requesting it be advised of any shortages the workers found.

The Citizens' Alliance seems here to have extended itself to see that signers satisfied the agreement with Local 574. Likely it wished to demonstrate its integrity, to show its members were men of their word. Equally as likely, it revealed that the power of the Citizens' Alliance had been successfully challenged and that its influence was on the wane.

The inertia of urban life soon prevailed over the labor difficulties that had arisen in three dramatic, sometimes violent strikes. Businesses and shops reopened and those who had jobs returned to work. The city turned to efforts to cope, to meet needs of citizens caught up in the Great Depression. The strike settlement established machinery that took disputes between Local 574 and EAC from the streets to bargaining tables.

Local 574's problems with Dan Tobin continued; he revoked its charter in April 1935, but the Union remained strong and unified. It lost some of its militancy, but the following year it held a mass meeting on the anniversary of Bloody Friday. It continued to support organization of all workers in Minneapolis and, indeed, in all Minnesota. Workers who organized other unions in the city looked to Local 574 for guidance. Some confronted their employers and even the city authorities in other violent clashes, but none approached the teamsters' organizing drive. All workers in Minneapolis may not have become union members after the teamsters strike of 1934, but Minneapolis was no longer know as an Open Shop city.

EAC published a pamphlet titled "The Truth Concerning the Two Truck Drivers' Strikes in Minneapolis" to vindicate their position during the conflict, and to warn again that Minneapolis was about to fall under the thralldom of the communist movement. Most employers settled in to work within the new framework of collective bargaining that avoided direct, violent confrontations with workers. Conflict did not disappear from economic life in Minneapolis, but it tended to occur in an orderly fashion within a framework the Minneapolis Teamsters strike of 1934 helped to build.

Notes

1. George H. Mayer, *The Political Career of Floyd B. Olson* (Minneapolis: University of Minnesota Press 1951), 202.
2. Sam Levy to W. W. Hughes, Citizens Alliance Papers, Minnesota Historical Society, St. Paul, Minnesota.
3. Employers' Advisory Committee to W. W. Hughes, Citizens Alliance Papers, Minnesota Historical Society, St. Paul, Minnesota.
4. Minneapolis *Tribune*, 3 July 1934.
5. Employers' Advisory Committee, *The Truth Concerning the Two Truck Drivers' Strikes in Minneapolis*, 1935.
6. "Preliminary Report of Commissioner of Conciliation", RG 25, Box 385 Folder 4, National Archives.
7. Memo, Day to Olson, June 28, 1934, Vince Day papers Minnesota Historical Society, St. Paul, Minnesota.
8. Minneapolis *Tribune*, 1 July 1934.
9. Harry deBoer (Executive Committee, Local 574), interview by Philip A. Korth, Philip Fishman, and Janet Topolsky, Minneapolis, 13 July 1974; Moe Hork, interview by Philip A. Korth, Philip Fishman, and Janet Topolsky, Minneapolis, 19 July 1974.
10. Ibid., July 3, 1934.
11. Ibid., July 4, 1934.
12. Minneapolis *Tribune*, 7 July 1934.
13. W. F. Dunne and M. Childs, *Permanent Counter-Revolution: The Role of the Trotsyites in the Minneapolis Strike* (New York, 1934).
14. Minneapolis *Tribune*, 8 July 1934.
15. Minneapolis *Tribune*, 14 July 1934.
16. Minneapolis *Journal;* Minneapolis *Star,* and Minneapolis *Journal.*
17. Mayer, *Floyd B. Olson*, 205.
18. *The Militant*, 30 June 1934.
19. Minneapolis *Tribune*, 10 July 1934; Minneapolis *Tribune*, 14 July 1934.
20. Joseph G. Rayback, *A History of American Labor* (New York: The Macmillan Company, 1961), 208.
21. Minneapolis *Tribune*, 10 July 1934; Minneapolis *Tribune*, 14 July 1934.

22. V. R. Dunne, interview with the author, Minneapolis, September 1964. Myrtle Harris Interview by Philip Fishman, and Janet Topolsky, Minneapolis, 24 July 1974.
23. Minneapolis *Tribune*, 11 July 1934.
24. Minneapolis *Tribune*, 15 July 1934.
25. Minneapolis *Tribune*, 16 July 1934.
26. Ibid.
27. Minneapolis *Tribune*, 17 July 1934.
28. Ibid.
29. Ibid.
30. Charles R. Walker, *American City* (New York: Farrar & Rinehart, 1937), 158.
31. Minneapolis *Tribune*, 18 July 1934.
32. Preliminary Report of Commissioner of Conciliation, filed by E. H. Dunnigan 7 July 1934. RG 25 Box 385 Folder 4, National Archives.
33. Minneapolis *Tribune*, 19 July 1934.
34. Minneapolis *Tribune*, 20 July 1934.
35. Ibid.
36. Minneapolis *Tribune*, 21 July 1934.
37. *The Organizer*, 5 September 1934.
38. New York *Times*, 21 July 1934, pages 1-2.
39. Mayer, *Floyd B. Olson*, 209.
40. Minneapolis *Journal*, 21 July 1934.
41. Ibid.
42. New York *Times*, 22 July 1934, page 3.
43. Mayer, *Floyd B. Olson*, 208.
44. Walker, *American City*, 168.
45. Minneapolis *Tribune*, 22 July 1934.
46. Minneapolis *Tribune*, 1 August 1934.
47. Farrell Dobbs, *Teamster Rebellion* (New York: Monad Press, 1972), 134.
48. Meridel LeSueur, "I Was Marching," *New Masses*, 18 September 1934.
49. Dobbs, *Teamster Rebellion*, 130.
50. Ibid., 134; V. R. Dunne, interview with the author, Minneapolis, September 1964.
51. Minneapolis *Journal*, 20 July 1934.
52. Minneapolis *Tribune*, 26 July 1934.
53. Minneapolis *Tribune*, 27 July 1934.
54. Minneapolis *Tribune*, 26 July 1934.
55. Minneapolis *Tribune*, 28 July 1934.

56. Wire from Francis J. Haas to Benedict Wolf, Executive Secretary, NLRB, 28 July 1934, RG 25, National Archives.
57. Wire from Lloyd K. Garrison to Rev. Francis J. Hass, 28 July 1934, RG 25, Box 385, Folder 4, National Archives.
58. Minneapolis *Tribune*, 27 July 1934.
59. Ibid.
60. Minneapolis *Tribune*, 29 July 1934.
61. Ibid.
62. Minneapolis *Tribune*, 1 August 1934.
63. Ibid.
64. Ibid.
65. Ibid.
66. Ibid.
67. Minneapolis *Tribune*, 2 August 1934.
68. Memo from BMS reporting telephone conversation with Father Haas, August 1, 1934, 3:30 p.m. RG 25, National Archives.
69. Mayer, *Floyd B. Olson*, 217.
70. Minneapolis *Tribune*, 4 August 1934.
71. Letter, Cochran to Haas dated 3 August 1934, Minnesota Historical Society, St. Paul, Minnesota, M494.
72. EAC Proposal, Section 2, dated 3 August 1934, Minnesota Historical Society, St. Paul, Minnesota, M494.
73. Olson's statement dated 3 August 1934, Minnesota Historical Society, St. Paul, Minnesota, M494.
74. Letter to Joseph Cochran from Haas and Dunnigan, dated 5 August 1934. RG 25, Box 385, folder 4, National Archives.
75. Minutes, Strike Committee Meeting 7 August 1934, Minnesota Historical Society, St. Paul, Minnesota, M494.
76. Injunction petition, Citizens Alliance Papers, Minnesota Historical Society, St. Paul, Minnesota.
77. Minneapolis Trucking Strike report dated 28 August 1934, RG 25, Box 385 Folder 4, National Archives.
78. R. D. Cramer to author, and letter dated 8 August 1934, Collection OF 4076, Minneapolis Truckers Strike 1934, Roosevelt Library, Hyde Park.
79. Memorandum from Benedict Wolfe dated 8 August 1934. RG 25, National Archives.
80. Ibid.
81. Minneapolis Truckers Strike Report dated 28 August 1934, RG 25 Box 385 Folder 4, National Archives. The number was actually 86.
82. Ibid.
83. Ibid.

84. Minutes, Committee of 100, 13 August 1934, Minnesota Historical Society, St. Paul, Minnesota, M494.
85. Memorandum, from Benedict Wolfe dated 13 August 1934, RG 25, National Archives.
86. Minneapolis *Tribune*, 13 August 1934.
87. Memorandum from Benedict Wolfe dated 14 August 1934, RG 25, National Archives.
88. Minneapolis Truckers Strike Report dated 28 August 1934, RG 25 Box 385 Folder 4, National Archives.
89. RG25, Box 385, National Archives.
90. Memorandum from Benedict Wolfe reporting phone call from P.A. Donoghue dated 18 August 1934. RG 25, National Archives.
91. Minneapolis Truckers Strike Report dated 28 August 1934, RG 25 Box 385 Folder 4, National Archives.
92. Ibid.
93. Wire to Roosevelt at Mitchell, Indiana on his B & O Train from Jesse S. Jones dated 28 August 1934 at 8:03 A.M., File 407-B; Minneapolis Truck Strike, Roosevelt Library, Hyde Park.
94. Terms of Strike Settlement as Amended September 15, 1934. Citizens Alliance Papers, Minnesota Historical Society, St. Paul, Minnesota.
95. *The Organizer*, 12 September 1934.
96. Walker, *American City*, 178.
97. Fruit Association Audit, Citizens Alliance Papers, Minnesota Historical Society, St. Paul, Minnesota.

9 | Voices

Voices of July

Harry deBoer (Executive Committee member, Local 574)

We didn't choose the market for the strike; the majority of the inside workers were in this market area. Now when the first contract was signed in May it included all inside workers. The contract read so. After we agreed and we settled the strike they refused to recognize the inside workers and so the result was we were forced out on another strike. The July strike was because the employees reneged on the contract they signed. They said we will only recognize the drivers and the helpers. Half of the membership were inside workers. So that's what brought on the second strike and that's how it happened to be the market.

There were hundreds of workers in the market area hauling fruit and unloading cars in the warehouses, and ice boxes, which is a dirty and tough job and them workers were only getting twelve to fifteen dollars a week. Let's say a carload of strawberries would come in and they should switch by railroad at 6:00 at night. Well these workers would have to stay if they knew that load of strawberries was waiting for them. They would have to stay and wait for that load, and no extra pay. At that time they were more liberal and if the workers had to stay late to unload any load of vegetables that would come in after 6:00, they would give them 20 cents to go and buy supper so they wouldn't have to go home. That's the compensation they got for maybe 3 or 4 hours work unloading a car or two cars. Those workers were on the weekly scale: 12 dollars a week. Gamble-Rob was the best pay and they were paying $15. That was a big chain outfit, Gamble-Rob, American Fruit. That's what brought on this second strike. They didn't want to recognize these workers.

All the employees that came under the jurisdiction, all the drivers, regardless. I might add before we get any further. They thought that by not recognizing the inside workers that they could strip this union. They didn't think the drivers would go on strike to meet these conditions. They had a contract and so the bosses thought they could strip the union. But instead the drivers by this time with the leaders that understood like Skoggy and Ray, the drivers understood where the power was. Split them up and they've got nothing. So that's what brought on the strike in July. But in the main the Citizens Alliance was the power. They told the bosses what to do, and they done it. They had to.

Rainbolt was in charge of issuing permits. If anybody that felt they were justified in moving their product whatever was the emergency, they could get a permit from him. And if he gave a permit for somebody to move, then the pickets would go right along with the permit to see to it that nothing happened. For instance, if some outfit got a permit to move a truck, they would do it for two reasons: to see that this particular load would be delivered to where they said that it would be. American Fruit got a permit to deliver some oranges to one of the hospitals. Well then we'd give them a permit to do it but we'd also check to see that it went there rather than some big store. If it looked like some poor people needed some medicine or some food.

They painted "Hospital Supplies" all over a truck. That's just one of their methods of trying to show the public how unreasonable we were, in spite of the fact they didn't need it. That's the reason that was done: to try and get public support, showing how unreasonable these strikers are. They wouldn't even let a load of medicine go to the hospital without police protection. Do you understand? That is one of the reasons why the strike bulletin was one of the most efficient vehicles we had to win the strike. The workers understood that what was in that organizer was true. The newspapers were carrying all of the employers arguments. They would come down to the Union headquarters and pick up The Organizer and take it home.

The Communist party, they were Stalinists of course and we were Trotskyists. The day we were shot, Sam Davis, the organizer for the communist party, come to me and said, "What are you doing here with all these pickets stopping one truck? Meaningless. Why don't you with all these pickets go over and take over the court house?" Well, fortunately I had already known differently between Stalin and Trotsky and I knew what they were trying to do. They were trying to break the strike and that would have been one way to break the strike. What business would we have, the trade labors union, of going over and taking over the city hall? And all the way through, we would have problems with them. They would try one way or another to discredit us.

Then of course we had the bureaucrats in the trade labor movement too. We finally had to tell them to fight. You see actually what happened, we had this contract and we were getting these conditions. The workers from various other towns particularly drivers that come in, they also recognized that we were getting better wages than they were and they wanted to join and so we started to organize. We told them go back to your local and get workers to join and we'd support you. There wouldn't be any problems. So that's how we started to organize the area committee, a twelve state area. Dobbs was put in charge of it. As a matter of fact Tobin hired Dobbs after we had it organized. He thought that he could persuade Dobbs to listen to him rather than organize. The St Paul drivers, they were ten cents behind us. They would negotiate. Union 120 was recognized and for a couple of years we had ten cents an hour more. Then finally Murphy Transportation started to move over to St. Paul to get away from 574 contracts and wages and then we went over and we had a strike over there. We supported it and got the wages up over there in order to protect our wages scale. After we got the agreement that their wages should be equal to ours, we had fairly good working arrangements with them.

Harvey Boscoe (laundry driver)

Then the military stepped in saying that any hospital or soldier home or anything like that, it was imperative that they had clean linen and anything that was needed. So I serviced one little hospital in Wayzata and by that reason I got a military permit for my truck. I think the Gross Brothers applied for it and gave a reason that we were applying for it that I was servicing the hospital. Then it seemed to me that I went and picked up the permit: a sticker about 12" by 3" that stuck on the windshield. So I sailed into town with a military permit plastered across my windshield, pulled up to Gross Brothers and load, because I took a few towels into this hospital. They used any angle they could to get a military permit and that made it legal. The strikers didn't bother me. In fact, I drove into town a couple of days when we couldn't move anything. I got down to the court-house the day they had the big hassle where they surrounded the court house and police would throw tear gas out in the crowd. These boys would run out and pick up the gas before it would go and throw it back into the windows of the courthouse and they had the courthouse filled with tear gas. We were in the crowd. It covered the entire block around there, from the telephone building all across the front hall down the side streets. Just a mass of people, the full width of the street. You couldn't move. Just all curious and of course a lot of the 574 boys

They wanted to go in and have a group meet with the Mayor and whoever was in charge of council at that time. And they wouldn't agree to it. They would allow only two or three of the head men in. They said nothing doing; they all wanted to come in and have a little show of strength. That's when they started lobbing canisters back and forth at each other. They had all the police that were in the courthouse at that time on duty.

The city drivers, I can't remember how they got by with their orders. You see we had a man who would cover just Dayton's and Donaldson's department stores. Even their new garments were tried on enough that they showed soil and the new garments came in ever so often to be dry cleaned and back on the racks. Now how those men got by with that, or whether Dayton's would bring them up in private cars, or how they got by servicing all the city routes, or whether people brought them in themselves and picked them up, maybe that's what they did. Of course I would leave in the morning, cover my entire Lake Minnetonka area (about one hundred miles a day) and end up in Spring Park. We lived in a cottage at Spring Park on the lake, from early spring to late fall 'til the water would freeze, and then we would come into an apartment for the winter. So I wasn't really there other than just in and out twice a day, or once every morning so I don't know how they fared in town. They did start a curb service at Gross Brothers where you could swing in with your car and they would have a little note with your name and address and say "Dry Clean" and hand the bundle and swing out. A boy would be out there and pick it up. So they had a curb service.

Bernard M Koski (striker)

I was getting two dollars a day. One unemployed offered to take my job for one dollar a day. One of my bosses was for it, and the other was against it because I knew the route. In September of '33 I joined the union. I wasn't involved in the coal strike. In May everyone went out.

We got called out again in July because the employers weren't living up to the agreement. I went down about 10:30 a.m. Friday with a bunch of guys. There was already pickets there. There was a truck backed up to the dock at Winston-Newell. There were no license plates on it. Chicken netting over the windshield and on the glass. It was all painted one color: yellow. There was a row of police on each side of the truck, armed with shotguns besides revolvers.

They came out of the warehouse and threw three small boxes on the truck, and the driver and a helper jumped in and they took off, and turned left on Third Street. I was on the opposite side of Third Street. A fellow with a dump truck full of pickets rammed into the side of this truck and stopped it. That's when this shooting started.

One fellow went down in the street and we went out there, three of us, to pick him up, and we had him up and taking him off, and then I went down too. The other two fellows, I don't know who they were, whether they were shot, so I crawled under a car so I wouldn't get hit anymore, and stayed there until after the shooting subsided. A car came driving down there then that wasn't involved in it, and they seen this fellow lying in the street, and they stopped to pick him up. There was two cars. They both stopped. They put him in one car, and I got in the other, and he was kinda surprised to see me. I was bleeding; the seat was all full of blood. He was going to take me to General Hospital, but I said no, I'd be placed under arrest there. I had him take me to strike headquarters on Eighth and Marquette across from the Athletic Club. The place was filled with people that had been shot and they were placing them in ambulances and were hauling them off to the hospital. I laid on a cot there for about an hour trying to stop the bleeding. Finally they got an ambulance and took me over to Swedish Hospital where I was for three weeks.

I got hit five times, two went through me and three are still in me. One went through my upper right arm, I got one in the left leg between my knee and left ankle and that broke my leg there, the smaller bone, one in my hip that's still there. One went through my right leg, and one went into my right shoulder. Its been in there a long time. Buckshot.

The one in my leg was from the side. That was after I fell down. The others were in the back.

Frank Forestal (policeman)

The only trucks that rolled were the newspaper trucks. We always sent a motorcycle escort with them. I remember one occasion, the driver was in a hurry to get going and the escort wasn't handy. He said "Aw, nobody's going to bother me." He got out as far as Loring Park and somebody tipped his truck over and the papers were in Loring Park.

I don't think we had any direct connection with anybody that the Citizens Alliance hired. They undoubtedly had informers.

I succeeded Johannes. I knew him for years. He was a strict disciplinarian. Everything had to be just exactly so. He was rigid on that. When he walked down the hall and passed a policeman he wanted a salute. He'd acknowledge that.

Friday, July 20, there wasn't anybody hit. It was over their heads. A policeman should try to be neutral.

Ed Ryan (Minneapolis policeman 1925-1947; Hennepin County Sheriff, 1947-1967)

It was a bad situation which should never have happened. these business people were so determined that this city wasn't going to be organized.

The final act of the strike was when the police were ordered by the Chief of police, Michael J. Johannes to shoot. They were going to move some trucks out of Gamble Robinson. "If you're attacked, shoot." They had sawed off shotguns.

Harry Pfaff (striker)

I was lucky. A cop gave me a shove and I backed up. I said, "Let me have it. I'm going to see who's shooting me." He didn't have guts enough to shoot me. He walked away, so I was lucky. I didn't get it.

Harry deBoer (Executive Committee member, Local 574)

I was captain at this particular spot when they were going to move this truck early in the morning. We heard they were going to move this truck through the workers, the grapevine, we'd say. The workers were all over and watching and so I was sent down and I seen they had five hundred or six hundred police so I called back for more pickets and so it wasn't only about an hour we had a couple, three thousand pickets. Then this police captain he seen he didn't want anything to do with moving that truck against these pickets so he come to me and wanted to know who was in charge and I said I was. He was right off Washington Avenue, and that was a through street. He said, "Look, we don't want these people going through town. Can't you send your men away?"

I said "Yeah, you send your cops away and don't move no truck and there won't be any problem."

So he went and he come back and he said, "We want to leave one squad here."

I said "OK, we'll leave a squad here. You can leave and we can leave and you can leave a squad here and we can leave a squad here to see that everything stays as it is." So we all went back and I reported back to Farrel. (I think he was dispatch at that time) 2:00 in the afternoon we get a call from the squad we left there and they said the police were coming, and so we started to send pickets. To make a long story short, it took only about an hour and they had all the police force in town, I suppose, there with guns. They started to move the truck and that's when they fired first; they just fired point blank. They just went wild. Actually they shot at anybody that moved.

The truck was just a decoy. I don't think they had but two cases of fruit on the darn thing. They just wanted to break the picket line so they showed to the rest of the employers that you can put your truck on the street. That's what they were trying. Obviously the Citizen's Alliance was watching.

I was down on the ground. We had a truck standing at a location in order to be able to block that truck from moving so we could stop it. There were several pickets in the truck and they all got shot. One of the strikers when they got to the hospital, they took a package of cigarettes out of his lung. They shot the cigarettes right into his lung; that's how close they were.

Before the police had night sticks. This was the first time we encountered the police shooting. The time we were going over the deputy run, then they used night sticks. They probably had guns, but they didn't have instructions to shoot just then. I think that's why they went back in the morning. They seen that they weren't going to be able to handle the strikers with clubs. They had experience with that, so they went back and got permission to shoot. There were even shots coming from the second and third story windows in the warehouse. They really loaded the whole area up with police and guns and whoever was in the warehouse upstairs, we don't know if they were police or what, but bullets came from all over. It really was organized.

Naturally we didn't expect them to shoot like that, right at you, not even a chance, no warning at all. They just started shooting.

There were trucks and various companies had tried and stopped. This definitely was a decoy; there's no question about that. The police were there before the truck had even come out of the warehouse. It was a company truck; it was a company on the market. Maybe it was Winston-Newell, some grocery place. At that time, there were a lot of companies.

I was shot. I crawled. I almost lost a leg. As a matter of fact I had to fight with the doctor to keep him from operating. They were scared of poison. In those days you didn't have the junk you've got today. They were scared of lead poisoning for one, but gangrene. My leg here is all wired up. I insisted that they do something rather than cut it off, the intern that was active around strike headquarters, he went and seen the x-ray of how the bullet was lodged in there. He went to a blacksmith shop and took a needle or something and had it bent just right and they got in there and hooked it out on the second operation. When they got it out my fever went down.

It was a slug; it smashed that whole bone. That bone now is all wired up. There was lots of parts of bullets. It took so long because I had forty-five pounds hanging on there so that the leg wouldn't shrink, for the leg bone to grow into the steel and wires. I was in traction better than six months. Then I was in a cast for about three months after that.

One of the things we were cautious about was having the police ambulance pick you up and bring you into General Hospital. You didn't know what kind of care you would get, so I crawled under the loading dock and I laid there for a while and finally a kid went by and I told him to call headquarters and they sent the same dump truck to pick me up. It wasn't a very comfortable ride. Of course they didn't know how bad; I knew my leg was broken. I could feel it. I laid in the Union headquarters there until they got the ones shot worse than I was, the ones that were bleeding. I'm fortunate I didn't bleed very much. It was just a matter of laying there. By this time my leg was numb anyway. I wasn't in much pain. So I waited until they got some of the more severe ones to the hospital. I was taken to St. Barnabas. They had several ambulances. By this time it was very amusing: they called out the National Guard and they had a guard at my door watching me, and there I am laying there with forty-five pounds of weight on my leg and they're still watching me scared I'm going to run out or something.

Just to show you the feeling of the strikers, several of them would come up and would say, "You know who shot you? We'll get the asshole who shot you." If I had wanted to get somebody shot, that's all I would have had to do was name somebody and they would have gone after him.

As a matter of fact you didn't see too many cops on the street after it happened. It was a couple of days before the cops were out in full fledged. It wasn't too healthy to be a cop after that shooting, I'll tell you that. I'm sure there was a few of them that got roughed up a bit. Of course we didn't hear about them. I say that because of the feeling of the workers. They came up to see me to see if I knew.

You see there were at least five thousand to six thousand pickets there by the time they started shooting. You can visualize almost a whole block of pickets. So they shot at random, anywhere; anywhere there was a worker moving they shot. They just didn't shoot at the truck and then quit, they just kept on shooting until all the pickets had either hid or got shelter somewhere. Oh, they meant business.

I was like on the executive board while I was in the hospital. They gave me a driver when I got that cast around my waist. I went out organizing. I was assigned mainly the coal yard workers. They all knew me and when you're shot like that, you know them too. There was a lot of grievances, and I took them. Got all the workers in and getting them paid up, withdrawal cards so they could get away.

In July of the following year, I was walking with a cane. I was getting around. Ever since then I've been an organizer.

Iver Swanson (policeman)

Well, the trucks were loaded and rolled out of the warehouse and the strikers just mobbed them. They climbed on the trucks like they were going to stop the drivers and drag them out of the trucks when they were fired on by the police.

I wasn't there at that instant. Somehow or another I had another assignment at that time, so I wasn't there. It was after that incident that the National Guard was brought in.

The police department was relieved to have martial law because it kind of cooled things off and kind of took them out of the conflict. Naturally the union didn't like it, but summing it all up in spite of all the hardships that went with it and all the people that got hurt, I still maintain that the union organization in Minneapolis was one of the best things that ever hit town. You had to admit the Citizen's Alliance was biased at that time and that the employers used the employee.

When the union took over of course, the pendulum swung the other way and they were just as unreasonable. It never equalizes you know, it is either way over here or way over there, so that the union was just as unreasonable when they got the upper hand as the employers had been when they were in control.

At the first incident in May, that was hand-to-hand combat. The policemen had guns then, but no one used them. Nobody used them. You know as things went on, the situation got more serious and finally of course it came to the point where the only way you could protect yourself, or even enforce any kind of a regulation, was with firearms, but there was none used in the first incident at all. We also had another one at Eleventh Avenue South and Washington, at a Salt Company that I was at. There was no firearms used there either. About the only time there was any shooting was at Third Street and Sixth Avenue North at the produce warehouse, that I recall.

Oscar Winger (striker)

There used to be a very prominent restaurant down in the stock market or Wall Street down there on Second Avenue and I think it was Ninth Street. There was a popular eating place where, you know, the stock brokers, businessmen down there, they called it Freddies. Of course he wasn't getting deliveries so he took his car, a great big Cadillac one day and the pickets were at the rear of the restaurant, and knocked two of them down. So of course, following that incident we sent about forty guys down there and I was one of them. I'm patrolling out in the street in front of the place, the establishment, and all of a sudden I get knocked to the ground. I didn't know what happened. Then the next thing I'm dragged into a police patrol and we wind up at the city jail. I was mugged and fingerprinted and thrown in a cell.

Well, there were twelve or thirteen and strike headquarters sent down great big cans of chicken, mash potatoes, peas, bread, three or four cartons of cigarettes, newspapers. We had just got through with our meal and were going to smoke and read the papers and relax, even though it was pretty uncomfortable, then we all got called down into the entrance, to the desk. There was a captain in the National Guard and he told us that we were going by orders of General Walsh. We were to be released, but we had to report back to strike headquarters and if we were found on the street again we were going to be sent out. The National Guard had set up a stockade out at the fairgrounds. There were several hundred men sent out there. I remember we got released and we got down from the fourth floor of the jail quarters. The elevator took us down to the basement which passed the police headquarters and the corridor was just jammed with people, sympathizers. Michael Johannes, the chief of police, was standing in the doorway. Everybody yelled at him, shouted at him "Bloody Johannes." That was the name they gave him then because of the shooting.

The day of the incident down on the Slocum-Bergren warehouse which was a wholesale food warehouse on Third Street and Sixth Avenue, they pulled this truck out. The cab was all enclosed with mesh, heavy gauge mesh wire, they had painted over the identity of the truck and they removed the license plates. The truck pulled up to the warehouse dock and of course we were warned. We were told that this was going to happen and about twenty gun squads, or police squads came down with four policemen in a squad, with sawed off shotguns and we stood behind the railroad track right adjacent to the warehouse. This truck pulled up and started putting a couple sacks of sugar and a case of vegetables and something else that they were supposed to deliver to a hospital.

A few days before we had a very heavy rain storm and in most of Minneapolis we didn't have concrete or asphalt pavements, we had these tar blocks, and after a real heavy storm these tar blocks would wash up. So on this occasion the city was removing these tar blocks in an area in North Minneapolis. It so happened that the day of this incident at Slocum-Bergren, this city maintenance truck came by with this load of tar blocks and it stopped behind our picket line. When this delivery truck started to move away, about twenty guys got on this maintenance truck and started throwing tar blocks. Two other fellows, one by the name of Ness and I forget the other chap's name, but they got on this truck and the police opened fire and killed them both. Then they turned on us. I think maybe I got one or two pellets which was very little but a chap named Red Hastings ran down the tracks and through some woods, I followed him and he collapsed. He was pretty well shot up. I got him out on the sidewalk, on the curb and an old chap in a Chevrolet touring car—must have been about a 1925 or '23 Chevy—I told him to drive me down to strike headquarters. We got this Hastings in the car and picked up another guy to go down to strike headquarters to the first aid station. He wouldn't go, so I knocked him out of the car and took the car and drove down to strike headquarters. Both of them were taken to St. Barnabas Hospital. There were about sixty of the pickets that were shot.

They'd take them to the first aid station at strike headquarters and then from there the doctors would look at them, examine them, and if it were serious enough they'd send them to the hospital. In the first place, you didn't know whether they'd be put under arrest, so this had to be checked out at the strike headquarters.

The truck was only to incite some action or some violence or what-have-you because it was two sacks of sugar and a case of vegetables and something else. There was no necessity of taking a truck, sealing the windows, the windshield and side windows in the cab with heavy gauge mesh wire and painting out the name of the truck, which was Slocum-Bergren, to deliver two sacks of sugar to a hospital. That could have easily been done in a car, or a case of vegetables but this was only to create a situation. Why call twenty squad cars comprising of about eighty, or hundred men. That situation certainly could have been avoided.

It was a set up to force Governor Olson to call for martial law, which he subsequently did. The National Guard raided the strike headquarters, which didn't make us too happy, but subsequent to that they also raided the Citizens Alliance office and I guess they didn't find too much there. They of course had taken stuff out that would have been very pertinent to their activities and their plans. That had all been taken out. One day we got a call that the police were going to march from the courthouse down to strike headquarters and raid the strike headquarters. They had called off-duty policemen and the deputies that they had deputized. I never saw so much action in that matter of a few minutes, clubs and bats, even weapons on top of this two-story garage. I mean, the men just got on top of the roof of that thing and they were all ready. Of course then the police were tipped off that they were gonna hit into a big battle so they disbanded and it was called off. It was following that I believe, Governor Olson declared martial law.

I think one of the saddest days during that whole strike was the day that they had the funeral for Otto Ness who was one of the strikers killed on that truck. I think the cortege must have been at least two miles long, tied up all the traffic going all the way from Loop out to Crystal Lake Cemetery which is a distance of about eight miles. During the busiest time of the day too, but it was really a sad occasion.

Harry deBoer (Executive Committee member, Local 574)

I was chairman of this grievance board. If a member had a complaint, or he wasn't getting wages, his duty was to come before the grievance board and we took it down in writing of what was wrong so we had a record. We done it for two reasons. Also we kept the record for the following year when it came to negotiating another contract and some of these employees would use some argument, well we had the record, just what they tried to pull and why we needed a new provision. For instance, well we pretty near struck the industry in '37. See our first contracts we agreed to arbitration clause, but after we got stronger, we got away from compulsory arbitration. On this clause was just one word: may or shall. Any dispute *may* go to arbitration or *shall*, and we said we want "may." Maybe we'll go to arbitration, and maybe we won't. Depends on what the problem is. If it is an out-and-out violation of the contract, we are not going to arbitrate, we are going to get straight or else. We pretty near come to a general strike over just that one provision. You see they wanted compulsory arbitration. The boss has got the upper hand. They got two from the union and two from employer and they don't agree. Well who does the judge appoint? You got two strikes against you, and of course we understood that and we explained it to the members and they understood it. If you accept a contract like that you're putting yourself at the mercy of the employers to settle.

I forget which one of the comedians it was, but one of them says when Hitler was getting power, he says, well, we don't have to worry about Hitler. Let him come over here til he gets to the Mississippi River and when he gets to the Mississippi, 544 will take care of him. That puts me in mind of the finance company. The first thing they asked a worker when they borrow money is whether they belong to 544. If he did, they knew that if he had a job, he would be protected and it would help him get a loan.

But that just goes to show you an honest leadership and the correct program. The first meeting I tried to organize of the coal workers was in October 1933 and there was seven members which

Skoggy, Nicky Grana and myself, and in July 1934, 100,000 workers demonstrated behind Nestle Sugar to give you an indication of how quick workers will support you. The workers are finding out every day how crooked these capitalist politicians are.

So from the time of the second strike, I joined Communist League: Trotsky Movement. And I've been a member ever since.

I was fortunate, I've been with Trotsky, spent a couple of weeks with him down in Mexico. Well, my best description of him would be like if you'd been away from home for ten years and go home: he greeted you like a father. There was two couples, and the first thing he asked was how my wife felt, how they made the trip and if they shouldn't have a *bacita*. He was a real guy, just like sitting down talking to us; no different. You would imagine talking to a man like that. He was common and easy to talk to as we are.

Moe Hork (Committee of 100 member)

Well a lot of these people brought in their shotguns and every-thing else when they heard about the shooting, but we wouldn't let them go on the picket line with a gun. This is what the whole trou-ble was. After the shooting a lot of them demanded to be on, but we wouldn't let them carry guns. It really would have started a civil war.

Governor Olson raided strike headquarters, and they raided the Citizens Alliance headquarters. You see all the bosses were orga-nized and that's what they called Citizens Alliance. They were determined to break the strike, so he raided ours and then they went in with the National Guard and raided theirs so we couldn't say he favored the working cause. The labor movement put him in office. Olson was up for re-election, you see and so there he turned right around and without giving them notice or anything, he went in there and he raided that Citizens Alliance for all their records.

There was a lot of meetings with the labor mediators. The Committee of 100 was elected all the time. You see before we called the meeting we elected a committee. We had a membership meeting; it was just packed. You couldn't get in no more and we elected a strike committee of a hundred, that any negotiations or anything else had to go through and be reported through this committee through the executive board before the executive board took final action on it. It was an advisory board of the rank and file. I just don't remember who suggested that we elect a committee of one hundred as a strike committee. You see to conduct the strike, everything had to go through this committee. When there were any negotiations or anything new popped up, the first thing they had to do was to be reported to the Committee of 100, before it was reported to the rank and file and before it was publicized.

They brought in Father Haas. Governor Olson worked with Haas, and this is where the settlement was made, was between Father Haas and Floyd Olson. There were four or five of us at the Nicollette Hotel, I'm trying to think of the room number that Father Haas was in, where this whole settlement was made. Then we took this back to the Union and that's when we settled the strike. Father Haas was there, Floyd Olson was there, Dunnigan, and we went up there with this committee. The employers already accepted it and there was a question of whether we would accept it. We knew they were in trying to draw a meeting together and we went up there to see what they had to offer. This is what they offered us and this is what we brought back to the strikers—42 $1/2$ cents an hour.

After the strike we had a lot of meetings with the employers, after, but not before.

In other words, it was put before the rank and file to accept or reject and then this was the way it was carried out. The rank and file was really the power of the whole movement but they still needed that leadership to lead them. I don't care how good the army is, without a general they're no good.

These people moved in gradually from the Socialist Workers Party to help and I say without them there wouldn't have been no victory. You see the Communist Party expelled the Dunne brothers. They were actually fighting the Communist Party themselves, but still the Citizens Alliance picked that up and branded every one of us as Communists. I never was a follower or a sympathizer. It just so happened, that the Socialist Workers Party came in through their help; they joined the Socialist Workers Party. It still did not make me a Communist or a Socialist Workers Party member. I never joined them, I never was a follower of them, yet I had to accept them for what they did in the labor movement. This is what I was interested in: the labor movement.

It didn't never bother me at all that they were in the Socialist Workers Party. Socially they were very nice people, but their political belief was different than mine. I always felt that your nationality, your religion and your political belief was your personal thing that didn't concern me a bit. I had to accept you for what you were. You come in here as a man, you talk to me, I accept you as such. This was my belief and I have lived seventy-six years that way.

10 Lessons

Epilogue

MINNEAPOLIS EMPLOYERS WHO believed that the historic past revealed the triumph of individual enterprise over community regulation were ill equipped to create new policies to cope with the emergence of an industrial working class. In fact the myth which defined this world of entrepreneurial freedom prevented them from cooperating with government to develop new policies. In their statement of *Policy and Principles* the Citizens Alliance of Minneapolis invoked American tradition with a familiar, hallowed text:

> The principles and ideals of the Citizens Alliance are embodied in those of the founders of this nation as expressed in the Declaration of Independence and the Constitution of the United States: viz, that all men, without regard to race, color, or previous conditions, are entitled to an equal right and opportunity to enjoy life, liberty and the pursuit of happiness. . . . [1]

The Alliance did not consider the army of rebels who banded together in 1776 to create a revolutionary community the most attractive feature of that tradition. Rather, it chose to defend economic individualism, asserting that the "right and opportunity to enjoy life, liberty and the pursuit of happiness . . . should be exercised by each individual in a spirit of fairness and recognition of the rights of every other individual."[2] This prescription for individual exercise of rights, implicitly rejecting a group as a legitimate agent in that exercise, resulted from a powerful myth underpinning Alliance behavior.

187

"Myth," unfortunately, has in common parlance come to mean something unreal. A myth is in reality an historical narrative that creates a cognitive and emotional context which integrates the chaos of experience, which creates order and meaning out of the ebb and flow of daily events. Myth creates a structure that interprets the past and the present, and promises a comprehensible future, and it carries within it a moral compass to guide behavior. It is profoundly real because it defines the parameters of reality and meaning. Myth assumes the stature of a self-evident truth.

It is therefore useful to interpret the myth within which these Minneapolis employers lived. The great drama of modern life, they would assert, unfolded in a series of events that liberated mankind from a handful of aristocrats who had bent government and economic policy to their will in order to exploit others. The economic policies of mercantilism had stifled the economic energies of able and adventurous individuals by distorting for the benefit of a few the natural operation of the market. The great challenge mankind faced was to permit the forces of the market to direct economic life. Adventurous and able individuals would align themselves with those forces and create abundance. This abundance would circulate through society eliminating both poverty and class. All would benefit. The American Revolution, then, was the essential act liberating Americans from these overweening and arbitrary manipulations of the British government.

The myth further asserted that the Founding Fathers created, through the Constitution, protections for enterprising and adventurous individuals from government itself. Defining the role of government negatively, the Founding Fathers believed that government posed the greatest threat to the individual, and that collective organizations, like factions, threatened to undo the Revolution. Vigilant entrepreneurs, recognizing attempts to limit the freedom of markets and to subordinate the enterprising and adventurous to the collective will, would resist. These entrepreneurs would monitor signs of collective or community activity and warn each other of impending threats to their autonomy. And they would resist, not because it was prudent to do so, but because they had the moral responsibility to do so. If these entrepreneurs failed to resist they would, in their own eyes, fail in their duty to bar the door against forces which would return mankind to a time when the human spirit was enslaved. They would have betrayed history.

It follows from this myth that these entrepreneurs could not join other community members in a search for compromise, for new ways to bring businesses, government and groups of workers together to find a cooperative solution to their relationships. To do so would mean loss of autonomy and abandonment of their historical mission. They would become engaged in a way that would make them responsible for their own regulation. They could, of course, freely join with other like-minded people in purely social and cultural organizations, such as the Minikahda Club, the Lafayette Club, or the Athletic Club. Participation in economic associations was far more circumscribed; it had to be justified as a reluctant acquiescence to necessity. For example, the Employers Advisory Committee interpreted Section 7a as government imposition. Its members could, as patriotic citizens, acquiesce to it and endeavor to accommodate its requirements so long as it left them free to manage their businesses as they saw fit. This posture absolved them from any responsibility for Section 7a or for its consequences. Thus they could accede to the Regional Labor Board's orders, but not to negotiations. They could autonomously file a declaration of wages with the Regional Labor Board, which they agreed to do in May, and they could, as good citizens, acquiesce in the Board's order. Neither action would compromise the autonomy of able and adventurous individual businessmen; neither would threaten the myth.

For the Citizens Alliance, American history was the history of entrepreneurial liberty. The function of the state, at best, was to facilitate the development and growth of business. Primarily, however, the adventurous and able individual, without state intervention, would guarantee social and economic progress through pursuit of enlightened self interest. The greatest danger to that pursuit lay in collective activities, whether by government or by unions. For example, we can see this concern for individual autonomy in the employers' strike preparations. Initially the employers formed a "committee" that designated certain committee members to act as spokespersons for them. These spokespersons carried all proposals back to committee members who judged them independently. The organization remained very loose. The final agreement was, from these employers' point of view, a product of the Regional Labor Board's order, which affected their individual firms. It was not the product of negotiations between an organization they had created—

for there was none—and a union; thus they sustained the fiction of individual, autonomous powers, by reserving finally their freedom of action.

Union organizers Vincent Dunne and Carl Skoglund brought to their activities in Minneapolis a myth derived from their experience as workers, and from reading socialist authors. This myth accepted Karl Marx's declaration that history was the record of class struggle. Workers in Minneapolis, they believed, faced bourgeois capitalists who opposed workers' attempts to create a life of dignity based on adequate wages, job security, and independent power through a union. Like the Citizens Alliance members, these leaders suspected the state and so did not trust it as an ally in their confrontation with employers, for the state, they asserted, was itself an agent of capitalism. Workers could succeed only if they united solidly to assert their rights as Americans to a just reward for their work. In the course of that struggle they would not be surprised if they met violent opposition. Cooperation, loyalty to fellow workers, solidarity, and determination could overcome that opposition.

This myth empowered union leaders by articulating a principle of organization and an interpretation that explained to workers their social position and the nature of their opposition: class struggle. The idea of class struggle glossed over differences in work roles and status that might have divided workers. It also glossed over the fact that many employers the union faced had built the firms which bore their names, had even begun as workers, and had developed their firms through their own skill and determination. But the idea of class struggle identified the basis of their unity. Workers were of the same class. The idea of class struggle also explained to workers why employers would quibble over a few cents per hour, and why they would refuse to recognize the union, and why they would organize against them. The Citizens Alliance in its words and actions added credibility to the organizers' myth.

Although some of the original eleven firms that the Union sought to organize supported the Citizens Alliance, this fact did not prove to workers the class nature of the struggle. However, when those eleven firms rallied one hundred fifty-five additional firms to their side, and when the Citizens Alliance began to take a visible role, the class nature of the struggle emerged to convince workers that the Dunne brothers and Carl Skoglund truly understood the forces arrayed against them. The historical drama unfolded before their eyes, and they were agents in it.

The immediate historical context for the organizers' myth was created by the Industrial Workers of the World, a union which, following socialist analysis, understood history as class struggle, and carried that understanding into the forests, fields and factories during its most effective years from 1905 to the early 1920s. As we have seen, Vince Dunne and other workers encountered the IWW during their early work experiences and sifted through its history to find principles they believed to be sound. The essential principle they adopted was the need and possibility of forming industrial unions.

Objectively, the I.W.W. was a casualty of the First World War. Few of its locals survived the Red Scare which after the War raged across the country intent on exterminating radicals, and those locals that survived turned into study associations more than unions. One could argue, then, as the AFL argued, that the I.W.W. had demonstrated the ineffectiveness of organizing industrial unions. Leaders in Minneapolis saw instead the I.W.W.'s successes; the principle of industrial unionism, they believed, was sound. All difficulties were tactical. Not all I.W.W. principles found ready acceptance from union leaders, though many did, including the central importance of solidarity and of rank and file control.

Among the principles the I.W.W. followed, one evokes an irony, for the I.W.W. took the same position with respect to contracts that the Citizens Alliance took, and for a similar reason: history. The I.W.W. held that as a matter of principle it should neither negotiate nor sign contracts with employers. Employers, it argued, had historically, and illegitimately, expropriated from the community for their own use the means of production. Capitalists had the moral standing of thieves. The workers' objectives, then, must be to displace these thieves and recapture for workers their rightful ownership of the means of production. While pursuing their ultimate goal, however, they would autonomously announce a wage rate and working conditions which they would accept. If an employer refused to pay or to improve conditions, then the I.W.W. might strike until the employer publicly announced and in fact implemented conditions the union demanded. Wobblies might also "soldier" on the job, slowing production or sabotaging machinery until the employer acceded to their demands, but they would not sit down at a bargaining table with an employer, because that very act would imply that the union recognized the employer's legitimacy as owner. Does one choose freely to sit down with thieves?

However logically consistent and morally correct this posture, it did not find support among strike leaders in 1934. Union leaders had available a logically consistent element within their myth that would have led them to assert in dealings with employers a militant, revolutionary position that mirrored the employers' position. The result would have been complete impasse. Instead Union leaders rejected the I.W.W. view on negotiations when they insisted on a written contract, and held out in the face of bitter resistance until they got one.

Union rhetoric was often militant and even inflammatory, but it belied the practical judgment union leaders had reached concerning negotiations. A collective bargaining contract is a compromise. It is appeasement. It is also litigable in the court system. To enter into a contract one must accept the legitimacy of the system that will adjudicate disputes over that contract: the state. One must be willing to submit one's judgments, one's interpretations to the scrutiny of others and to subordinate one's own will to the will of those adjudicating the dispute. However dramatically this process changes relationships between employers, workers, and government, it is not a revolution. In fact it relies upon the existing system of law and thus acquiesces to a conservative tradition. These observations are particularly important for Minneapolis, since the strike leadership was accused of plotting the overthrow of the existing order, of planning to establish soviets throughout Minneapolis. Organizers were radicals, both Dan Tobin and the Citizens Alliance charged, whose only purpose was revolution. Union rhetoric, particularly in *The Organizer*, offered frequent flourishes that both could quote.

The charges of radicalism had credibility with the public because a number of strike leaders were members of the Communist League which asserted the historical right and duty of workers to overthrow capitalism. This idea was central to the union organizers' myth. It was a principle they would defend, but as we have seen, that principle yielded to pragmatic considerations. This Red baiting in the heat of the campaign had little effect on workers, but the revolutionary ideal of the Communist League did have dramatic consequences later. When Local 574 turned its back on the AFL and Dan Tobin and joined the CIO, its leaders confronted again charges of revolutionary radicalism. The union was only a front for their subversive activities, the federal government charged, when it brought in indictments against Vince Dunne, Carl Skoglund, and sixteen others, most of whom were associated with Local 574. In 1941 under the Smith Act, federal prosecutors charged the Socialist Workers Party, successor to the Communist League, headquartered in New York City, with conspiracy, with advocating the overthrow of the United States Government by force and violence, and brought its national leaders and Local 574 members to trial in Minneapolis. This trial focused national attention on Minneapolis as Socialist Workers Party chairman James P. Cannon testified about the Party's revolutionary principles and strategies. Union leaders were effectively removed from leadership when they were convicted on a lesser charge of "advocating the desirability" of overthrowing the government. On December 8, 1941, Vince Dunne, Carl Skoglund, Farrel Dobbs, Harry deBoer and fourteen others were sentenced to up to sixteen months in federal prison. Sandstone prison became their home. Grant Dunne escaped the trial and conviction when he committed suicide October 24, 1941, while in jail awaiting trial. Sadly, the war to defend democracy began in Minneapolis with suppression.

The Communist League's perception of the workers' right and duty to overthrow capitalism certainly provided an historical framework and a tactical analysis that helped direct the strike and win recognition. However, the strike neither resulted in nor led to the kind of revolutionary overthrow the League supported, and the Citizens Alliance warned against. Rather, the strike produced a conventional collective bargaining contract enforceable in the courts of the capitalist state. Clearly the strike leaders' myth, modified by pragmatic considerations, proved an effective guide to their planning and actions, but they knew how to remember the past in the context of their own realities, and so they were not doomed to repeat it.

The role of both state and federal government in industrial relations evolved into new policies in part as a result of this strike. Although the government would continue to play the role of honest broker between workers and employers, it would do so within a new framework and with greater vigor. Governor Olson virtually became a mediator attempting to reach a settlement; he refused to use the state's powers to enforce the employers' will. Nationally, the experience in Minneapolis contributed to a new climate of opinion in Congress that led to a major statement of American industrial relations policy. The Wagner Act, passed in 1935, established collective bargaining as national policy for regulating employer-employee relations, and a strengthened National Labor Relations Board emerged as the heir of the four national labor boards appointed during 1933-34.

Minneapolis in 1934 was not unique in its suffering, in its response, or in its historical context. It was unusual in the mix of employers, of a patrician class, of imaginative union leaders, of a rich political history, and of a liberal governor. Although the Minneapolis Teamsters strike of 1934 resulted in victory for Local 574, it was not an end, but a beginning. The Citizens Alliance disintegrated within two years, its staff forming Associated Industries, an industrial relations consulting firm, but the Union grew, as did other unions in the city. The debate over craft vs. industrial unionism intensified. Within a year the industrial union movement, gaining encouragement and momentum from the Minneapolis Teamsters' strike, the Toledo Auto-Lite strike and the San Francisco Longshoremen's strike, coordinated its organizing efforts nationally, forming the Committee for Industrial Organizing within the American Federation of Labor. The disagreement over organizing strategy and philosophy, which had colored relations between Local 574 and the International Teamster president Dan Tobin, divided the craft and industrial unionists further in the ensuing year, and in 1936 the Committee separated to become the Congress of Industrial Organizations under the leadership of coal miner John L. Lewis.

Collective bargaining became the conventional way in Minneapolis to regulate employer-employee relations, but the struggle to bring it about did not occur peacefully. Within a year of the teamsters' victory, strikers and police clashed at the Strutwear factory during an organizing strike. However, the level of violence in the teamsters strike was never duplicated in Minneapolis in an industrial dispute.

The Minneapolis teamsters' strike makes several contributions to our understanding of strikes and of American life. Unions can look to the importance of careful planning and of the importance of a firm, dedicated leadership. In many ways Local 574 offers a model of how to organize a strike. Several tactics proved central to its success. Leaders recognized the importance of communications and of rank and file involvement. Frequent public meetings helped counter employers' propaganda and newspaper accounts. The Committee of 100 provided a broad base of involvement. Workers could feel they had a voice or had access to someone who would speak on their behalf in the highest circles of leadership. Good communications and involvement reduced the impact of "Red scare" tactics on workers.

The strike demonstrated the efficacy of organizing industrial unions, undermining conservative labor traditions that relied on craft organization alone. It persuaded workers that they must be involved in politics, and could be through organization; that Floyd B. Olson sat in the governor's chair proved very important. Workers also learned that local authorities who owed their elections to the employing class would yield to employers' wishes. The police, they learned sadly, follow orders. From this the Union concluded that they must involve themselves in local politics if they hoped to neutralize local government.

Employers learned valuable lessons as well. The strike did not persuade employers that they should welcome unions, but it did discredit the militant open shop position of the Citizens Alliance. The strike also revealed a changing climate of opinion in Minneapolis and the nation with respect to economics. Unwilling to allow employers the autonomy they had abused, elected officials, particularly at the national level, set about establishing new relationships between employers, workers, and government through the National Labor Relations Board.

Government learned how to play a neutral, honest broker's role. It discovered the will to discipline the business community to accept new economic, social, and political relationships. It could not rely entirely on good will and voluntary compliance to regulate industrial relations. It had to intervene in industrial relations to preserve order and facilitate the search for justice. Local authorities could not be relied upon to act even-handedly, for they were too close to the emotions and the politics of the conflict. Harmony could only come through balancing the power of business by the power of the worker, on a playing field umpired by government.

Minneapolis citizens who had paid little attention to relationships between workers and employers discovered a fundamental interest in the nature of industrial relations. To rely on private parties alone to make agreements threatened to disrupt the life of the community; the parties' self-restraint would not suffice. There were no limits to the excesses one or the other party might commit in order to prevail. Community leaders began to create a new climate of opinion that defined acceptable behavior in industrial disputes, and employers who had followed the militant Citizens Alliance turned to more accommodating attitudes toward unions. Central to all these discoveries, Minneapolis learned that economics is the business of the entire community.

In sum, we should conclude from this study that a strike is a profoundly human event evoking clashes of values that may lead to violence unless mediated by the community. Individuals are profoundly conflicted in these situations. We should also stand willing to subject our own values, our own assumptions to careful analysis and review lest we find ourselves, like the Citizens Alliance, locked into uncompromising positions that lead to actions we condemn.

The public's interest in law and order must rest upon justice, upon accommodation of separate, even conflicting interests within the community. We must address anew perennial questions about the relationship between the individual and the collective, private enterprise and public regulation. We must reassess the proposition that normalcy and harmony rule and that they are disrupted only by "outsiders." We must accept that organizing to defend an interest is a legitimate, effective and even desirable activity. By regulating economic life, we can, ironically, move closer to fulfilling this original vision of social and economic justice promised by a market economy.

Notes

1. *Policy and Principles of the Citizens Alliance of Minneapolis*, issued by the Citizens Alliance of Minneapolis, 812 Builders Exchange, O. P. Briggs, President, J. W. Schroeder, Secretary," undated, Citizens Alliance Papers, Minnesota Historical Society, St. Paul, Minnesota.
2. Ibid.

Bibliography

Articles and Books

Aikin, Charles. *National Labor Relations Board Cases*. New York: J. Wiley and Sons, Inc., 1939.

American Civil Liberties Union. *Liberty under the New Deal: The Record for 1933-34*. New York: American Civil Liberties Union, 1934.

Bauman, John F., and Thomas H. Coode. *In the Eye of the Great Depression: New Deal Reporters and the Agony of the American People*. Dekalb: Northern Illinois University Press, 1988.

Beecher, John. *Tomorrow Is a Day: A Story of the People in Politics*. Chicago: Vanguard Books, 1980.

Behind the 544 Suit: The Truth about the Fink Suit against the Minneapolis General Drivers Union. Minneapolis: Northwest Organizer, 1940.

Berle, A. A., et al. *America's Recovery Program*. New York: Oxford University Press, 1934.

Bernstein, Irving. *Turbulent Years: A History of the American Worker 1933-1941*. New York: Houghton Mifflin, 1970.

Blantz, Thomas E. *A Priest in Public Service: F.J. Haas and the New Deal*. Notre Dame: University of Notre Dame Press, 1982.

Blegen, Theodore Christian. *Building Minnesota*. New York: D.C. Heath and Company, 1938.

———. *Minnesota: A History of the State*. Minneapolis: University of Minnesota Press, 1963.

Boddy, Francis Murray. *Federal Expenditures in Minnesota: Their Significance for the Economic Welfare of the State*. Minneapolis: University of Minnesota Press, 1935.

Brill, Steven. *The Teamsters*. New York: Simon and Schuster, 1978.

Brinkley, Alan. *Voices of Protest: Huey Long, Father Coughlin, and the Great Depression*. New York: Alfred A. Knopf, 1982.

Brook, Michael. *Reference Guide to Minnesota History: A Subject Bibliography of Books, Pamphlets, and Articles in English*. St. Paul: Minnesota Historical Society, 1974.

————. *A Supplement to Reference Guide to Minnesota History: A Subject Bibliography, 1970-80*. St. Paul: Minnesota Historical Society, 1983.

Canon, James P. *The History of American Trotskyism*. New York: Pioneer Publishers, 1944.

Casper, Dale E. *Public Regulation of Work Stoppages: Journal Articles, 1983-1988*. Monticello, Ill.: Vance Bibliographies, 1989

Clark, Gordon L. *Unions and Communities under Siege: American Communities and the Crisis of Organized Labor*. New York: Cambridge University Press, 1989.

Dale Kramer. "The Dunne Boys of Minneapolis." *Harpers*, March 1942.

Daniel, Pete, et al. *Official Images: New Deal Photography*. Washington, D.C.: Smithsonian Institution Press, 1987.

Dearing, Charles L. *The ABC of the NRA*. Washington, D.C.: The Brookings Institution, 1934

Dobbs, Farrell. *Teamster Power*. New York: Monad Press, 1973.

————. *Teamster Rebellion*. New York: Monad Press 1972.

Dunne, W. F., and M. Childs. *Permanent Counter-Revolution: The Role of the Trotsyites in the Minneapolis Strike*. New York, 1934.

Edwards, Paul K. *Strikes in the United States, 1881-1974*. New York: St. Martin's Press, 1981.

Employers' Advisory Committee. *The Truth Concerning the Two Truck Drivers' Strikes in Minneapolis*, 1935.

Faue, Elizabeth. *Community of Suffering & Struggle: Women, Men, and the Labor Movement in Minneapolis, 1915-1945*. Chapel Hill: The University of North Carolina Press, 1991.

Filipetti, George. *The Economic Effects of the NRA: A Regional Analysis*. Minneapolis: University of Minnesota Press, 1935.

Fleming, R. W. *The Labor Arbitration Process*. Urbana: University of Illinois Press, 1965.

Fraser, Steven. *Labor Will Rule: Sidney Hillman and the Rise of American Labor*. New York: The Free Press, 1991.

Geroge D. Tselos. "The Minneapolis Labor Movement in the 1930s."
Ph.D. diss., University of Minnesota, 1970

Gieske, Millard L. *Minnesota Farmer-Laborism: The Third-Party
Alternative.* Minneapolis: University of Minnesota Press, 1979.

Goldbloom, Maurice. *Strikes under the New Deal.* New York: League
for Industrial Democracy, 1935.

Goldston, Robert C. *The Great Depression: The United States in the
Thirties.* Greenwich, Conn.: Fawcett Premier Books, 1970.

Green, James R. "Working Class Militancy in the Depression."
Radical America 6 (November-December 1972).

Gross, James A. *The Making of the National Labor Relations Board: A
Study in Economics, Politics, and the Law.* Vol. 1 (1933-1937).
Albany, N.Y.: New York State School of Industrial and Labor
Relations Cornell University, State University of New York Press,
1974.

Gutman, Herbert. *Power and Culture.* New York: Pantheon Books,
1987.

Hansen, Alvin Harvey. *The Duluth Casual Labor Group.* Minneapolis:
University of Minnesota Press, 1932.

———. *Occupational Trends in Minnesota.* Minneapolis: University of
Minnesota press, 1933.

Haskett, William. "Ideological Radicals: The A.F.L. and the Federal
Labor Policy in the Strikes of 1934." Ph.D. diss. University of
California, 1957.

Hurd, Rick. "New Deal Labor Policy and the Containment of
Radical Union Activity." *Review of Radical Political Economy* (Fall
1976).

Hyman, Collete A. "Workers on Stage: An Annotated Bibliography
of Labor Plays of the 1930's." *Performing Arts Resources* 12 (1987).

Jesness, Oscar Bernard. *A Program for Land Use in Northern
Minnesota: A Type Study in Land Utilization.* Minneapolis:
University of Minnesota Press, 1935.

Jones, Jesse, and Edward Angly. *Fifty Billion Dollars: My Thirteen
Years with the RFC 1932-1945.* New York: The Macmillan Co.,
1951.

Joseph G. Rayback. *A History of American Labor.* New York: The
Macmillan Co., 1961.

Kaltenborn, Howard S. *Governmental Adjustment of Labor Disputes.*
Chicago: The Foundation Press, Inc., 1943.

Koch, Raymond. "The Development of Public Relief Programs in Minnesota, 1929-1941." Ph.D. diss. University of Minnesota, 1967.

Kochan, Thomas A. *The Transformation of American Industrial Relations*. New York: Basic Books, 1986.

Koepke, Charles Augustus. *A Job Analysis of Manufacturing Plants in Minnesota*. Minneapolis: University of Minnesota Press, 1934.

Korth, Philip A., and Margaret Beegle. *I Remember Like Today: The Auto-Lite Strike of 1934*. East Lansing: Michigan State University Press, 1988.

Korth, Philip A. "The Yeoman and a Market Economy." Ph.D. diss., University of Minnesota, 1967.

Lass, William E. *Minnesota: A Bicentennial History*. New York: W.W. Norton, 1977.

Le Sueur, Meridel, *North Star Country*. Lincoln: University of Nebraska Press, 1984.

Leither, Robert David. *The Teamsters Union, A Study of its Economic Impact*. New York: Bookman Assoc., 1957.

LeSueur, Meridel. "I Was Marching." *New Masses*, 18 September 1934.

Lorwin, Lewis L., and Arthur Wubnig. *Labor Relations Board: The Regulation of Collective Bargaining under the National Industrial Recovery Act*. Washington, D.C.: The Brookings Institution, 1935.

Magee, James Dysart. *Collapse and Recovery*. New York: Harper & Brothers Publishers, 1934.

Matters, Marion E. *Minnesota State Archives Preliminary Checklist*. St. Paul: Minnesota Historical Society, Division of Archives and Manuscripts, 1979.

Mayer, George H. *The Political Career of Floyd B. Olson*. Minneapolis: University of Minnesota Press, 1951.

McCulloch, Frank W. *The National Labor Relations Board*. New York: Praeger, 1974.

McGrath, John S., and James J. Delmont. *Floyd Bjornsterne Olson*. St. Paul, Minn.: McGrath and Delmont, 1937.

Milkman, Ruth, ed. *Women, Work and Protest:A Century of Women's Labor History*. Boston: Routledge & Kegan Paul, 1985.

Minnesota Department of Jobs and Training. *Annual Report*. St. Paul: Minnesota Department of Jobs and Training, 1986-.

Mitau, G. Theodore. *Politics in Minnesota*. Minneapolis: University of Minnesota Press, 1960.

Montgomery, David. *The Fall of the House of Labor: The Workplace, the State, and American Labor Activism, 1865-1925*. New York: Cambridge University Press, 1987.

———. *Workers' Control in America: Studies in the History of Work, Technology, and Labor Struggles*. New York: Cambridge University Press, 1979.

Nass, David, ed. *Holiday: Minnesotans Remember the Farmers' Holiday Association*. Marshall, Minn.: Plains Press, Southwest State University, 1984.

Nelson, Bruce. *Workers on the Waterfront: Seamen, Longshoremen and Unionism in the 1930s*. Urbana: University of Illinois Press.

Neufeld, Maurice F. *American Working Class History: A Representative Bibliography*. New York: Bowker 1983.

O'Dell, John. *The Great American Depression Book of Fun*. New York: Harper & Row, 1981.

Painter, Clara Searle. *Minnesota Grows Up*. Minneapolis: University of Minnesota Press, 1936.

Perkins, Frances. *The Reminiscences of Frances Perkins Microform 1951-1955*.

Picturing Minnesota, 1936-1943: Photographs from the Farm Security Administration. St. Paul: Minn.: Historical Society Press, 1989.

Rayback, Joseph G. *A History of American Labor*. New York: The MacMillan Co., 1961.

Romer, Sam. *The International Brotherhood of Teamsters: Its Government and Structure*. New York: J. Wiley Bros., 1962.

Roosevelt, Franklin D. *Looking Forward*. New York: The John Day Co., 1933.

Schuyler, Michael W. *The Dread of Plenty: Agricultural Relief Activities of the Federal Government in the Middle West, 1933-1939*. Manhattan, Kans.: Sunflower University Press, 1989.

Sellin, Johan Thorsten. *Research Memorandum on Crime in the Depression*. Prepared under the direction of the Committee on Studies in Social Aspects of the Depression. Social Science Research Council. New York, 1937.

Severeid, Eric. *Not So Wild a Dream*. New York: A. A. Knopf, 1946.

Short, Lloyd Milton. *The Minnesota Commission of Administration and Finance, 1925-1939; and Administrative History*. Minneapolis: University of Minnesota Press, 1942.

Simkin, William E. *Mediation and the Dynamics of Collective Bargaining*. Washington, D.C.: The Bureau of National Affaris, Inc., 1971.

Stevenson, Russell Alger. *Balancing the Economic Controls: A Review of the Economic Studies of the Employment Stabilization Research Institute*. Minneapolis: University of Minnesota Press, 1935.

Taylor, George W. *Government Regulation of Industrail Relations*. New York: Prentice-Hall, Inc., 1948.

Thiebolt, Armand J. *Union Violence: The Record and the Response by Courts, Legislatures, and the NLRB*. Industrial Research Unit, The Wharton School. Philadelphia: Vance Hall/CS, University of Pennsylvania, 1983.

Tselos, George. "Self-help and Sauerkraut: The Organized Unemployed Inc., of Minneapolis." *Minnesota History* 45 (1977).

Tweton, D. Jerome. *Depression: Minnesota in the Thirties*. Fargo: North Dakota Institute for Regional Studies, 1981.

U.S. Department of Commerce. *Historical Statistics of the United States: Colonial Times to 1970*. Part 1. Washington D.C.: Government Printing Office, 1975.

U.S. Department of Labor. *The Monthly Labor Review* 39, no. 1 (May 1934).

Vaile, Roland S. *Impact of the Depression on Business Activity and Real Income in Minnesota*. Minneapolis: University of Minnesota Press, 1933.

Valelly, Richard M. *Radicalism in the States: The Minnesota Farmers Labor Party and the American Political Economy*. Chicago: University of Chicago Press, 1989.

Vorse, Mary Heaton. *Labor's New Millions*. New York: Modern Age Books, Inc., 1938.

Walker, Charles R. *American City*. New York: Farrar & Rinehart, 1937.

Oral Histories

Robert C. Alexander, interview by Janet Topolsky, Minnetonka, 5 August 1974.

Arnold S. Anderson, interview by Philip A. Korth and Janet Topolsky, St. Louis Park, 18 July 1974.

August Bartholomew (Minneapolis striker), interview by Philip Fishman and Janet Topolsky, 20 August 1974.

John H. Bosch (head of the Minnesota Farm Holiday Assocition), interview by Philip A. Korth, Philip Fishman, and Janet Topolsky, Minneapolis, 9 July 1974.

Harvey Boscoe (laundry driver in 1934 Minneapolis), interview by Philip A. Korth, Philip Fishman, and Janet Topolsky, 1 July 1974.

Harold M. Boyd, interview by Philip Fishman and Janet Topolsky, Minneapolis, 13 July 1974.

Frank J. Brace, interview by Philip A. Korth, Minneapolis, 15 July 1974.

Howard Carlson, interview by Philip Fishman and Janet Topolsky, Shakopee, 10 July 1974.

Jake Cooper (union activist; Trotsky bodyguard), interview by Philip A. Korth, Philip Fishman, and Janet Topolsky, Chaska, 11 July 1974.

R. D. Cramer (editor, *Minneapolis Labor Review*), interview by Philip A. Korth, Minneapolis, September 1964.

William and Fannie Curran, interview by Philip Fishman, and Janet Topolsky, Minneapolis, 5 August 1974.

Harry deBoer (Executive Committee, Local 574), interview by Philip A. Korth, Philip Fishman, and Janet Topolsky, Minneapolis, 13 July 1974.

Clara Dunne (union activist; wife of Grant Dunne), interview by Philip A. Korth, Philip Fishman, and Janet Topolsky, Minneapolis, 3 July 1974.

Isabelle G. Dunne (wife of Miles Dunne), interview by Philip A. Korth, Philip Fishman, and Janet Topolsky, Minneapolis, 3 July 1974.

V. Raymond Dunne, Jr., interview by Philip A. Korth, Philip Fishman, and Janet Topolsky, Minneapolis, 11 July 1974.

V. R. Dunne, interview by Philip A. Korth, Minneapolis, September 1964.

Vincent R. Dunne, Sr., interview by George Tselos, Minneapolis.

Oscar Eidem, interview by Philip Fishman and Janet Topolsky, Minneapolis, 16 July 1974.

Walfrid Engdahl, interview by Philip Fishman, and Janet Topolsky, Minneapolis, 30 July 1974.

Alice Pearson Fahr, interview by Philip A. Korth, Philip Fishman, and Janet Topolsky, Minneapolis, 2 July 1974.

George S. Favorite, interview by Philip Fishman and Janet Topolsky, Minneapolis, 15 July 1974.

Frank Forestal, interview by Philip A. Korth, Philip Fishman, and Janet Topolsky, Minneapolis, 20 August 1974.

Myrtle Harris, interview by Philip Fishman and Janet Topolsky, Minneapolis, 24 July 1974.

Totton P. Heffelfinger, interview by Philip A. Korth, Philip Fishman, and Janet Topolsky, Minneapolis, 2 July 1974.

Arthur C. Hesle (policeman), interview by Philip Fishman and Janet Topolsky, Minneapolis, 23 July 1974.

Happy Holstein, interview by Philip Fishman and Janet Topolsky, Minneapolis, 1 August 1974.

Moe Hork, interview by Philip A. Korth, Philip Fishman, and Janet Topolsky, Minneapolis, 19 July 1974.

Rodney Jacobson, interview by Philip Fishman and Janet Topolsky, Minneapolis, 3 August 1974.

Earling O. Johnson, interview by Philip Fishman and Janet Topolsky, Minneapolis, 10 July 1974.

Bernard M. Koski, interview by Philip A. Korth, Philip Fishman, and Janet Topolsky, Minneapolis, 17 July 1974.

Meridel LeSueur, interview by Philip A. Korth, Minneapolis, 19 December 1974.

Martin O. Lillejord, interview by Philip Fishman and Janet Topolsky, Minneapolis, 5 August 1974.

Lloyd M. MacAloon, interview by Philip A. Korth, Minneapolis, 21 December 1974.

Clarence A. Moe, interview by Philip Fishman and Janet Topolsky, Minneapolis, 13 August 1974.

Chris Moe, interview by Philip A. Korth, Philip Fishman, and Janet Topolsky, Minneapolis, 1 August 1974.

Clarence Moeglein, interview by Philip A. Korth, Philip Fishman, and Janet Topolsky, Minneapolis, 17 July 1974.

Orrie W. Norton, interview by Philip A. Korth, Philip Fishman, and Janet Topolsky, Minneapolis, 18 July 1974.

George T. O'Brien, interview by Philip A. Korth, Philip Fishman, and Janet Topolsky, Minneapolis, 10 July 1974.

Francis P. O'Connor, interview by Philip A. Korth, Philip Fishman, and Janet Topolsky, Minneapolis, 8 July 1974.

Frank Ondrey, interview by Philip A. Korth, Philip Fishman, and Janet Topolsky, Minneapolis, 5 August 1974.

Sam Petrie, interview by Philip A. Korth, Philip Fishman, and Janet Topolsky, Minneapolis, 19 August 1974.

Harry G. Pfaff, interview by Philip Fishman and Janet Topolsky, Minneapolis, 2 August 1974.

Ed Ryan (born across the street from the Court House in Minneapolis), interview by Philip Fishman and Janet Topolsky, Minneapolis, 6 August 1974.

Mrs. I. G. Scott, interview by Philip Fishman and Janet Topolsky, Minneapolis, 30 July 1974.

August Seeber, interview by Philip Fishman and Janet Topolsky, Minneapolis, 31 July 1974.

Pearl and John Shugren, interview by Philip Fishman and Janet Topolsky, Minneapolis, 22 July 1974.

Nels A. Sorenson, interview by Philip A. Korth, Philip Fishman, and Janet Topolsky, Minneapolis, 18 July 1974.

Iver Swanson (policeman), interview by Philip A. Korth, Philip Fishman, and Janet Topolsky, Minneapolis, 16 July 1974.

Peter Warhol (union activist), interview by Philip A. Korth, Philip Fishman, and Janet Topolsky, St. Paul, 11 July 1974.

Oscar Winger, interview by Philip Fishman and Janet Topolsky, Minneapolis, 7 August 1974.

Dominic Zappia (Upholsterer's Union business agent), interview by Philip A. Korth, Philip Fishman, and Janet Topolsky, Minneapolis, 31 July 1974.

Manuscript Collections

Citizens Alliance Papers. Minnesota Historical Society, St. Paul, Minnesota.

Minnesota Historical Society. *The Oral History Collections of the Minnesota Historical Society*. St. Paul: Minnesota Historical Society Press, 1984.

O. P. Briggs file. Local History Collection, Minneapolis Public Library.

Record Group 25. National Archives, Washington, D.C.

A. W. Strong. Local History Collection, Minneapolis Public Library.

Index

43, 184, 192; and Congress of
Industrial Organizations (CIO),
191-92; employer recognition of,
59, 60, 61-65, 67, 76-78, 81, 82, 83,
87, 92-93, 98-99, 101, 102-3, 137,
140, 151, 152, 162; Federal Workers
Section, 131, 135; and Floyd B.
Olson, 103; gains from May strike,
135; general labor union support
for, 97, 102, 130, 144, 150; and
Haas-Dunnigan Plan, 151, 156-57,
160; industrial union philosophy
of, 90, 140, 143-44, 191; and
Industrial Workers of the World
(IWW), 191-92; and July strike settlement, 160, 161-62; July strike
strategy of, 146, 150, 152, 154, 155;
Ladies' Auxiliary of, 91, 115-16,
132; lessons from strikes, 194-95;
and martial law, 153, 155, 178;
May strike strategy of, 80, 81-82,
86-87, 88, 90; membership of, 23,
66-67, 79-80, 135-36, 138, 140-41;
raid on headquarters of, 155-56,
181, 183; rhetoric of, 192; strike
headquarters of, 90, 91, 115, 116,
117, 128, 132, 146, 181; and
Teamsters International Union, 88;
union council of, 23, 24, 30, 56; and
union elections, 60, 64, 161, 162-63
Lotz, Rubin, 141
Lyman, Arthur, 99, 121, 123, 129

M

MacAloon, Lloyd, 15
MacFarlane, C., 46
McNutt, John G., 20
Mahady, Dan, 16-17
Market Gardeners' Association, 146
Marshall, Leon C., 45
May teamsters strike: accomplish-
ments of, 135; and Citizens'
Alliance, 81, 85, 104; Communist

Party role in, 96, 126-27; General
Advisory Committee strategy for,
81-82, 85, 86, 87-88, 89, 91-93, 99,
101; general labor union support
for, 97, 102, 130; Local 574 strategy
for, 81-82, 86-87, 88, 90;
Minneapolis-St. Paul Regional
Labor Board role in, 82-83, 85, 86,
97, 98, 101, 102; National Guard
mobilization in, 101, 125-26;
National Labor Board role in, 97,
101-2; negotiations leading up to,
80-88; settlement of, 102-4; special
police forces during, 90, 91, 93, 94,
95, 97, 99, 114, 117, 118, 128, 129-30,
132-33; violence during, 92, 93, 94,
97-98, 99, 113-15, 117-18, 121, 129-30
Merrill, Keith, 99-100
Militant, The, 8, 143
Minneapolis Civic and Commerce
Association, 92
Minneapolis-St. Paul Regional Labor
Board: and arbitration negotia-
tions, 137, 138, 142; and the coal
strike, 58-60, 61, 62, 64; and
General Advisory Committee, 82-
83, 84, 85; ineffectiveness of, 63, 65,
101, 136, 138-39; and May strike,
82-83, 85, 86, 97, 98, 101, 102;
membership of, 46-47; and union
elections, 60, 64
Minnesota Farm Holiday
Association. *See* Farm Holiday
Association
Minnesota Federation of Labor
(MFL), 38, 39, 59
Moe, Chris, 30, 67, 71, 116
Muste, A. J., 8
Myers, Fred, 16-17

N

National Industrial Recovery Act
(NIRA), 4-7, 9, 42-43, 44, 46, 53